Also by Tyler O'Neil

Making Hate Pay: The Corruption of the
Southern Poverty Law Center

Advance Praise for *The Woketopus*

"Tyler O'Neil, talented when he was a college student, has now immersed himself in the troubled civic affairs of our time. In this insightful analysis, he has compared the contemporary distortions of our Constitution against its text and its proper and hallowed operation. If your eyes are closed, it will open them. At the end, Tyler recommends what to do. I hope we do it."
  –Dr. Larry Arnn, President of Hillsdale College

"Tyler O'Neil's book *The Woketopus* provides a definitive account of how the Left's vast patronage network funds the woke pressure groups manipulating the administrative state. O'Neil pulls back the curtain on how America's elites promote far-left ideologies like Critical Race Theory using the federal government, and how to combat this effort. This book will be a useful guide as the next conservative administration seeks to reign in the sprawling, radical bureaucracy of the federal government."
  –Chris Rufo

"Tyler O'Neil exposes how the radical Left has infiltrated the structures that make up permanent Washington. By shining light on how the deep state truly operates, Tyler provides much-needed accountability. The corporate media is desperate to hide the facts in this book. Arm yourself with the truth by reading this book today."
  –Ted Cruz

"Conservatives are desperately in need of a wake-up call. The Left has infiltrated every part of American life with its sinister agenda. Tyler O'Neil's compelling new book, *The Woketopus: The Dark Money Cabal Manipulating the Federal Government*, exposes the far-left's infiltration of the administrative state. There is a revolving door between the left-wing foundations funding anti-Israel protests on our college campuses and the federal bureaucrats circumventing our elected officials to craft policies that upend America's way of life. This nefarious campaign underscores the urgent need to rein in the deep state and restore the form of government our Founders wisely envisioned."

–Heritage President KEVIN D. ROBERTS, PHD.

"O'Neil has relentlessly burrowed into the schemes launched by left-wing megadonors like George Soros and Hansjörg Wyss with the help of unions and the Left's nonprofit industrial complex. Together they collude with the deep state to reshape our lives. If you disagree with their agenda of forcing men into women's sports, shutting down school choice for parents, and blowing out border security, you need to see what O'Neil has uncovered in this netherworld."

–SCOTT WALTER, President, Capital Research Center

THE
WOKETOPUS

THE
WOKETOPUS

The Dark Money Cabal Manipulating
the Federal Government

TYLER O'NEIL

BOMBARDIER
BOOKS

Published by Bombardier Books
An Imprint of Post Hill Press
ISBN: 979-8-88845-767-2
ISBN (eBook): 979-8-88845-768-9

The Woketopus:
The Dark Money Cabal Manipulating the Federal Government
© 2025 by Tyler O'Neil
All Rights Reserved

Cover Design by Jim Villaflores

Post Hill Press
New York • Nashville
posthillpress.com

Published in the United States of America
2 3 4 5 6 7 8 9 10

To my brave son Tristan,

May you grow into the wisdom to learn what to fight for and the courage to stand firm to the end. I see so much heart in you, even before your second birthday. As you sing along with the "Hallelujah" in the Battle Hymn of the Republic, I pray that America would remain strong as you grow—that my generation will fight to restore what is good in this country so that your generation may enjoy the fruits of our heritage as I knew them. This book exposes the major forces holding our country back in the hope that we can reverse course. I pray that it will secure an America in which you can live your values, prosper, and make your mark on the world.

Contents

Author's Note

Conservatives who note the broad influence that George Soros has had on the Left often face a rather disingenuous accusation. I hesitate to even give it the dignity of a response, but current events suggest I should. Soros, a Hungarian American hedge-fund billionaire who has bankrolled almost every leftist group you've ever heard of, comes from a non-observant Jewish family and survived Nazi-occupied Hungary during the Holocaust.

Some on the Left have wielded Soros's Jewish ancestry as a cudgel against conservatives who dare criticize the way he directs his billions to prop up leftist causes. In an ironic twist of fate, a U.S. senator faced accusations that he was spreading an "antisemitic trope," because he criticized Soros for supporting anti-Israel protests and riots on college campuses, where protesters had reportedly harassed Jews (more on this funding in Chapter 7).

The Southern Poverty Law Center (an organization that will feature prominently in Chapter 6) decided to accuse Texas Republican Ted Cruz of being antisemitic…by condemning the funding going to support antisemitic rioters. The SPLC's Alon Milwicki noted that conservatives portray Soros "as a boogeyman" and "a puppet master behind the scenes." Milwicki went on condemn "Soros conspiracy theories" and suggest that criticism of the ties between Soros funding and the riots is ipso facto antisemitic. (The SPLC has a financial incentive to protect Soros, of course, since it is among the many organizations that have benefitted from the hedge fund billionaire's largesse.)

Soros may not himself support antisemitic harassment of Jews on college campuses, but the fact remains that the foundations he established and funds directed money to organizations that supported the riots. This isn't antisemitic to point out—it is simply true.

"The SPLC is a chief smear apparatus of the modern Left, and it dutifully attacked me for citing *Politico*'s investigative report linking George Soros's money to the antisemitic riots at college campuses across the country," Cruz said in response to the SPLC attack. "Instead of attacking people for speaking the truth, the SPLC should investigate why George Soros was financially supporting rioters who used horrific antisemitic slurs and attacked Jewish students."[1]

Speaking as a conservative journalist and the descendant of Eastern European Jews who came to the U.S. fleeing persecution, I can assure you that my interest in Soros has everything to do with the ideological bent of his funding and what he's getting for his money, and nothing to do with his ancestry. I am also sure that Soros would criticize me for my opinions and analysis, not my own Jewish ancestry.

It is perfectly legitimate for conservatives to note Soros's funding and to wonder about what he's getting as a return on his investment.

Charles and David Koch, brothers and majority owners of Koch Industries, funded a right-of-center network of nonprofits impacting American politics. Their critics on the Left used the term "Kochtopus" to describe the infamous Koch brothers' influence. It would be absurd to attack reporting on the Koch brothers' influence as rooted in anti-German racism. It is also the height of hypocrisy for liberals who attack the "Kochtopus" to cry foul when the Woketopus receives similar scrutiny.

---

1   O'Neil, Tyler. "EXCLUSIVE: Ted Cruz Sets the Record Straight After SPLC Claims He Spread 'Antisemitic Trope.'" *The Daily Signal*. May 21, 2024. https://www.dailysignal.com/2024/05/21/exclusive-ted-cruz-slams-splc-calling-criticism-george-soros-funding-antisemitic/

THE HERITAGE FOUNDATION

On a similar note, I will be citing The Heritage Foundation throughout this book. Heritage established my employer, *The Daily Signal* in 2014, and I regularly work closely with Heritage staff. Heritage publishes research from a conservative perspective, but that research has rightly gained a reputation for accuracy and rigor. Even if you disagree with Heritage's conclusions, please consider the data and what it means before dismissing Heritage's findings out of hand.

The Heritage Foundation does not disclose its donors, and therefore counts as a "dark money" organization. As I stated in the introduction, I do not believe that dark money is inherently nefarious. I focus on the Left's dark money network because so few Americans seem familiar with its impact, but I do not support efforts to force nonprofits like Heritage or the Center for American Progress to reveal the identities of their donors. The ability to anonymously send money to organizations you agree with is a fundamental aspect of the right to free speech in the First Amendment.

I do not deny that my conservative perspective informs my work in this book, but please consider my research and my arguments, as I asked for Heritage, before dismissing what I write. I firmly believe that all Americans should be concerned about the way the Woketopus operates—even those who agree with some of its policy commitments.

The Woketopus represents a threat not just to conservative or commonsense policy, but to America's integrity as a country.

Reference Note

Throughout this book, I will repeatedly reference a few sources of data that shine a light on the Left's dark money network and the administrative state. I am explaining them here so that I can declutter the footnotes throughout the rest of the book for easier reading.

Tax-exempt entities under 501(c)(3) and 501(c)(4) of the tax code must file returns with the Internal Revenue Service. The Form 990 includes a reference of all tax-exempt organizations that received grants from the organization filing the form. These forms are public, and I have used ProPublica's Nonprofit Explorer to track them down.[1]

I will repeatedly cite the Form 990s available at the following links. I'll be citing these major players the most:

- Arabella Advisors

    o Hopewell Fund EIN: 47-3681860 https://projects.propublica.org/nonprofits/organizations/473681860

    o New Venture Fund EIN: 20-5806345 https://projects.propublica.org/nonprofits/organizations/205806345

    o North Fund EIN: 83-4011547 https://projects.propublica.org/nonprofits/organizations/834011547

    o Sixteen Thirty Fund EIN: 26-4486735 https://projects.propublica.org/nonprofits/organizations/264486735

---

1   https://projects.propublica.org/nonprofits/

- o Windward Fund EIN: 47-3522162 https://projects. propublica.org/nonprofits/organizations/473522162

- The Proteus nexus

  - o Proteus Fund EIN: 04-3243004 https://projects.pro-publica.org/nonprofits/organizations/43243004

  - o Proteus Action League EIN: 22-3888268 https:// projects.propublica.org/nonprofits/organizations/ 223888268

- The Tides Nexus

  - o Tides Foundation EIN: 51-0198509 https://projects. propublica.org/nonprofits/organizations/510198509

  - o Tides Advocacy EIN: 94-3153687 https://projects. propublica.org/nonprofits/organizations/943153687

- Open Society Policy Center EIN: 52-2028955 https://projects.propublica.org/nonprofits/organizations/522028955

- Rockefeller family foundations

  - o Rockefeller Philanthropy Advisors EIN: 13-3615533 https://projects.propublica.org/nonprofits/ organizations/133615533

  - o Rockefeller Family Fund EIN: 13-6257658 https:// projects.propublica.org/nonprofits/organizations/ 136257658

  - o Rockefeller Brothers Fund EIN: 13-1760106 https:// projects.propublica.org/nonprofits/organizations/ 131760106

I will also cite these secondary players:

- Amalgamated Charitable Foundation EIN: 82-1517696 https://projects.propublica.org/nonprofits/organi zations/821517696

- American Federation of Labor & Congress of Industrial Orgs EIN: 53-0228172 https://projects.propublica.org/ nonprofits/organizations/530228172

- American Federation of State County & Municipal Employees EIN: 53-0237789 https://projects.propublica. org/nonprofits/organizations/530237789

- Center for American Progress Action Fund EIN: 30-0192708 https://projects.propublica.org/nonprofits/orga nizations/300192708

- Demos A Network For Ideas And Action EIN: 13-4105066 https://projects.propublica.org/nonprofits/orga nizations/134105066

- Human Rights Campaign Foundation EIN: 52-1481896 https://projects.propublica.org/nonprofits/orga nizations/521481896

- National Education Association EIN: 53-0115260 https://projects.propublica.org/nonprofits/organizations/ 530115260

- Natural Resources Defense Council EIN: 13-2654926 https://projects.propublica.org/nonprofits/organizat ions/132654926

- Nature Conservancy EIN: 53-0242652 https://projects. propublica.org/nonprofits/organizations/530242652

- Nextgen Climate Action EIN: 46-1957345 https://proj- ects.propublica.org/nonprofits/organizations/461957345

I will also cite reports from the Department of Labor's Office of Labor-Management Standards (OLMS), where labor unions pub- licize the money they send to external organizations. The page to search for OLMS union spending reports can be accessed at this link (https://olmsapps.dol.gov/olpdr/#Union%20Reports/Payer/Payee%20Search/).

I will also cite the grants that the Open Society Foundations publishes on its website (https://www.opensocietyfoundations.org/grants/past), as well as the grants that the Rockefeller Foundation publishes on its website (https://www.rockefellerfoundation.org/grants/).

Finally, I will frequently cite the White House visitor logs, which are available for searching and downloading here (https://www.whitehouse.gov/disclosures/visitor-logs/).

Preface

President Joe Biden stunned America by announcing his withdrawal from the 2024 presidential race on July 21.[1] His withdrawal followed a weeks-long pressure campaign after a disastrous debate performance against former President Donald Trump—a debate performance that revealed the truth of Biden's mental decline, despite the White House and legacy media efforts to cover it up.

I wrote this book before Biden's withdrawal, but the president's decision to drop out of the race underscores the basic point of *The Woketopus*: the Left's elites have a stranglehold on the federal government and they often relegate the people's elected president to the status of figurehead.

Many of my chapters note that if Biden remains in office or leaves before January 20, 2025, the Woketopus' tentacles will remain throughout the federal government. If Vice President Kamala Harris replaces him in the Oval Office, as the result of the November election, or if Biden resigns before January 20, 2025, she will keep many of his old associations in place.

In fact, the manner of Biden's withdrawal underscores my main point. After the debate, while the legacy media and even some prominent Democrats started calling for Biden to drop out of the race, the president stubbornly insisted that he would stay in it—and

---

1   Mitchell, Elizabeth Troutman and Mary Margaret Olohan. "Joe Biden Withdraws From 2024 Race, Endorses Kamala Harris." *The Daily Signal.* July 21, 2024. https://www.dailysignal.com/2024/07/21/joe-biden-drops-2024-presidential-race/ Accessed July 24, 2024.

he started showing his face in public more frequently in a stance of defiance.[2]

Only after anonymous sources leaked that former President Barack Obama and former House Speaker Nancy Pelosi had pressured Biden to drop out of the race did the president belatedly make his announcement.[3] He didn't even bother to hold a press conference, but blasted the news out on X, as if it were a humdrum affair like responding to the latest jobs numbers.

Shortly after Biden announced he would withdraw, he also endorsed Harris. On the heels of his endorsement, Alex Soros—son of leftist billionaire philanthropist George Soros and head of his father's Open Society Foundations—posted a photo endorsing Harris. "It's time for us all to unite around Kamala Harris and beat Donald Trump," Alex Soros posted. "She is the best and most qualified candidate we have. Long live the American Dream!"[4]

Alex Soros' quick support for Harris suggests that he had been part of the cabal behind the Democrats' sudden switcheroo.

Similarly, many of the left-wing groups that make appearances in this book fell in line nearly immediately behind Harris. The American Federation of Teachers, the American Federation of Labor and Congress of Industrial Organizations, the American Federation of State, County, and Municipal Employees, the Human Rights Campaign, and the Service Employees International Union have already backed Harris.[5]

The Woketopus, it seems, is more in control than President Biden.

2   "Defiant Biden vows to stay in race despite growing revolt." *Agence France Press.* July 20, 2024. https://www.timesofisrael.com/liveblog_entry/defiant-biden-vows-to-stay-in-race-despite-growing-revolt/ Accessed July 24, 2024.

3   Mascaro, Lisa; Zeke Miller; Michael Balsamo; and Aamer Madhani. "Biden is isolated at home as Obama, Pelosi and other Democrats push for him to reconsider 2024 race." The Associated Press. July 18, 2024. https://apnews.com/article/biden-democrats-drop-out-election-2024-3f9e3d15431f-d4974771a54e1d0e4ea7 Accessed July 24, 2024.

4   X Post. @Alexander Soros. July 21, 2024. 3:34 p.m. Eastern. https://x.com/AlexanderSoros/status/1815108202499027417 Accessed July 24, 2024.

5   Djordjevic, Patrick; Damita Menezes; and Devan Markham. "List of Democrats endorsing Kamala Harris." News Nation. July 23, 2024. https://www.newsnationnow.com/politics/2024-election/endorsing-kamala-harris/ Accessed July 24, 2024.

Introduction

OUR GOVERNMENT IS A LIE

What if I told you that our government is a lie? It's not a small lie, either, but a con on a monumental scale.

That federal government you learned about in school, with its nice Constitution and its nifty checks and balances—that's not how the government adopts policies today. Instead, a cabal of far-left donors props up a system of woke nonprofits that help staff bureaucratic government agencies, and essentially write the laws Americans have to live by, all in the name of priorities that have nothing to do with improving your everyday life.

The same left-wing network of donors that supported the anti-Israel riots on college campuses in the spring of 2024 bankrolls the phenomenon I refer to as "the Woketopus," the left-wing non-profits that manipulate the federal government.

You may call me a conspiracy theorist, but I have the receipts. In this book, I will reveal the real forces behind how the federal government operates, and why the "deep state" has a mind of its own—a mind obsessed with the agenda of a leftist elite that lives in a bubble and doesn't have to face the concerns of everyday Americans.

While this "shadow government" has been developing for decades, it burst into the open most clearly in the Biden administration, so this book will focus on the past four years.

"RESTORING THE SOUL OF AMERICA"

Joe Biden campaigned on "restoring the soul of America," but three years of his presidency have left Americans struggling to make ends meet, mistrustful of authority, and more divided than ever. He promised to be a president "for all Americans," but under his leadership the federal government seems ever more disconnected from the concerns of the working class, and ever more wedded to interests that strike Americans as downright bizarre.

In March 2021, slightly less than half of Americans (48 percent) said they were "very" or "somewhat" confident in Biden's ability to "bring the country closer together," but that number declined to less than a quarter (24 percent) by December 2023, according to the Pew Research Center. Even Democrats—most of whom (74 percent) trusted Biden to bring Americans together in March 2021—largely lost faith in his uniting abilities by December 2023, when only 42 percent still expressed hope he could unite the country.[1]

Biden's governing strategy appears to have no relation to his promises of unity.

Rather than trying to make goods more affordable in a time of record inflation, he's transitioning to electric cars. Rather than investing in Americans, he's opening the border and helping resettle illegal aliens throughout the country. Rather than beefing up America's armed forces after the embarrassing withdrawal from Afghanistan, Russia's invasion of Ukraine, and the horrors of Hamas's October 7 terrorist attack on Israel, he's using the government to promote transgender identity and scapegoat conservatives as a domestic terror threat. Rather than trying to mend the mistrust between teachers' unions and parents that grew from the COVID-

---

1   "In GOP Contest, Trump Supporters Stand Out For Dislike of Compromise." Pew Research Center report. December 14, 2023. Page 2. https://www. pewresearch.org/politics/2023/12/14/assessments-of-joe-biden/   Accessed May 7, 2024.

19 pandemic, he's demonizing the moms and dads who want a say in their kids' education.

How did everything go so wrong?

First, "restoring America's soul" was little more than campaign rhetoric for Joe Biden, who had championed increasingly far-left policies in order to unite the Democratic Party during the 2020 presidential election.

Second, America's system of government and the ideological leaning of our elites, tip the scales away from sanity and toward the "woke" interests of major left-wing donors. The "conspiracy theorists" who see Biden as a figurehead for powerful interests, pulling the strings behind the scenes, may actually be on to something.

How does our government work today? Most of us learned in elementary school that our government has three branches: the Legislative, the Executive, and the Judicial. According to the Founders' vision, Congress passes laws, the president signs them and carries them out, and the courts—headed by the Supreme Court—resolve disputes. The Founders set up an elaborate system of checks and balances to restrain tyranny, while allowing the government to function.

That's not how it works today. During the twentieth century, two Democratic presidents upended the system in the name of pursuing "progress," and they created a vast bureaucracy that today helps elites circumvent the people's elected leaders. Presidents Woodrow Wilson and Franklin Delano Roosevelt believed the government should act in a more "scientific" fashion, with "experts" making policy. Through his "New Deal," FDR urged Congress to outsource more of its lawmaking authority to administrative agencies that issued regulations to achieve Congress's broader goals.

Congress tried to restore checks and balances through the Administrative Procedure Act of 1946, which established some rules agencies had to follow in order to release new regulations. Even so, this law did not reverse the fundamental change that took place under FDR.

Today, a fourth branch of government—the administrative state—promulgates the vast majority of rules that affect Americans' lives. According to the Competitive Enterprise Institute study *Ten Thousand Commandments*, Congress only enacted 247 laws in the 2022 calendar year, while agencies promulgated 3,168 rules and published 80,756 pages of rules in the Federal Register (the massive compendium of government rules) for 2022.[2]

Technically, the administrative state falls under the president's authority as chief executive, but certain rules insulate the administrative state from the president's control. Former President Donald Trump attempted to weaken these rules through a reform called Schedule F, but the Office of Management and Budget under Biden has issued new rules to prevent Trump's attempt to bring the administrative state to heel.[3]

It is no surprise that federal government employees skew liberal. The Washington, D.C., area is a hotbed for radical leftist ideas, and conservatives often feel like an embattled minority in the city I affectionately refer to as "Mordor."

A 2022 poll found that 46 percent of federal workers planned to vote for the Democratic nominee in House races that year, while 35 percent planned to vote for the Republican.[4] A Daily Caller News Foundation analysis of Federal Election Commission records found that over 60 percent of federal government employee contributions went to support President Biden and Democrats in 2023. Federal

---

2 Crews, Clyde Wayne. *Ten Thousand Commandments 2023: An Annual Snapshot of the Federal Regulatory State.* Competitive Enterprise Institute. November 29, 2023. https://cei.org/studies/ten-thousand-commandments-2023/ Accessed May 8, 2024.

3 Lucas, Fred. "Biden Protects Deep State Bureaucrats With 'Anti-Democratic' Rule." *The Daily Signal.* April 8, 2024. https://www.dailysignal.com/2024/04/08/bidens-anti-democratic-personnel-regulation-could-insulate-deep-state/ Accessed May 8, 2024.

4 Katz, Eric. "Poll: Federal Employees Slightly Prefer Democrats in Upcoming Midterms." Government Executive. November 1, 2022. https://www.govexec.com/workforce/2022/11/poll-federal-employees-slightly-prefer-democrats-upcoming-midterms/378843/ Accessed May 8, 2024.

employees donated nearly $200,000 to Democratic campaign groups, while they only gave $116,000 to Republican committees.[5] The largest government employee union, the American Federation for Government Employees, has endorsed Biden for reelection.[6]

Federal employees' liberal bias aligns with the leftward slant of America's elites in business, academia, entertainment, and other commanding heights of culture.

The elites who are focused on the problem of overpopulation may be surprised that America is facing the opposite crisis. Elites who benefit from investments in green technology may be surprised to hear that Americans mistrust their doom-and-gloom narrative about the coming fossil fuel Armageddon. Elites obsessed with "racial justice" may be surprised to hear that working-class Americans—of all races—are struggling to make ends meet and fearful that the schools their tax dollars fund may be trying to indoctrinate their children.

At some point, the elites' insistence that their climate and diversity agenda will save the rubes who just aren't enlightened enough to grasp their own self-interest sounds a lot like the statement (falsely) attributed to the French Queen Marie Antoinette: "If the peasants have run out of bread, why, let them eat cake!" If the rubes have lost their jobs, can't afford a house, and mistrust the public schools, can't they at least celebrate the glorious inclusion of drag queens at the White House? After all, they don't have to worry about the president's mean tweets, anymore, right?

5   Schmad, Robert. "Federal Employees' Political Donations Largely Went To Biden, Other Dems in 2023." *The Daily Caller News Foundation.* January 5, 2024. https://dailycallernewsfoundation.org/2024/01/05/federal-employees-political-donations-largely-went-to-biden-other-dems-in-2023/ Accessed May 8, 2024.

6   "AFGE Endorses President Biden for Reelection." American Federation of Government Employees news release. June 16, 2023. https://www.afge.org/publication/afge-endorses-president-joe-biden-for-reelection/ Accessed May 8, 2024.

HOW DOES OUR GOVERNMENT ACTUALLY WORK?

A separation between the needs of the people and the interests of the government shouldn't be possible in what Americans often call a "democracy." After all, government officials are ultimately accountable to the people, with elections every two, four, and six years. Yet America's governing structure barely resembles the Founders' vision. The federal bureaucracy now operates more like a classical monarchy, with a king as the figurehead and a massive court of officials determining policy. That court, and the "dark money" network behind it, helps to explain why the Biden administration pushes policies that harm the American people.

Sure, Congress still makes the laws that must pass both the House of Representatives and the Senate, then receive the president's signature to become law, but this process is mostly for show.

Here's how it works today. Congress passes a bill like the Clean Air Act of 1970, which declares that America must have clean air. Who can oppose clean air? The act doesn't lay out the specific regulations to attain clean air, however. Instead, it gives authority to a third party—an executive agency called the Environmental Protection Agency (EPA)—to write those rules. This allows Congress to say that it is trusting the "experts," while it shifts responsibility to an agency that Americans can blame when they don't like the trade-offs that they are forced to make, in order to get "clean air."

When an influential American complains to her representative, the representative makes a call to the EPA, asking for an exception or a loosening of the rules.

This system represents a win-win for the elites in power, and a hidden loss for the voters. Congress gets to say, "Look, we're doing something," while the agency gets to exercise the real power by making the rules. When a constituent complains loudly enough, the representative tells the agency to back down, and the representative seems like a hero.

Americans sense that something is very wrong. Most Americans mistrust Congress, with 72 percent saying they have an unfavorable view of the representative body, and only 26 percent saying they view it favorably, according to the Pew Research Center.[7] Most Americans also express concern about the influence of money in politics. A whopping 73 percent of respondents told Pew that "lobbyists and special interest groups" have too much influence on members of Congress, while 80 percent said that "the people who donated a lot of money to their political campaigns" have too much sway on representatives in the House and Senate.[8]

Congress gets a lot of flak because it is the most representative branch of the federal government. After all, every member of the House of Representatives faces reelection every two years, as does a third of the U.S. Senate, and the Constitution puts Congress in the very first article for a reason. The Founders intended Congress to be the most powerful branch of the government, giving it both the power to make laws and the power to make spending decisions. Yet Americans shouldn't overlook the vast impact of the administrative state. Our tax dollars fund a sea of bureaucrats who have the real power to make regulations in this country, and Congress can only stop them if it is united in doing so.

President Biden has been able to shepherd big legislation through Congress, but a great deal of every recent president's impact comes through executive orders to the administrative state.

Polls rarely ask Americans if they think money in politics has too much impact on the administrative state, even though activist and lobbying groups on both the Left and the Right know that they can achieve a concrete impact by going directly to the bureaucrats who write the regulations that impact Americans' daily lives. Many organizations also publish drafts of executive orders and recom-

---

7   "Americans' Dismal Views of the Nation's Politics." Pew Research Center's American Trends Panel survey. July 10-16, 2023. p. 3. Published September 19, 2023. https://www.pewresearch.org/politics/2023/09/19/how-americans-view-congress-the-president-state-and-local-political-leaders/ Accessed April 15, 2024.

8   Ibid. p. 5

mendations for the president to implement their preferred agendas. Much of this takes place in the open, for all Americans to see.

Yet many on the Left warn that the Right's attempts to influence the system are untoward and evil, and they often use the term "dark money" to suggest that those nefarious conservatives are up to no good.

"DARK MONEY"

Senator Sheldon Whitehouse (D-RI) arguably represents the most prominent example of "dark money" fearmongering on the Left. Whitehouse highlighted what he described as "a sprawling network of organizations that is funded by at least a quarter-billion dollars of largely anonymous money and is spearheaded by the Federalist Society's Leonard Leo." He warned that this network helped President Donald Trump confirm his Supreme Court justices.

> This dark money network applies its influence at all levels of the judiciary and all phases of the process.... The Supreme Court is now mired in dark money. Dark money influences the selection of the justices. Dark money funds political campaigns for their confirmation. Cases are brought to the Court not just by regular real litigants, but by dark-money funded litigation groups that shop for, or manufacture, plaintiffs of convenience to bring strategic cases before the Court. The Court is swarmed with amicus groups funded with dark money.[9]

Yet Whitehouse seems oblivious to the Left's dark money network, which dwarfs the spending on the Right.

As *The New York Times*'s Ken Vogel and Shane Goldmacher explained, "There is no legal definition of 'dark money,' but it gener-

---

9   Whitehouse, Sheldon. "With Supreme Court Mired in Dark Money, Time for Large Dose of Transparency." Just Security. December 4, 2019. https://www.justsecurity.org/67591/with-supreme-court-mired-in-dark-money-time-for-large-dose-of-transparency/ Accessed April 11, 2024.

ally has been understood to mean funds spent to influence politics by nonprofits that do not disclose their donors.... These groups are usually incorporated under the tax code as social-welfare and advocacy groups or business leagues. Legally, these groups are allowed to spend money on partisan politics, but it is not supposed to be their primary purpose." [10]

Vogel and Goldmacher analyzed the dark money impacts in the 2020 election and discovered that—despite the Left's loud protestations about the money on the Right—donors and operatives allied with the Democratic Party surpassed the Republican equivalents in 2020 spending. Their analysis showed that fifteen of the most politically active nonprofit organizations that generally align with Democrats spent more than $1.5 billion in 2020, compared to only $900 million spent by comparable politically active groups aligned with Republicans.

Dark money is not inherently nefarious. Americans have the right to come together and form civic associations that present certain messages in the public sphere. Nonprofit organizations, unions, schools, and other civic associations exist to promote the interests and beliefs of members, and the Supreme Court has upheld their right to speak on political issues.

The Supreme Court case *Citizens United v. Federal Election Commission* (2010) struck down restrictions on political speech and arguably helped empower citizens to wrest political control from entrenched party and media elites. Bradley Smith, a former chairman of the Federal Election Commission, noted in 2020 that "since *Citizens United*, party outsiders such as [Donald] Trump and Bernie Sanders have raised to national prominence," and "money hasn't been able to buy elections as predicted." Instead, *Citizens United* "made it easier to promote (or criticize) a candidate without help from party leaders or media elites." [11]

---

10   Vogel, Kenneth P. and Shane Goldmacher. "Democrats Decried Dark Money. Then They Won With It in 2020." *The New York Times*. January 22, 2022. Updated August 21, 2022. https://www.nytimes.com/2022/01/29/us/politics/democrats-dark-money-donors.html Accessed April 12, 2024.

11   Smith, Bradley A. "Celebrate the Citizens United Decade." *The Wall Street Journal*. January 20, 2020. https://www.wsj.com/articles/celebrate-the-citizens-united-decade-11579553962 Accessed April 12, 2024.

America has a proud tradition of anonymous speech, tracing back to the Federalist Papers (written by Alexander Hamilton, James Madison, and John Jay, and published anonymously to support the Constitution of 1789) and Benjamin Franklin's "Silence Dogood" columns. Americans have the right to contribute funds to organizations preaching a message that resonates with them, even if that message is unpopular.

Yet some donors on the Left have found new ways to obscure their funding, often while demanding transparency from their political opponents. A particularly secretive left-wing dark money network, recently exposed by the Capital Research Center, sheds important light on the way that woke elites spread their tentacles into the administrative state.

WHAT IS ARABELLA?

When Justice Anthony Kennedy announced his resignation from the Supreme Court in 2018, allowing President Donald Trump to appoint a successor, a new organization called "Demand Justice" suddenly appeared on the scene, loudly condemning Trump's nominees. This organization's structure raised alarm bells even in the left-leaning outlet Open Secrets.

Open Secrets explained that, unlike its counterpart on the Right, Judicial Crisis Network,

> …which follows the well-established 'dark money' model of incorporating as a tax-exempt nonprofit organized under Section 501(c) of the Internal Revenue Code that is required to file annual 990 tax returns, Demand Justice is a non-tax-exempt entity organized by a fiscal sponsor—making their finances even more opaque.
>
> According to a May 2018 addition to the list of trade names on file with [the] D.C. Department of Consumer and Regulatory Affairs, Demand Justice

was organized by a fiscal sponsor called the Sixteen Thirty Fund. As a fiscal sponsor, the Sixteen Thirty Fund is an existing 501(c)(4) nonprofit organization that has agreed to provide a legal home and support for Demand Justice as a non-tax-exempt entity.

Donors who steer money to Demand Justice would report donations to the fiscal sponsor rather than Demand Justice itself, adding an extra layer of secrecy that further obscures the source of the funds.... Sixteen Thirty Fund acts as a fiscal sponsor for over 45 initiatives that lack tax-exempt status or do not exist as separately incorporated entities. Because Sixteen Thirty Fund consolidates all of its fiscally sponsored projects into a single tax return, information about the project's activities, funding, and spending [remains] largely hidden among all of its other projects.[12]

Yet Sixteen Thirty Fund itself represents only one tentacle of a vast dark money enterprise. Scott Walter, the president of the nonprofit watchdog group Capital Research Center, lays out the larger network in his book *Arabella: The Dark Money Network of Leftist Billionaires Secretly Transforming America*. He traces left-leaning groups to a puppet-master organization: the for-profit consulting firm Arabella Advisors, LLC:

Just as Sixteen Thirty spun into existence dozens of groups like Demand Justice to wage political war, simultaneously lending its nonprofit status to those pop-up groups and cloaking their donors more darkly than any normal nonprofit group could hope to do, the three 'sister' umbrella nonprofits to Sixteen

---

12   Massoglia, Anna and Geoff West. "Kennedy's resignation sparks millions in conservative, liberal ad campaigns." Open Secrets. June 28, 2018. https://www.opensecrets.org/news/2018/06/kennedys-resignation-sparks-seven-figure-ad-campaigns-from-conservative-liberal-groups/ Accessed April 12, 2024.

Thirty—the New Venture Fund, Hopewell Fund, and Windward Fund—likewise launched dozens, nay *hundreds*, of not-quite-real groups into the fray.

In reality, each of these groups was little more than an accounting code at one of the sister nonprofits and (usually) a website on the same server. But in the unreality of our current politics, policed by media that are sympathetic to the goals pursued by the Arabella empire and ignorant of the means it employs, these groups could pretend to be grassroots Americans demanding 'justice' on all kinds of issues, from climate change to abortion to Obamacare to the election process.[13]

Walter explains how the Capital Research Center discovered the vast Arabella network, in part by realizing that many of the pop-up activist groups shared the same address on Connecticut Avenue in Washington, D.C.

At its head is Arabella Advisors, an influential philanthropic consulting firm in Washington, D.C., catering to donors various ways, whether that be by adding justices to pack the Court, or in forcing term limits on existing members, or harassing the Court with new 'ethics' rules, or simply delegitimizing it in the eyes of citizens in hopes of weakening the wills of sitting justices to do their duty and strike down unconstitutional power grabs by the president and Congress.

Demand Justice protested Trump's Supreme Court nominees, even going so far as to print multiple signs with the names of different potential nominees before Trump ultimately picked Brett Kavanaugh. The Arabella network also propped up a similar group, "Fix the Court," through Sixteen Thirty's "sister" organization, New

---

13   Walter, Scott. *Arabella: The Dark Money Network of Leftist Billionaires Secretly Transforming America*. New York: Encounter Books, 2024. ebook pp. 13–14.

Venture Fund. As Walter noted, Senator Whitehouse's website cited Fix the Court at least six times, and *The New York Times* has repeatedly cited the group and allowed its executive director, Gabe Roth, to publish editorials.

Roth later revealed just how secretive the Arabella network is when he lost his composure during an interview with *The Washington Examiner*'s Gabe Kaminsky.

Fix the Court launched in 2014 with a six-figure advertising campaign condemning a "disdain for openness and transparency" among Supreme Court justices. After the Senate confirmed Kavanaugh, it came to light that Fix the Court owned both the internet domains BrettKavanaugh.com and BrettKavanaugh.net, and used them to host sexual assault resources with the message, "We Believe Survivors." This strategy bolstered the many women who came forward with claims that Kavanaugh had sexually assaulted them—claims Kavanaugh emphatically denied and for which the women presented no evidence. (Fix the Court did not stop with Kavanaugh. It has joined a public campaign to delegitimize Supreme Court Justice Clarence Thomas, condemning him for not formally disclosing certain gifts, particularly from Texas billionaire Harlan Crow.[14])

Kaminsky reached out to Roth, asking why Fix the Court did not initially file a Form 990 when it split off from New Venture Fund in 2021. Nonprofit groups that disclose receiving $50,000 or less in a year may file a smaller version of a Form 990, which Fix the Court did in 2021. Yet New Venture Fund disclosed on its 2021 tax forms that it granted Fix the Court $111,677.

Roth responded that he "misunderstood the filing instructions" and sent *The Washington Examiner* full copies of his nonprofit's 2021 and 2022 financial disclosure forms. One minute after he sent that email, however, he replied with a follow-up email: "S***, I'm

---

14   Kaplan, Joshua, Justin Elliott, and Alex Mierjeski. "Clarence Thomas and the Billionaire." ProPublica. April 6, 2023. Updated April 7, 2023. https://www.propublica.org/article/clarence-thomas-scotus-undisclosed-luxury-travel-gifts-crow Accessed May 20, 2024.

not legally allowed to send you those. I really messed up. Can you call me now?"

Tax attorneys told Kaminsky that it is not illegal for nonprofit groups to provide this information to the public. Yet Roth's follow-up call with Kaminsky revealed a great deal about the secrecy of the Arabella network. "As you can see if you've reviewed the forms, I'm not a good fundraiser," Roth told Kaminsky on the phone. "I'm not a good CPA. I'm a klutz. Schedule B is not something that is sent out, right? It's not made public. Like, if you're donating to a 501(c)(3), the IRS gets to see who donates to you, but the general public doesn't."

"I mean, basically, I've tried to donate money; I have failed," Roth added. "I tried to raise money; I have failed. I have only two foundations that give me money, and if their names become public, they're never going to talk to me again, and Fix the Court is over. My screwup this morning probably cost me my job."

Roth told Kaminsky he hadn't spoken with New Venture Fund "in years." He described himself as "lucky enough to get a grant from them when we started in 2014 and that was renewed up until 2019, and then they said they didn't want to support Fix the Court anymore. I said, 'Fine, I'll start my own 501(c)(3) nonprofit.' That's what I did."[15]

In addition to New Venture Fund's $111,000, Fix the Court received $175,000 from the William and Flora Hewlett Foundation in 2021. (Hewlett-Packard co-founder William R. Hewlett has used the left-leaning foundation to donate large sums to Planned Parenthood.) Roth earned $162,138 in 2022—not far from the group's reported $195,512 in revenue that year.

Parker Thayer, an investigative researcher at Capital Research Center, noted the irony of Roth's terror about financial disclosure

---

15   Kaminsky, Gabe. "Supreme Court 'transparency' charity director panics over IRS donor leak: 'I just f***ed up.'" *The Washington Examiner.* May 17, 2023. https://www.washingtonexaminer.com/news/2201699/supreme-court-transparency-charity-director-panics-over-irs-donor-leak-i-just-fed-up/ Accessed April 12, 2024.

regarding Fix the Court. "They have attempted to smear honorable men like Justice Thomas over his own financial disclosures but are apparently terrified at the thought of someone obtaining their own," he told the *Examiner*.

Most nonprofit organizations do not disclose their donors, so they can be characterized as a form of "dark money," but the Arabella network goes to extreme lengths to cloak its funding. In the wake of the Capital Research Center's efforts to expose the network, many Arabella pop-up groups have become separate 501(c)(3) nonprofits, and the network also contributes to other established nonprofits that align with its objectives.

Speaking to me in remarks for this book, an Arabella Advisors spokesperson described the company as "a consulting business that supports the philanthropic sector" and touted helping its clients to solve "some of the most important issues facing our world today."

Sixteen Thirty Fund told me that it strictly follows the law in advocating for "policies that advance our progressive values."

Hansjörg Wyss

Many conservatives may be familiar with George Soros, the Hungarian American hedge fund billionaire whose Open Society Foundations funds much of the Left's nonprofit ecosystem. They may also know Tom Steyer, an American hedge fund manager and climate activist investor who unsuccessfully ran for president in 2020. Fewer know of Hansjörg Wyss, a Swiss billionaire whose funding for the Arabella network drew the attention of *The New York Times*'s dark money reporter Ken Vogel.

Wyss lives in Wyoming, and he has not publicly disclosed whether he holds citizenship or permanent residency in the U.S. Foreign nationals without permanent residency cannot legally donate directly to federal political candidates or political action committees, but they can bankroll groups that seek to influence public policy. Wyss founded two large nonprofits that direct money to left-wing causes: the Wyss Foundation and the Berger Action Fund.

In 2022, the Berger Action Fund funneled $35 million to the Arabella entity Sixteen Thirty Fund and $5 million to the League of Conservation Voters, an environmentalist group.[16] That same year, the Wyss Foundation gave $11.5 million to Arabella's New Venture Fund (dedicated to the "Andes Amazon Fund"). That foundation also sent hefty checks to The Nature Conservancy ($5.6 million), Demos ($550,000), and The Sierra Club ($150,000)—which I will discuss in chapters 4 and 8.[17] Wyss also sits on the board of the Center for American Progress, a central hub of the Woketopus's efforts.[18] According to Americans for Public Trust, Wyss has pumped at least $475 million into the arena of U.S. politics and discourse.[19]

Sixteen Thirty Fund, one of the Arabella entities that Wyss funds, poured nearly $164 million into super PACs and other political organizations to influence elections in 2020. Much of that money supported America Votes, a voter turnout operation for the Left, and super PACs backing Biden and Senate Democrats.[20]

While Wyss's foundations, like Sixteen Thirty Fund, support left-leaning causes and organizations that directly lobby for Democratic candidates, Berger Action Fund spokesman Price Floyd told Vogel that the fund has an internal policy banning "any of its funding from being used to support or oppose political candidates or electoral activities."[21]

16 "Grants Paid Schedule," page 32 of "Berger Action Fund Inc." Form 990 for 2022, published by Politico Pro. https://subscriber.politicopro.com/f/?id=0000018d-b27c-dff1-a7df-f7fd1ab90000 Accessed May 20, 2024.

17 Wyss Foundation 2022 grants page. https://www.wyssfoundation.org/grants Accessed May 20, 2024.

18 Center for American Progress Board of Directors page. https://www.americanprogress.org/about-us/c3-board/ Accessed May 20, 2024.

19 *Foreign Influence in U.S. Elections: How Swiss Billionaire Hansjörg Wyss and the Arabella Advisors Network Uses Foreign Dark Money to Sway American Politics and Policy.* Americans for Public Trust. July 2023. https://americansforpublictrust.org/wp-content/uploads/2023/07/APT-Wyss-Report.pdf Accessed May 31, 2024.

20 Ibid.

21 Vogel, Ken. "Swiss Billionaire Quietly Becomes Influence Force Among Democrats." *The New York Times.* May 3, 2021. https://www.nytimes.com/2021/05/03/us/politics/hansjorg-wyss-money-democrats.html Accessed May 20, 2024.

However, in May 2021, the nonprofit Americans for Public Trust filed a complaint with the Federal Election Commission, claiming that Wyss "indirectly funded federal electoral advocacy through his nonprofit organizations, the Wyss Foundation and the Berger Action Fund," likely violating campaign finance laws.[22] In July 2022, the FEC dismissed the complaint, though the commission split 3–3 on whether Wyss and the groups he funded made foreign national contributions.[23]

Wyss's sister Hedi wrote a book about her brother in 2014. That book, obtained by Americans for Public Trust and shared with me for this book, revealed some of Wyss's intentions to influence the U.S.

"What was important for him was to find out that he could exert an influence [on America] through his foundations," Hedi Weiss wrote.[24]

> Behind the scenes a Swiss plays an important part in American politics, with money, though, that in great part he earned in the United States.... Whenever I attend board meetings of my brother's foundations, I'm once again made aware of the fact that he is an important man. Quite often I don't fully grasp what is going on because I live in Switzerland and thus am not close enough to the issues of current American politics that are being discussed, but I am made aware of the magnitude of these issues and to what extent my brother can exert an influence on American domestic politics through his foundations.[25]

22 Complaint Against Hansjörg Wyss, his foundations, New Venture Fund and Sixteen Thirty Fund. Americans for Public Trust. https://14n.815. myftpupload.com/wp-content/uploads/2021/05/Wyss-Foundation-FEC-Complaint-.pdf Accessed May 20, 2024.

23 Federal Election Commission in the matter of Hansjörg Wyss; The Wyss Foundation; Berger Action Fund, Inc.; New Venture Fund; Sixteen Thirty Fund. MUR790400084. July 28, 2022. https://www.fec.gov/files/legal/murs/7904/7904_15.pdf Accessed May 30, 2024.

24 Wyss, Hedi. *Hansjörg Wyss—My Brother.* Bozen, Italy: Longo AG, 2014. p. 48.

25 Wyss, p. 49.

Hedi Wyss also notes her brother's close relationship with John Podesta, the former chief of staff to President Bill Clinton who founded the Center for American Progress. Wyss helped Podesta found CAP and has served as one of its "sponsors." Podesta also serves as a trustee of Wyss's foundations.

The book mentions many policy issues Wyss supports, from working with the American Civil Liberties Union on weakening immigration laws, to protecting the American West from "a growing Republican right—the Tea Party and Congress dominated by a growing number of radical Republicans—[that] sounds the attack on any kind of protection of the environment."[26]

In another section of the book, Hansjörg Wyss reveals his efforts to support voter registration in lieu of direct participation in politics.

> I can only try to influence things indirectly.... For example, by making sure that organizations that have a focus on so-called voter education have the necessary means to do so. They inform voters about their rights. They don't come up with recommendations which party they should vote for but help them to register as voters, which for many people in the States is not easy. So I can do my bit to ensure that a greater number of people go and cast their vote.

As explained in Chapter 8, registering voters is a key part of election campaigns, and Wyss is supporting an effort to turn federal agencies into a get-out-the-vote machine.

Other Dark Money Sources

Arabella Advisors did not come up with the idea of "fiscal sponsorship" to hide the exact projects donors' money supports. That model originated with the Tides Foundation, the center of the Tides Nexus—a collection of San Francisco-area nonprofits that brought

---

26 Wyss, pp. 50–53.

in more than $1.6 billion in 2020. In 1996, Tides passed its financial sponsorship services to a separate nonprofit, the Tides Center. Yet the foundation has become a pass-through funder on the Left thanks to its donor-advised funds, a kind of charitable "savings account" in which donors make grants to Tides, which invests the money and passes it on to other nonprofits at the donors' direction. "Anonymity is very important to most of the people we work with," Tides Founder Drummond Pike stated.

The Tides Nexus incorporates eight nonprofits, including the Tides Network, the Tides Foundation, the Tides Center, and Tides Advocacy, among others.[27] Donors include eBay founder Pierre Omidyar's Democracy Fund, George Soros's Open Society Foundations, and the foundations associated with the Ford family, the Rockefeller family, W. K. Kellogg, and Hewlett.[28]

Many nonprofit groups that influence policy in the administrative state have received money through the Tides Nexus or the Arabella network, and some of them began as Arabella projects. The Left also has smaller pass-through groups, such as the Proteus Fund, which funneled $41 million from foundations and donors to left-leaning groups in 2020, often to boost mail-in voting.[29]

In this book, I hope to show how woke nonprofits have shaped administration policies in ways that harm America, often fitting into the Left's dark money network of Arabella, Tides, and Proteus. I refer to the confluence of left-wing funding through the Open Society Foundations, the Proteus Fund, the Arabella Advisors nonprofits, and the Tides Nexus as "the Left's dark money network." While some of the network's donors are not dark money engines like Arabella and Tides, they work in concert with these dark money pass-throughs to prop up the Woketopus.

---

27 "Tides Nexus." Capital Research Center's Influence Watch. https://www.influencewatch.org/organization/tides-nexus/ Accessed April 12, 2024.

28 "The Tides Foundation." Capital Research Center's Influence Watch. https://www.influencewatch.org/non-profit/tides-foundation/ Accessed April 12, 2024.

29 Ludwig, Hayden. "'Dark Money' Networks on the Left Pulled In $3.7 Billion in 2020." Capital Research Center. May 12, 2022. https://capitalresearch.org/article/dark-money-networks-on-the-left-pulled-in-3-7-billion-in-2020/ Accessed April 12, 2024.

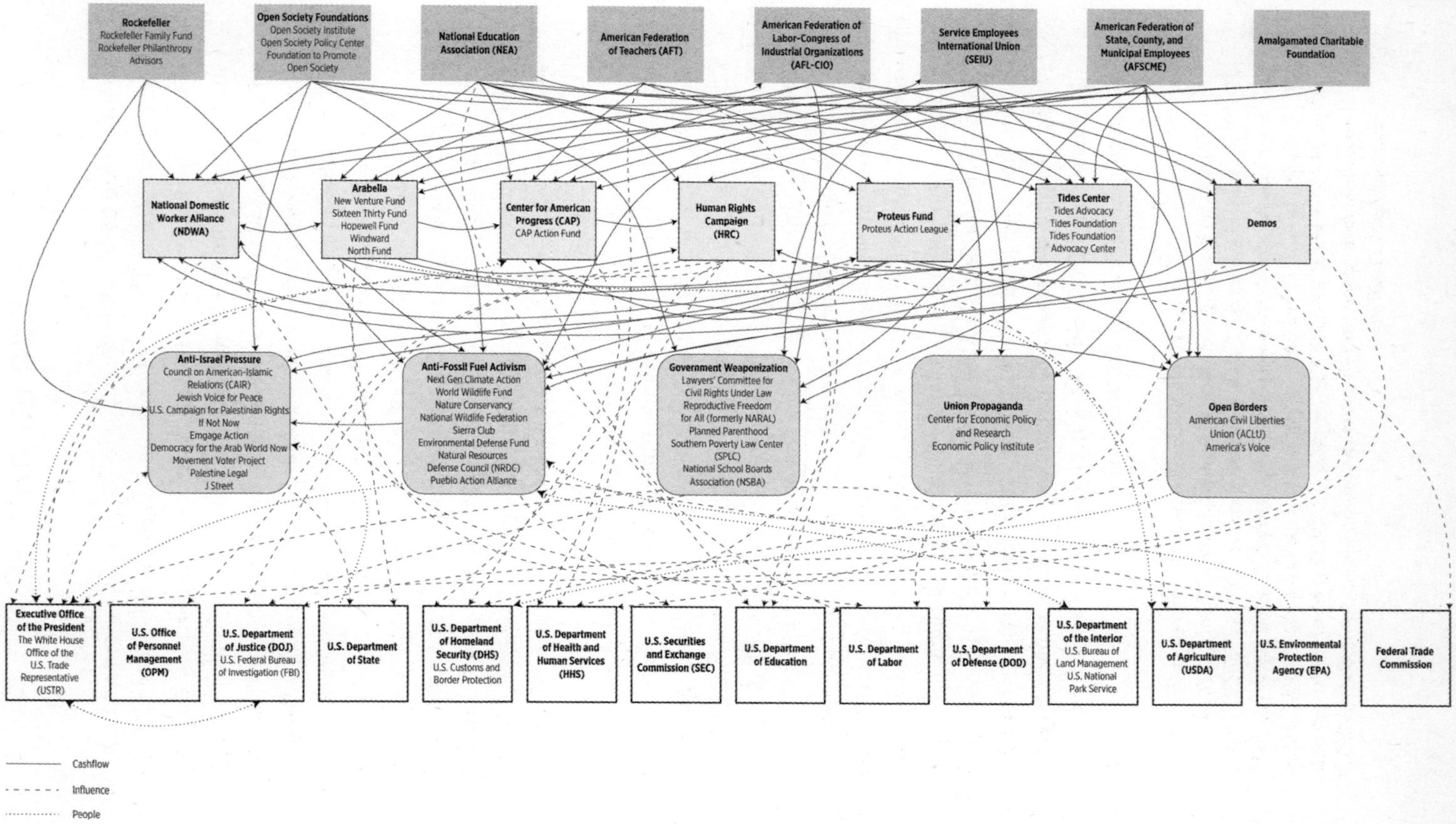
Rockefeller
Rockefeller Family Fund
Rockefeller Philanthropy Advisors
Open Society Foundations
Open Society Institute
Open Society Policy Center
Foundation to Promote Open Society
National Education Association (NEA)
American Federation of Teachers (AFT)
American Federation of Labor-Congress of Industrial Organizations (AFL-CIO)
Service Employees International Union (SEIU)
American Federation of State, County, and Municipal Employees (AFSCME)
Amalgamated Charitable Foundation
National Domestic Worker Alliance (NDWA)
Arabella
New Venture Fund
Sixteen Thirty Fund
Hopewell Fund
Windward
North Fund
Center for American Progress (CAP)
CAP Action Fund
Human Rights Campaign (HRC)
Proteus Fund
Proteus Action League
Tides Center
Tides Advocacy
Tides Foundation
Tides Foundation Advocacy Center
Demos
Anti-Israel Pressure
Council on American-Islamic Relations (CAIR)
Jewish Voice for Peace
U.S. Campaign for Palestinian Rights
If Not Now
Emgage Action
Democracy for the Arab World Now
Movement Voter Project
Palestine Legal
J Street
Anti-Fossil Fuel Activism
Next Gen Climate Action
World Wildlife Fund
Nature Conservancy
National Wildlife Federation
Sierra Club
Environmental Defense Fund
Natural Resources Defense Council (NRDC)
Pueblo Action Alliance
Government Weaponization
Lawyers' Committee for Civil Rights Under Law
Reproductive Freedom for All (formerly NARAL)
Planned Parenthood
Southern Poverty Law Center (SPLC)
National School Boards Association (NSBA)
Union Propaganda
Center for Economic Policy and Research
Economic Policy Institute
Open Borders
American Civil Liberties Union (ACLU)
America's Voice
Executive Office of the President
The White House
Office of the U.S. Trade Representative (USTR)
U.S. Office of Personnel Management (OPM)
U.S. Department of Justice (DOJ)
U.S. Federal Bureau of Investigation (FBI)
U.S. Department of State
U.S. Department of Homeland Security (DHS)
U.S. Customs and Border Protection
U.S. Department of Health and Human Services (HHS)
U.S. Securities and Exchange Commission (SEC)
U.S. Department of Education
U.S. Department of Labor
U.S. Department of Defense (DOD)
U.S. Department of the Interior
U.S. Bureau of Land Management
U.S. National Park Service
U.S. Department of Agriculture (USDA)
U.S. Environmental Protection Agency (EPA)
Federal Trade Commission
Cashflow
Influence
People

THE STRUCTURE OF THIS BOOK

The first chapter of this book will zero in on one of the Arabella pop-up groups: Governing for Impact. This chapter will explain the basic concept of the Woketopus, acting as a case study in how the dark money cabal works. It will also mention the ties that two major dark money funders, Arabella Founder Eric Kessler and Open Society Foundations Chairman Alex Soros, have to the White House and the administrative state.

The second chapter will focus on the teachers' unions that have Biden's ear and direct money through the Arabella network. These unions directly influence policy as well as direct members' dues to prop up the Left's dark money network fueling the other parts of the Woketopus.

The third chapter will delve into the labor unions that spearhead rules making it harder for Americans to find work. As with teachers' unions, these labor unions abuse their members by using their dues to breathe oxygen into the financial network that keeps the Woketopus alive.

The fourth chapter will expose the green revolving door: how environmental activists pass in and out of the administrative state to various arms of the Woketopus. It will reveal how radical green groups manipulate policy at federal agencies by leveraging these activists embedded in them as bureaucrats, and by employing a nefarious strategy to cut the American people out of the process through activist lawsuits.

The fifth chapter will reveal the Human Rights Campaign's impact in pushing Biden and the administrative state to embrace transgender policy, in ways that undermine legitimate government objectives and leave Americans baffled and outraged.

The sixth chapter will zero in on the perverse way federal law enforcement has painted conservatives as akin to lawbreakers and terrorists. It will expose the Left's dark-money fingerprints on the terrifying weaponization of government, which aims to frighten the Left's ideological opponents into silence.

The seventh chapter will raise important questions about the forces driving Biden away from supporting Israel in the wake of the Hamas October 7, 2023, terrorist attacks on the Jewish state. It will reveal the Left's dark money funding for groups that team up with a deep state cabal and arms of the Woketopus, pressuring Biden to punish Israel while it fights a war for its survival.

The eighth chapter will reveal how the Woketopus influenced Biden-Harris border policy, allowing unprecedented numbers of illegal aliens to enter the U.S. It will also explain the Immigration Industrial Complex, a network of non-profit organizations that help resettle illegal aliens across the U.S. in the name of charity.

The ninth chapter will explain how the Woketopus aims to deputize the federal government in a last-gasp effort to hold on to power, as the American people become aware of its schemes. It will zero in on Biden's executive order on elections, which directs every federal agency to help register voters in what amounts to a massive get-out-the-vote operation.

A WORD ON 'WOKE'

For purposes of this book, I define "woke ideology" to include four different major aspects: Critical Race Theory, gender ideology, climate alarmism, and a preference for technocratic government.

"Woke" ideology traces back to cultural Marxism. Karl Marx created a philosophy built around the idea that history proceeds as a struggle between the forces of labor and the forces of capital (ownership of the means of production) in which the working class will finally revolt against oppressive capitalists and usher in socialism or communism. Thinkers like Herbert Marcuse applied this framework to cultural issues, suggesting that various ostensibly oppressed minorities need to throw off the ostensibly oppressive system of capitalism. In this framework, "whites" are oppressors, while non-whites are oppressed. Men tend to be oppressors and women tend to be oppressed. Heterosexual people and those who live according to their biological sex tend to be oppressors, while homosexuals, transgender people, and those who otherwise identify as LGBTQ are oppressed.

This ideology has seeped into American culture through the universities, but it became hypercharged after Donald Trump's election in 2016 and after the death of George Floyd in police custody in 2020. Radical ideas previously discussed mainly on college campuses burst into the mainstream, and K-12 teachers began applying this worldview in their classes, while hiding it from parents.

This is the root of the battle over Critical Race Theory. I do not use that term to mean the academic discipline of Critical Race Theory—which includes scholars who challenge the very concept of race as meaningless—but the political version popularized by the likes of Ibram X. Kendi and Robin D'Angelo. Critical Race Theory in this sense refers to a lens through which teachers tell students to analyze the world according to an oppressor-oppressed binary, and encourage students to advocate for social and political change to "liberate" these so-called oppressed groups.

This worldview includes gender ideology, which claims that a person's inherent sense of gender overrides his or her biological sex. Surveys have repeatedly found that most Americans oppose gender ideology and the many policies that it entails, but the elites behind the Woketopus support it.[30][31]

Gender ideologues treat transgender identity as the norm, referring to biological sex by the euphemistic term "sex assigned at birth," as though doctors were *imposing* a sex category on a baby rather than *acknowledging* the biological reality of the person's male or female body. Gender ideologues treat the "acceptance" of trans-

30 Cosgray, Mary Elise. "Supermajorities Oppose 'Gender-Affirming Care' for Minors, Against Biological Males Playing Female Sports, Poll Finds." *The Daily Signal.* March 12, 2024. https://www.dailysignal.com/2024/03/12/new-survey-finds-most-voters-dont-support-gender-affirming-services-minors/ Accessed May 20, 2024.

31 O'Neil, Tyler. "The Silent Majority Opposes Transgender Activism in Schools, Supports Parents' Rights." *The Daily Signal.* October 31, 2022. https://www.dailysignal.com/2022/10/31/silent-majority-opposes-transgender-activism-schools-supports-parents-rights/ Accessed May 20, 2024.

gender people as paramount, willing to sacrifice fairness in women's sports, privacy and safety in women's bathrooms and changing rooms, and even safety in women's prisons and shelters, to honor a person's claimed transgender identity. They also champion experimental transgender medical interventions, which they euphemistically refer to as "gender-affirming care," even though there is no evidence that these interventions improve quality of life in the long run, and many transgender people later reject their identities and transition back to their biological gender.

"Climate alarmism" refers to the belief that human beings are causing catastrophic changes to the global climate, and any climate disaster can be attributed to the malign influence of human activity. This ideology has taken many forms, from a fear of "global cooling" in the 1970s to "global warming" in the 1980s, 1990s, and 2000s. The latest jargon "climate change" has the virtue of being vague enough to fit changing circumstances, so that ideologues can interpret either warming trends or cooling trends as the result of supposedly malign human activity.

Most catastrophic climate predictions have failed, however, and there is no concrete evidence that burning fossil fuels has impacted the global climate. Even so, this ideology props up a massive, often government-funded, "green" energy industry that competes with cheaper and more reliable energy sources like oil, gas, and nuclear.

Finally, woke ideology often involves a preference for government by experts, rather than by the people's elected representatives. Many on the Left hail the concept of democracy, but in practice they want bureaucrats to make policy decisions, trusting that career staff in Washington, D.C., will better understand the technical problems of government. This preference for "experts" translates to a willingness to trust institutions that have demonstrated bias in recent years. It extends to an arguably irrational trust in medical institutions, despite their confessed lies during the COVID-19 pandemic. It extends to trusting teachers and their unions when parents raise concerns. It extends to a preference for union organizers, rather than employers and employees working out the best deals on their own.

Woke ideology blends Critical Race Theory, gender ideology, climate alarmism, and a preference for technocracy into a coherent worldview that often dismisses any disagreement as inherently suspect. Those who dare buck the narrative find themselves demonized, excluded, deplatformed, deboosted, debanked, demonetized—in a word, cancelled.

This ideology and its treatment of heretics carries negative consequences when applied to the federal government. It often leads agencies to run rampant over citizens' rights in the name of protecting what they perceive to be the public good. Worse, the elites that preach this ideology form an echo chamber that insulates them from hearing good arguments against their positions, coloring public policy and leading bureaucrats to harm the very people they intend to help.

It also explains how activists justify implementing their agenda by circumventing the people's elected representatives, all the while chanting slogans about protecting "democracy." This ideology forms the beating heart of the Woketopus, acting as the inspiration for its manipulation of the federal government.

1

CASE STUDY: GOVERNING FOR IMPACT

How does an organization that's barely two years old pull off a "listening tour" with one of the most important regulators in the federal government?

Before I delve into specific issues where the Woketopus impacts federal policy, I'd like to take a moment to highlight exactly how the Left's influence campaign operates. An organization you've likely never heard of, Governing for Impact, best illustrates how the Left's dark money network props up an organization and unleashes it on the federal government, to devastating effect.

Fox News's Joe Schoffstall stumbled upon a Governing for Impact presentation in April 2022, and at the time, the organization's website was invisible to internet searches like Google. (As of April 15, 2024, a Google search does turn up the organization's website.[1]) The presentation mentioned a "listening tour" with left-leaning legal scholars, policy activists, and current and former members of the Biden administration, the results of which demonstrate an astonishing level of access to the administrative state. According to the presentation, the Biden administration "has taken action on more than twenty of GFI's regulatory recommendations." Unfortunately, there are good reasons to take this boasting seriously.

---

1 Schoffstall, Joe. "Secretive Soros-funded group works behind the scenes with Biden admin on policy, documents show." Fox News. April 26, 2022. https://www.foxnews.com/politics/secretive-soros-funded-group-works-behind-scenes-biden-admin-policy-documents Accessed April 15, 2024.

The presentation quoted Biden administration officials' exuberant praise for Governing for Impact.[2] For example, Sharon Block said, "I'm jumping out of my seat with excitement about this idea." Block isn't just someone off the street. She served as acting administrator at the Office of Information & Regulatory Affairs (OIRA) at the White House Office of Management and Budget, from January 2021 to February 2022.[3] According to its website, OIRA serves as the federal government's "central authority for review of executive branch regulations, approval of government information collections, establishment of government statistical practices, and coordination of federal privacy policy."[4]

"Under Sharon's leadership, OIRA has played a crucial role in advancing the president's agenda—from powering our historic economic recovery and combating the pandemic, to tackling the climate crisis and advancing equity," Shalanda Young, acting Office of Management and Budget director, told *Politico*'s E&E News when Block resigned[5] in late January 2022, returning to teach at Harvard Law School and direct the school's Center for Labor and a Just Economy.[6]

The Governing for Impact presentation also mentions:

- o Joel McElvain, then a senior trial counsel at the Justice Department (currently serving as a special counsel with the Department of Health and Human Services)[7]

2   Governing for Impact (PowerPoint Presentation). The Capital Research Center's InfluenceWatch. https://www.influencewatch.org/app/uploads/2023/06/GFI-Mockup-Presentation-Screenshots.pdf Accessed April 15, 2024.

3   "Sharon Block." LinkedIn profile. https://www.linkedin.com/in/sharon-block-586583130/ Accessed April 15, 2024.

4   Information and Regulatory Affairs page. White House website. https://www.whitehouse.gov/omb/information-regulatory-affairs/ Accessed April 15, 2024.

5   Brugger, Kelsey. "White House acting regulations director to depart." *E&E News by Politico.* January 28, 2022. https://www.eenews.net/articles/white-house-acting-regulations-director-to-depart/ Accessed April 15, 2024.

6   "Sharon Block." Center for Labor & a Just Economy at Harvard Law School. https://clje.law.harvard.edu/team/sharon-block/ Accessed April 15, 2024.

7   "Joel McElvain." LinkedIn profile. https://www.linkedin.com/in/joel-mcelvain-23438a4/ Accessed April 15, 2024.

o   Raj Nayak, Assistant Secretary for policy at the Department of Labor[8]

o   K. Sabeel Rahman, then a senior counselor at OIRA

o   Narayan Subramanian, then a legal advisor to the general counsel at the Department of Energy (currently advising Energy Secretary Jennifer Granholm on clean energy projects and supply chains)[9]

o   Frances Maggie Thomas, then chief of staff at The White House's Office of Domestic Climate Policy[10]

o   Katie Keith, then a scholar at the O'Neill Institute for National & Global Health Law at Georgetown University, whom Biden tapped to become senior advisor for health policy to the White House Gender Policy Council in November 2022[11]

According to the affiliations listed in the presentation, the listening tour must have taken place between October 2021, when McElvain re-joined the DOJ, and February 2022, when Block stepped down from OIRA. It represents an impressive reach for an organization that only dates back to about 2019.

WHAT IS GOVERNING FOR IMPACT?

Governing for Impact claims to represent "everyday working Americans" who face an "imbalance" when squaring off against

---

8   "Rajesh Nayak." LinkedIn profile. https://www.linkedin.com/in/rdnayak/ Accessed April 15, 2024.

9   "Narayan Subramanian." LinkedIn profile. https://www.linkedin.com/in/ narayansub/ Accessed April 15, 2024.

10   "Frances Maggie Thomas." LinkedIn profile. https://www.linkedin.com/in/ francesmaggiethomas/ Accessed April 15, 2024.

11   "O'Neill's Katie Keith Named Health Policy Advisor to White House Gender Policy Council." O'Neill Institute for National & Global Health Law at Georgetown University Law Center. News release. November 15, 2022. https://oneill.law.georgetown.edu/press/oneills-katie-keith-named-health-policy-advisor-to-white-house-gender-policy-council/ Accessed April 15, 2024.

"corporate and other entrenched interests" that push their own policy agendas. The group claims it seeks to "fill this gap" to bring "successful advocacy" for working Americans, which "requires access to expertise about agency laws and the rulemaking process."[12]

Yet working-class Americans did not band together to form this group. Rather, it emerged from its fiscal sponsor, New Venture Fund. Governing for Impact is a nonprofit organization registered under Section 501(c)(3) of the IRS tax code. The 501(c)(3) status restricts the organization from lobbying for candidates or specific legislation, but its sister organization, Governing for Impact Action Fund, a 501(c)(4), faces fewer restrictions. The action fund grew out of yet another fiscal sponsor, Sixteen Thirty Fund.

Both New Venture Fund and Sixteen Thirty Fund are projects of the for-profit company Arabella Advisors. Arabella Advisors allows donors to fund projects like Governing for Impact through sponsors like New Venture Fund, in part to cloak how much money the donors are spending on specific projects. As explained previously, New Venture Fund's status as a fiscal sponsor allowed donors to fund Governing for Impact's activities covertly, disclosing the donations only to New Venture Fund, but not to Governing for Impact.

A New Venture Fund spokesperson told me in remarks for this book that the organization "does not engage in partisan activities or support any electoral campaigns, and we fully comply with all rules and regulations." The group provides "operational and administrative support to help advocates and philanthropists…launch new solutions to today's toughest challenges. Sometimes these solutions include policy changes."

Much of Governing for Impact's funding comes from the Open Society Foundations, a grant-making network established by George Soros, the Hungarian American billionaire hedge fund manager and philanthropist.

Between 2019 and 2021, Open Society Foundations funneled $9.98 million into GFI through New Venture Fund, and $7.45

---

12   About Governing for Impact. Governing for Impact. https://governingforimpact.org/about/ Accessed April 15, 2024.

million into GFI Action through Sixteen Thirty Fund. In total, the Open Society Foundations gave Governing for Impact and its action arm $17.43 million during those three years.[13]

GFI's staff also reveal its leftward tilt and political connections. Rachael Klarman, GFI's executive director, previously worked as a legal policy analyst at Democracy Forward, identifying and developing litigation challenging the Trump administration's actions on health care, labor, and education—according to her GFI bio.[14] She served as deputy chief of staff on the 2017 Virginia gubernatorial campaign of Tom Perriello, who served as a GFI board member.[15] Perriello, a former congressman, served as executive director for U.S. programs at the Open Society Foundations until July 2023. In 2024, Secretary of State Antony Blinken appointed him U.S. special envoy to Sudan.[16]

Perriello is a frequent White House guest, having visited at least sixteen times. He repeatedly met with John Podesta, a longtime Democratic operative who founded the Center for American Progress and who currently serves as Biden's senior advisor to the president for clean energy innovation (more on Podesta in Chapter 4).[17] Perriello also served as president and CEO of the Center for American Progress Action Fund from 2012 to 2014, shortly after Podesta stepped down as president of the Center for American Progress in 2011.

---

13 "Awarded Grants" page search results for "Governing for Impact." Open Society Foundations. https://www.opensocietyfoundations.org/grants/past?-filter_keyword=Governing+for+Impact Accessed March 22, 2024.

14 Rachel Klarman. Bio on About page. Governing for Impact. https://governingforimpact.org/about/ Accessed March 22, 2024.

15 GFI's website no longer lists Perriello as a member of its board of directors, but The Capital Research Center's Influence Watch entry on "Governing for Impact" mentions that the website previously did list Perriello as a board member. https://www.influencewatch.org/non-profit/governing-for-impact-gfi/ Accessed April 15, 2024.

16 Blinken, Antony. "Announcement of a Special Envoy for Sudan." State Department website. February 26, 2024. https://www.state.gov/announcement-of-a-special-envoy-for-sudan/ Accessed March 22, 2024.

17 White House Visitor Logs.

Governing for Impact provides a snapshot into how the Arabella Advisors network, Open Society Foundations, Center for American Progress, and others intersect with the Biden administration and the administrative state more broadly. That's how an organization that was barely two years old pulled off a "listening tour" with one of the most important regulators in the federal government.

THE ARABELLA APEX

Eric Kessler, the founder of Arabella Advisors, likely also enabled this access. While Kessler has not held an executive role at Arabella since 2020, he remains on the company's board, and he himself has shaped federal policy.

According to internal emails from the Department of Agriculture—obtained by Americans for Public Trust in 2023—Agriculture Secretary Tom Vilsack personally worked with Kessler in helping to "direct and lead" a food processing initiative.[18] Vilsack emailed Kessler—along with Marty Matlock, a USDA senior adviser, and Vilsack's senior adviser Matthew McKenna—expressing his excitement about the project on July 15, 2021: "Gentlemen—woke up very early this morning thinking about the processing project you are helping to direct and lead. I can tell you from the response I have received to date there is excitement over the possibility of this helping to create a more dynamic and competitive market."

Kessler responded, "This is striking a real chord and filling a huge need. The feedback I've heard has been 100% positive around the initiative and the Department's leadership."

Matlock wrote that he had been "in nearly daily conversation" with Kessler "about elements and strategies" regarding the project.

---

18 Catenacci, Thomas, and Joe Schoffstall. "Biden admin coordinated with liberal dark money behemoth on 'transforming food system,' emails show." Fox News. May 16, 2023. https://www.foxnews.com/politics/biden-admin-coordinated-liberal-dark-money-behemoth-transforming-food-system-emails-show Accessed May 17, 2024.

The project appears connected to a January 3, 2022, White House event in which President Biden announced steps to "increase processing options" for farmers and ranchers. After the event, Vilsack wrote to USDA officials and Kessler that "the President was extremely appreciative of your effort." A USDA spokesperson did not deny Kessler's involvement in the project, telling Fox News Digital that "external partners are critical in USDA's effort to maximize our investment in a way that creates new markets and increases income opportunities for producers."

"I am an advocate for a food system that supports rural economies, family farmers, farm workers, healthy soil and provides access to nutritious, delicious sustainably grown food for all," Kessler told me when approached for comment about his influence at the Department of Agriculture. "I am proud to reflect these values in my own communications with public officials."

Kessler visited the White House at least seven times between 2022 and 2024. Those meetings have involved State Department and Environmental Protection Agency officials.[19]

THE SOROS HEIR

Governing for Impact also benefits from the largesse and connections of the Open Society Foundations, through which George Soros has bankrolled much of the modern Left. His son, Alex Soros, took the reins in December 2022 and the foundations announced it would lay off up to 40 percent of its staff worldwide in the transition.[20]

George Soros's funding has enabled leftist groups to erode America's system of law and order in the name of criminal justice reform. Democracy PAC, a Soros super PAC, has backed the election campaigns of "rogue prosecutors" in what Heritage Foundation

---

19 White House Visitor Logs.

20 Beaty, Thalia. "George Soros' Open Society Foundations name new president after years of layoffs and transition." *The Associated Press*. March 11, 2024. https://apnews.com/article/george-soros-alex-soros-osf-open-society-542a23 88195d8605df68f6b9197fffb Accessed July 9, 2024.

scholars Zack Smith and Cully Stimson describe as "a devious scheme to replace law and order prosecutors with zealots opposed to the death penalty." In the thirty United States cities with the highest murder rates, at least fourteen have prosecutors backed or inspired by Soros. The murders in those fourteen cities accounted for 68 percent of the homicides in the thirty top homicide cities through June 2022.[21]

These "rogue prosecutors" took inspiration from a Marxist left-wing movement to abolish the death penalty and overhaul American society, redistributing wealth and rooting out capitalism, prisons, and corporations. These Marxists argue that America is "systematically racist" and requires "a radical transformation of our entire system of government, including the norms and practices of civil society."

The Marxist activist Angela Davis, who called on Americans to "imagine a world without prisons," inspired the movement. She equates prisons to modern-day slavery, calling them "racist institutions" and decrying the "prison industrial complex." Smith and Stimson write that "it's hard to overstate how influential Davis's advocacy and writings have been on the rogue prosecutor movement, and how she, in a way, is one of the intellectual bridges between the radicals of old and today."[22]

Alicia Garza, a co-founder of the Black Lives Matter movement, drew inspiration from Davis. She said, "It's not possible for a world to emerge where black lives matter if it's under capitalism. And it's not possible to abolish capitalism without a struggle against national oppression and gender oppression." She also said, "Criminalization is the way that black bodies have been forced from the formalized economy." She glorified cop killers like Mumia Abu-Jamal (also known as Wesley Cook), who shot and killed a

---

21   Smith, Zack and Cully Stimson. *Rogue Prosecutors: How Radical Soros Lawyers Are Destroying America's Communities.* New York: Bombardier Books, 2023. pp. x–xi.

22   Smith, pp. 3–4.

Philadelphia police officer during a traffic stop in 1981.[23] (Garza will make another appearance in Chapter 3.)

According to Smith and Stimson, George Soros employee Whitney Tymas took inspiration from Davis and Garza when she teamed up with American Civil Liberties Union attorney Chloe Cockburn and drafted a strategy to elect district attorneys who opposed the death penalty. "Like Angela Davis, the unabashed prison abolitionist, these authors of the rogue prosecutor movement sought to abolish the traditional concept of a prosecutor who enforced the law as written and to instead 'choose prosecutors who will open the locks' of prisons."[24] Smith and Stimson also cite Rachel Barkow, a New York University School of Law professor and a former member of the U.S. Sentencing Commission, who supports the progressive prosecutor movement. She described its goal as "to reverse-engineer and dismantle the criminal justice infrastructure" as it currently exists.[25]

George Soros has had a tremendous impact on the American Left by bankrolling the "rogue prosecutor" movement, and that impact may grow further as his son, Alex, takes over. The younger Soros has described himself as "more political" than his father. Alex Soros' Open Society Foundations directs about $1.5 billion per year to various nonprofits claiming to support human rights around the world and to build democracies.[26]

Alex Soros has had at least twenty-four meetings at the White House in the past three years, often including his special advisor, Yasin Yaquibe. He met with Principal Deputy National Security Advisor Jon Finer six times. He also met with Amos Hochstein, a senior adviser for energy and investment who has negotiated between Lebanon and Israel, a little more than a month after the October 7 terrorist attacks, and with National Security Advisor Jake Sullivan around the same time.[27]

23 Smith, pp. 5–6.
24 Ibid, pp. 7–9.
25 Ibid, p. 14–15.
26 Zuckerman.
27 White House Visitor Logs.

WHAT DOES GFI WANT?

Governing for Impact's presentation reveals the nexus between Arabella, the Open Society Foundations, and the Biden administration, exposing the Left's tentacles in government. It included a "Roadmap 2021 Transition Project" with "50+ legal policy memos" for the Departments of Education, Interior, Labor, Justice, Agriculture, Energy, Treasury, and more. The policies ranged from "protecting transgender students" at the Department of Education to applying new rules on carbon emissions, to allowing health care exchanges set up by the Affordable Care Act (better known as Obamacare) to include voter registration, to "racial equity" in programs administered under the Fair Housing Act.

Governing for Impact claimed that the Biden administration "has taken action on more than 20 of GFI's regulatory recommendations." The group claimed credit for a special enrollment period under Obamacare, $5.8 billion in debt relief for 300,000-plus borrowers who qualify as "totally and permanently disabled," and a policy of up to two days of paid leave that federal employees receive for getting a COVID-19 vaccine.

Single-Sex Shelter Rule

GFI's "roadmap" included policies on "transgender shelter protections," an area in which the Biden administration reversed a Trump administration rule. The Biden move substantially echoed GFI's recommendation.

Single-sex shelters exist in part to give women an opportunity to recover after they have suffered abuse, often at the hands of men. Yet a 2016 rule at the department of Housing and Urban Development required women's shelters to admit men who claim to identify as women, in the name of preventing discrimination. These "transgender women" may mean no harm to the vulnerable women in these shelters, but the rules did not require or explicitly allow vetting to ensure these men did not pose a threat to the women.

In July 2020, HUD under President Donald Trump proposed a change to the rule, allowing single-sex shelters to bar individuals of the opposite sex regardless of gender identity claims.[28] This rule would have allowed women's domestic abuse shelters to house women without also housing men who claim to identify as women. The 2020 HUD rule mandated that all single-sex shelters that turn anyone away must notify that person of other shelters in the area that can meet that person's needs. Similarly, the rule required any women's shelter that accommodates men who claim to identify as women to refer any woman seeking shelter who expresses concern about "transgender women" to a facility with a sex-based policy.

"This important update will empower shelter providers to set policies that align with their missions, like safeguarding victims of domestic violence or human trafficking," Ben Carson, then-secretary of HUD, said at the time. "Mission-focused shelter operators play a vital and compassionate role in communities across America. The Federal Government should empower them, not mandate a single approach that overrides local law and concerns."

After Joe Biden won the 2020 presidential election, Governing for Impact released a "proposed action memorandum" urging the incoming Biden administration to repeal "the Anti-Trans Single-Sex Shelter Rule." Governing for Impact urged the Biden administration to withdraw the 2020 rule and reinstate the Obama regulation.[29] On April 22, 2021, HUD Secretary Marcia Fudge announced that the department had withdrawn the 2020 rule, returning to the Obama version.

---

28 "HUD Updates Equal Access Rule, Returns Decision Making to Local Shelter Providers." Department of Housing and Urban Development. July 1, 2020. https://web.archive.org/web/20200702043736/https://www.hud.gov/press/press_releases_media_advisories/HUD_No_20_099 Accessed via Internet Archive March 21, 2024.

29 "Repealing the Anti-Trans Single-Sex Shelter Rule." Governing for Impact Proposed Action Memorandum. December 2020. https://govforimpact.wpengine.com/wp-content/uploads/2021/07/Single-Sex-Shelter.pdf Accessed April 15, 2024.

"Unfortunately, transgender and gender non-conforming people report more instances of housing instability and homelessness than cis-gender people," Fudge said at the time. "Today, we are taking a critical step in affirming HUD's commitment that no person be denied access to housing or other critical services because of their gender identity. HUD is open for business for all."[30]

Governing for Impact likely counted this rule as one of the twenty-plus recommendations the Biden administration fulfilled.

GFI has not just impacted the Biden administration, it has also taken in staff from the administration. Reed Shaw, a former voting law clerk at the Department of Justice's Civil Rights Division, joined Governing for Impact as a legal policy analyst in June 2022.[31]

Governing for Impact helps pull back the curtain on how the Left's dark money network manipulates the federal government. The figures at the top, like Alex Soros and Eric Kessler, spread their influence to long-established organizations and new front groups like Governing for Impact. Soros and Kessler influence policy, but their funding apparatus upholds a broader woke ecosystem of non-profits all moving the government in one direction: an ecosystem I call "The Woketopus."

30   "HUD Withdraws Proposed Rule, Reaffirms Its Commitment to Equal Access to Housing, Shelters, and Other Services Regardless of Gender Identity." Department of Housing and Urban Development News Release. April 22, 2021. https://archives.hud.gov/news/2021/pr21-069.cfm Accessed via archive on April 15, 2024.

31   "Reed Shaw." LinkedIn profile. https://www.linkedin.com/in/reed-shaw-66492128/ Accessed April 15, 2024.

2

TEACHERS' UNIONS

Teachers famously work hard for little pay, but America's top two teachers' unions add insult to injury by using their members' dues to bankroll far-left causes. They support Democrats in elections and help prop up the Left's dark money network funding the Woketopus. These unions also enjoy unique access to the president's ear, using that influence to secure vast sums of money from the federal government, in part by holding America's students for ransom. These unions lobbied to keep schools closed amid the COVID-19 pandemic for longer than they needed to be, and then lobbied for a student loan bailout that encourages students' reckless borrowing and universities' reckless spending. Both policies help protect an increasingly woke public education system at a time when Americans are growing increasingly disillusioned with it.

A WOKE AGENDA

The National Education Association (NEA)—America's largest teacher's union—and the second largest—the American Federation of Teachers (AFT)—claim to represent teachers on all sides of the political spectrum, but they both support woke left-wing political positions.

The American Federation of Teachers supports a bevy of left-wing causes, including abortion, "diversity, equity, and inclusion" programs, and climate alarmism. It has pledged to "work with public pension funds, state treasurers, policymakers and advocacy organizations to promote diversity, equity, and inclusion among asset managers, corporate leadership and boards of directors through engagement and shareholder activism."[1] AFT urged Biden to declare a national climate emergency and "build a robust, just and regenerative energy system,"[2] and condemned laws restricting abortion after the Supreme Court ruling *Dobbs v. Jackson Women's Health Organization* (2022) overturned the 1973 *Roe v. Wade* abortion precedent.[3]

The National Education Association has taken similar positions to AFT. NEA President Becky Pringle condemned the *Dobbs* decision, calling it "an attack on rights deeply rooted in the promise of America" and noting NEA's long advocacy for abortion.[4] NEA claims to recognize what it calls "the scientific consensus that global climate change is largely caused by human activity, resulting in significant, measurable damage to the earth and its inhabitants." It further claims that "humans must take immediate steps to change activities that contribute to global climate change," and warns that "black, Latino, indigenous, Asian American and Pacific Islander, and other communities of color, low-income communities, people

---

1   "DEI and Racial Justice in Investments." American Federation of Teachers resolution adopted July 17, 2022. https://www.aft.org/resolution/dei-and-racial-justice-investments Accessed April 15, 2024.

2   "Declaring a Climate Emergency and Developing Climate Action and Healthy Building Plans." American Federation of Teachers Resolution, adopted October 3, 2023. https://www.aft.org/resolution/declaring-climate-emergency-and-developing-climate-action-and-healthy-building-plans Accessed April 15, 2024.

3   "Abortion and reproductive healthcare." American Federation of Teachers position statement. https://www.aft.org/position/abortion-and-reproductive-healthcare Accessed April 15, 2024.

4   Jotkoff, Eric. "NEA President's Statement on Dobbs v. Jackson Women's Health Organization." National Education Association. News release. June 24, 2022. https://www.nea.org/about-nea/media-center/press-releases/nea-presidents-statement-dobbs-v-jackson-womens-health-organization Accessed April 15, 2024.

with disabilities, and under-resourced urban and rural communities bear the greatest burdens from negative climate impacts."[5]

On October 8, 2021, as parents were voicing their concerns about Critical Race Theory, NEA President Pringle sent a letter to the leaders of Facebook, Twitter, and TikTok, urging them to stifle opposition to CRT. Pringle bizarrely compared concerned parents protesting school boards to a TikTok trend among kids encouraging property damage at schools. She warned about "the alarming growth of a small but violent group of radicalized adults who falsely believe that graduate level courses about racism are being taught in K-12 public schools because of misinformation on social media."

Pringle was intentionally obscuring the issue. The critics of CRT whom she condemned as "radicalized" do not complain about "graduate level courses about racism," but rather that teachers are applying CRT in schools. Parents noted that the ideas of Critical Race Theory are leading teachers to treat students differently according to their race, to teach white kids that they are "oppressors" and black kids that they are "oppressed," and to denigrate American society as "systemically racist."

Pringle and her allies define Critical Race Theory narrowly, in order to deflect criticism. While CRT did originate in law schools and appears in graduate school curricula, the idea that American society is systemically racist has applications beyond law school, and advocates like Pringle know this. After all, the NEA has publicly embraced CRT. In January 2021, it published a "Governance Document" stating, among other things, that America suffers from "institutional racism" and even a "white supremacy culture." The document adds, "Racial and social justice in education is a stated priority for NEA.... Expanding our collective understanding of institutional racism, structural racism, and white supremacy culture is critical to achieving racial and social justice." The

5   "Climate & Environmental Justice." NEA position page. https://www.nea.org/climatejustice Accessed April 15, 2024.

document leaves no room for doubt about the union's stance on these issues:

> The National Education Association believes that the norms, standards, and organizational structures manifested in white supremacy culture perpetually exploit and oppress people of color and serve as detriments to racial justice. Further, the invisible racial benefits of white privilege, which are automatically conferred irrespective of wealth, gender, and other factors, severely limit opportunities for people of color and impede full achievement of racial and social justice.[6]

The NEA has also defended *The 1619 Project*, a *New York Times* initiative reframing American history around the arrival of the first black slaves in Virginia in 1619, an event the project described as America's "true founding." Historians have criticized the project for claiming that the Founders launched the Revolutionary War to protect slavery. Critics have also noted that black slaves first emerged in Florida in 1526, nearly a century before 1619, and that slavery as an institution is nearly universal in early human societies, including Indigenous North American tribes. *The New York Times* stealth-edited the project in 2020, removing the claim about 1619 being America's "true founding."[7]

In July 2021, the NEA adopted a resolution to devote staff to "fight back against anti-CRT rhetoric," stating that the union opposes "attempts to ban Critical Race Theory and/or *The 1619 Project*," and insisting that "it is reasonable and appropriate for curriculum to be informed by academic frameworks for understanding

---

6   "NEA and Racial Justice in Education." Governance Document. National Education Association. January 2021. https://www.nea.org/resource-library/nea-and-racial-justice-education Accessed April 23, 2024.

7   O'Neil, Tyler. "The New York Times Just Gave Definitive Proof the '1619 Project' Is a Fraud." PJ Media. September 22, 2020. https://pjmedia.com/tyler-o-neil/2020/09/22/the-new-york-times-just-gave-definitive-proof-the-1619-project-is-a-fraud-n954008 Accessed July 10, 2024.

and interpreting the impact of the past on current society, including critical race theory."[8]

Like Pringle, AFT President Randi Weingarten has simultaneously insisted that K-12 teachers do not teach CRT and has loudly condemned critics of CRT, claiming that "culture warriors are labeling any discussion of race, racism, or discrimination as CRT to try to make it toxic."[9]

Despite her organization's own support for ideas grounded in CRT, Pringle urged social media companies to "help put an end to the stream of propaganda fueling violence against our educators in our communities." She demanded that social media companies pledge "to regulate lies and fix your algorithms."

Nicole Neily, president of the parental rights group Parents Defending Education, condemned the letter at the time. "It's a strawman for NEA to falsely assert that 'graduate level courses about racism' are not being taught in K-12 schools; after all, the most important part of a child's Montessori education isn't making a four-year-old read the collected works of Maria Montessori, but rather the implementation of these ideas in the classroom," she said.[10]

BIG DONORS

Some of the 4.7 million teachers represented by America's two largest teachers' unions might be surprised to hear that their union dues

8   "New Business Item 39." National Education Association website. Acccssed via the Internet Archive. Archived on July 6, 2021. https://web.archive.org/web/20210706172057/https://ra.nea.org/business-item/2021-nbi-039/ Accessed on April 23, 2024.

9   Will, Madeline. "Teachers' Unions Vow to Defend Members in Critical Race Theory Fight." *Education Week*. July 6, 2021. https://www.edweek.org/teaching-learning/teachers-unions-vow-to-defend-members-in-critical-race-theory-fight/2021/07 Accessed April 23, 2024.

10   O'Neil, Tyler. "NEA urged social media giants to fight anti-CRT 'propaganda' stoking 'violent' 'radicalized' parents." Fox News. January 12, 2022. https://www.foxnews.com/politics/nea-teachers-union-social-media-crackdown-violent-radicalized-parents-crt Accessed April 23, 2024.

prop up the Left's dark money network. The National Education Association, America's largest teachers' union with 3 million members, has funded:

- o The American Federation of Labor and Congress of Industrial Organizations (more on this in Chapter 3)

- o The union-owned Amalgamated Bank and its charitable foundation (which also funds the Left's dark money network)

- o The Arabella network groups New Venture Fund and Sixteen Thirty Fund

- o The Center for American Progress and its action arm

- o The Human Rights Campaign

- o The Proteus Fund

- o The Tides Center

NEA notably sent $420,000 to Sixteen Thirty Fund, more than $1 million to Amalgamated Bank and its charitable foundation, and $424,000 to the AFL-CIO between 2019 and 2021. [11] Its members gave $2.44 million to Democrats and only $64,830 to Republicans, donating $200,957 to Biden's campaign, while giving $2,610 to Trump.[12]

Unions like NEA must file a form LM-2 with the Department of Labor that shows how much money they spend on specific items. NEA's LM-2 for the period between July 1, 2022, and June 30, 2023, shows that the NEA only spent 19 percent of its members' dues money on "representational activities"—a term that refers to the traditional function of a union, namely employees bargaining with employers. Much of the union's money went to overhead, union administration, and benefits for employees (34 percent), or

11   "National Education Association." Form 990, Schedule I for 2019–2021.

12   "National Education Association" Open Secrets. https://www.opensecrets.org/orgs/national-education-assn/recipients?candscycle=2020&id=D000000064&toprecipscycle=2020&t5-search=biden Accessed March 22, 2024.

to the NEA's state and local affiliates (30.4 percent), but the union also spent millions of its members' dues on politics and grants.[13]

The NEA spent $2.9 million on political activities and lobbying (4.6 percent of its budget) and another $2.4 million on "contributions, gifts, and grants" (3.8 percent of its budget). While these grants represent a small portion of NEA's cut of members' union dues, they nonetheless prop up the Left's influence network, helping to impact the administrative state on issues NEA members may disagree with.

Through the Arabella nonprofits, the Center for American Progress, the Human Rights Campaign, The Tides Foundation, and The Proteus Fund, NEA members unwittingly support efforts to restrict oil and gas, the push to force gender ideology through the federal government, a campaign to crack down on pro-life protesters, and more. These dark money outfits allow NEA to hide which projects the union is funding with its members' dues, and both Arabella and Tides direct funds to groups supporting anti-Israel protests and efforts to turn the federal government into a get-out-the-vote machine.

The American Federation of Teachers, the second largest teachers' union with 1.72 million members, is no better. It has funded:[14]

- o New Venture Fund ($240,000 in 2018 and 2019)

- o Sixteen Thirty Fund ($840,000 from 2020 to 2023)

- o Tides Advocacy ($100,000 in 2019)

- o The Center for American Progress ($75,000 in 2019) and its action fund ($100,000 in 2023)

- o The left-wing elections group Demos (more on this in Chapter 8)

---

13 National Education Association. Form LM-2, July 1, 2022 to June 30, 2023. https://olmsapps.dol.gov/query/orgReport.do?rptId=875367&rptForm=LM2Form Accessed May 29, 2024.

14 OLMS search results, accessed May 20, 2024. https://olmsapps.dol.gov/olpdr/#Union%20Reports/Payer/Payee%20Search/

o   The Lawyers' Committee for Civil Rights Under Law (more on this in Chapter 6)

o   NARAL Pro-Choice America

o   Planned Parenthood

According to Open Secrets, the AFT donated $2.54 million to Democrats and only $7,002 to Republicans in 2020. Its members gave $54,116 to Biden's campaign, but only $483 to Trump's campaign.[15]

The AFT's Form LM-2 for July 1, 2022, to June 30, 2023, shows that the union spent only 27.4 percent of its funds on representational activities, while spending 19.7 percent of its funds on overhead, administration, and employee benefits, and another 11 percent on state and local affiliates. However, the union spent 13.8 percent of its funds—$46.9 million of members' dues—on political activities and lobbying. It spent another 2.1 percent of its funds—$7.3 million—on "contributions, gifts, and grants," much of that funding left-wing pressure groups.[16]

Teachers think they are supporting a union that has their best interests at heart, but they are really funding the Woketopus. These unions have transformed their members' dues into a dark money funding apparatus masquerading as "charitable giving." Union members should demand transparency or consider leaving.

This grotesque funding apparatus does not represent the entire influence that these two teachers' unions have over the administrative state. In addition to funding other parts of the Woketopus, they have manipulated the federal government.

---

15   "American Federation of Teachers" Open Secrets. https://www.opensecrets.org/orgs/american-federation-of-teachers/recipients?candscycle=2020&id=D000000083&toprecipscycle=2020&t5-search=Trump Accessed March 22, 2024.

16   American Federation of Teachers. Form LM-2, July 1, 2022 to June 30, 2023. https://olmsapps.dol.gov/query/orgReport.do?rptId=873943&rptForm=LM2Form Accessed May 28, 2024.

WHITE HOUSE ACCESS

Both Weingarten and Pringle enjoy a great deal of access to the Biden White House. Biden and his wife Jill had met with Weingarten and Pringle at the White House on January 21, 2021. In that meeting, the first lady—an NEA member—told Weingarten and Pringle, "I said I was going to bring you with me into the White House, and on day one, you're here."[17]

Weingarten, whose legal name is Rhonda, visited the White House at least thirty-eight times under Biden. Pringle has visited the White House at least twenty-two times, meeting with Biden one-on-one on December 12, 2022.[18] In April 2023, Biden appointed Pringle to the Presidential Advisory Commission on Advancing Educational Equity, Excellence, and Economic Opportunity for Black Americans.[19]

The NEA and AFT enjoy a lasting access to the administrative state and the Democratic Party, access that is not likely to disappear when Biden ultimately leaves office.

KEEPING KIDS OUT OF CLASS

These unions used their access to hold American students back, pressuring the Biden administration to prevent the return to in-person learning amid the COVID-19 pandemic. The long delay wreaked havoc on America's kids, stunting their learning.

---

17 Christenson, Josh. "Biden backed teacher union head Randi Weingarten over honoring promise to get kids back in school during COVID: book." *New York Post*. September 8, 2023. https://nypost.com/2023/09/08/how-biden-caved-to-randi-weingarten-and-kept-schools-closed/ Accessed March 22, 2024.

18 White House Visitor Logs.

19 "President Biden Announces Key Appointments to Boards and Commissions." White House Briefing Room. April 21, 2023. https://www.whitehouse.gov/briefing-room/statements-releases/2023/04/21/president-biden-announces-key-appointments-to-boards-and-commissions-25/ Accessed April 23, 2024.

President Biden repeatedly claims that his administration was responsible for reopening schools coming out of the COVID-19 pandemic. "When President Biden took office, less than half of K-12 students were going to school in person," the White House noted in August 2023. "Today, thanks to the president's swift actions and historic investments, every school in America is open safely for in-person instruction. Since Day One, President Biden has worked to help every school open safely for in-person instruction, accelerate academic achievement, and build communities where all students feel they belong."[20]

The truth is that his administration actually hampered reopening, working closely with teachers' unions. Biden had pledged to reopen most of the nation's schools during his first one hundred days as president.[21] Yet on February 10, 2021, White House Press Secretary Jen Psaki significantly redefined the pledge. "His goal that he set is to have the majority of schools—so, more than 50 percent—open by day 100 of his presidency, and that means some teaching in classrooms," she said. "So, at least one day a week. Hopefully, it's more."[22]

According to the Department of Education's analysis, 46 percent of elementary and middle schools had opened by Biden's inauguration on January 20, 2021, and 95 percent of those schools had

20   "FACT SHEET: Biden-Harris Administration Highlights Efforts to Support K-12 Education as Students go Back-to-School." White House Briefing Room. August 28, 2023. https://www.whitehouse.gov/briefing-room/statements-releases/2023/08/28/fact-sheet-biden-harris-administration-highlights-efforts-to-support-k-12-education-as-students-go-back-to-school/ Accessed March 22, 2024.

21   Weissert, Will. "Biden vows to reopen most schools after 1st 100 days on job." *The Associated Press*. December 8, 2020. https://apnews.com/article/joe-biden-health-coronavirus-pandemic-80275870d7fca89b-d38992a611b26616 Accessed March 22, 2024.

22   Binkley, Collin. "Is one day a week enough? Biden's school goal draws blowback." *The Associated Press*. February 10, 2021. https://apnews.com/general-news-domestic-news-domestic-news-6de489a8be366b836067a6acd8528912 Accessed March 22, 2024.

opened by January 20, 2022.[23] Psaki's redefined goal of increasing the 46 percent to 50 percent was so modest as to be laughable.

According to the school data aggregator Burbio, over 60 percent of school districts had opened with at least a "hybrid" model—two to three days of in-person learning per week—by February 10, 2021.[24] In other words, Psaki's redefined "goal" wasn't met in Biden's first hundred days but in his first forty, though his actual promise did not get fulfilled until more than a year into his presidency, when Americans had already learned to live with COVID-19.

The teachers' unions advocated *against* returning to in-person instruction. After his pledge and before Psaki's clarification, the president called AFT President Weingarten on January 28, 2021, and—according to Franklin Foer's book *The Last Politician*—assured her, "I am not abandoning you on schools. I want you to know that."[25] He told her that "he knew she was taking a lot of heat around the reopening of schools" and reassured her that "he was an abiding friend."

Starting on January 29, 2021, then-CDC Director Rochelle Walensky emailed, called, and texted Weingarten to discuss the school reopening guidelines, according to documents obtained by Americans for Public Trust and first reported by *The New York Post*.

Kelley Trautner, AFT's senior director for health issues, sent an email to White House staff on Monday, February 1, 2021, thanking the office "for Friday's rich discussion about forthcoming CDC guidance and for your openness to the suggestions made by our

---

23   "FACT SHEET: In One Year of the Biden-Harris Administration, the U.S. Department of Education Has Helped Schools Safely Reopen and Meet Students' Needs." Department of Education press release. January 20, 2022. https://www.ed.gov/news/press-releases/fact-sheet-one-year-biden-harris-administration-us-department-education-has-helped-schools-safely-reopen-and-meet-students%E2%80%99-needs Accessed March 22, 2024.

24   Cooper, Rory. "President Biden Is Keeping Schools Closed." *National Review*. February 10, 2021. https://www.nationalreview.com/2021/02/president-biden-is-keeping-schools-closed/ Accessed March 22, 2024.

25   Christenson. "Biden backed teacher union head Randi Weingarten."

president, Randi Weingarten, and the AFT." In those meetings, Weingarten suggested language that halted a full return to schools.

On February 11, 2021, the day before the CDC released the guidance, Weingarten texted Walensky directly to say she had "heard something from a [*New York Times*] leak that seemed at odds with discussion. Do you have time for a call." Walensky said she did not have time, but asked the teacher's union boss to "ping what you learned."

Weingarten objected to a section in the guidance that read "all schools can provide in-person instruction (either full or hybrid), through strict adherence to mitigation strategies." When the CDC released the guidance, "all schools can provide in-person instruction" had changed to "all schools have options to provide in-person instruction." The guidance also included two other inputs from AFT, allowing for school closures based on high levels of community transmission and remote-work options for certain teachers based on their risk of contracting or spreading COVID-19.

Weingarten praised the guidelines on the same day the CDC released them. "For the first time since the start of this pandemic, we have a rigorous road map, based on science, that our members can use to fight for a safe reopening," she said in a news release. She added that "this set of safeguards should have been done 10 months ago," and blamed the Trump administration for having "meddled with the facts and stoked mass chaos and confusion."[26]

Corey DeAngelis, a senior fellow at the American Federation for Children, condemned Biden's attempts to take credit for reopening schools. "Biden should rename himself the gaslighter-in-chief," DeAngelis told *The Daily Signal* in February 2023.

> Teachers' unions—who own Democratic politicians—held children's education hostage to secure multibillion-dollar ransom payments from taxpayers. And it

---

26 "AFT's Weingarten on CDC's Schools Reopening Guidelines." American Federation of Teachers press release. February 12, 2021. https://www.aft. org/press-release/afts-weingarten-cdcs-schools-reopening-guidelines Accessed March 22, 2024.

worked for them. The federal government allocated about $190 billion in so-called COVID relief to K-12 schools since March 2020. The push to keep schools closed was always more about politics and power than safety and the needs of children. Parents aren't dumb. They'll never forget how teachers' unions hurt their children by fighting to keep schools closed for so long.[27]

Indeed, federal funding for schools increased substantially under Biden. The Elementary and Secondary School Emergency Relief Fund, set aside to help schools address the impact of the COVID-19 pandemic, began under Trump but ballooned under Biden. On March 27, 2020, Congress passed the Coronavirus Aid Relief and Economic Security (CARES) Act, setting aside $13.2 billion for the fund. On December 27, 2020, Trump signed the Coronavirus Response Relief and Supplemental Appropriations Act, adding $54.3 billion for the fund. President Biden signed the American Rescue Plan Act into law on March 11, 2021, more than doubling the amount for the fund by adding $122 billion, bringing the total to approximately $200 billion. The window for the use of these funds does not close until September 30, 2024.[28]

Generational Learning Loss

The results are in: "remote learning" wreaked havoc on American children.

Eighth grade students' math scores dropped eight points from 2019 to 2022, according to The National Assessment of Educational Progress, a measure of student achievement released by the Education Department. A mere 26 percent of eighth grad-

27 Kinnett, Tony. "FACT CHECK: Biden Touts Reopening of Schools After COVID-19, but Republicans Were a Year Ahead of Him." *The Daily Signal.* February 7, 2023. https://www.dailysignal.com/2023/02/07/fact-check-biden-touts-re opening-schools-covid-19republicans-were-yearhim/ Accessed March 22, 2024.

28 "Elementary and Secondary School Emergency Relief Fund." Office of Elementary & Secondary Education, U.S. Department of Education. https://oese.ed.gov/offices/education-stabilization-fund/elementary-second ary-school-emergency-relief-fund/ Accessed April 15, 2024.

ers performed math at grade level in 2022, down from 33 percent in 2019. Fourth graders saw a five-point decline, from 41 percent down to 36 percent proficient.

Reading scores also plummeted. Only 33 percent of fourth graders could read at grade level in 2022, down from 35 percent in 2019. Less than a third of eighth graders (31 percent) could read proficiently, down from 34 percent in 2019.

Catholic schools, however, did not suffer these declines, likely because fewer of them remained closed.[29]

A 2024 *New York Times* analysis of NAEP data found that

> …students in districts that were remote or hybrid the longest—at least 90 percent of the 2020–21 school year—still had almost double the ground to make up compared with students in districts that allowed students back for most of the year…. As districts shifted toward in-person learning as the year went on, students that were offered a hybrid schedule (a few hours or days a week in person, with the rest online) did better, on average, than those in places where school was fully remote, but worse than those in places that had school fully in person.[30]

Ron DeSantis, the Republican governor of Florida, released on June 11, 2020, recommendations to open up schools at full capacity for the start of the traditional 2020-21 school year.[31]

---

29   Burke, Lindsey. "New NAEP Test Scores Are a Disaster. Blame Teachers Unions." *The Daily Signal.* October 24, 2022. https://www.dailysignal. com/2022/10/24/new-naep-test-scores-are-a-disaster-blame-teachers-unions/ Accessed April 15, 2024.

30   Mervosh, Sarah, Claire Cain Miller, and Francesca Paris. "What the Data Says About Pandemic School Closures, Four Years Later." *The New York Times.* March 18, 2024. https://www.nytimes.com/2024/03/18/upshot/pandemic-school-closures-data.html Accessed March 22, 2024.

31   "Governor Ron DeSantis Announces Recommendations to Safely Reopen Florida's Education System." Governor Ron DeSantis news release. June 11, 2020. https://www.flgov.com/2020/06/11/governor-ron-desantis-announces-recommendations-to-safely-reopen-floridas-education-system/ Accessed March 22, 2024.

AFT's Pushback

The AFT has pushed back on claims that it had "uncommon access" to the CDC guidelines for reopening, noting that other organizations also had access to the document before it was published. In October 2023, the AFT accused the Republican-majority House Select Subcommittee on the Coronavirus Pandemic of twisting the facts to "demonize and scapegoat educators and their unions—including most notably, the AFT and its president Randi Weingarten." AFT noted that other organizations also collaborated with the CDC on the guidelines and claimed that AFT's suggested edits were minor. Yet the AFT report did not contest the teachers' union's efforts to delay school reopening.[32]

AFT has separately cited its April 2020 school reopening plan as evidence that the union preferred to reopen schools.

However, that document undercuts AFT's argument. The April 2020 plan actually reveals an attempt to milk the pandemic for political gain, as it ties reopening schools to many left-wing priorities that are not directly related to education or safety. This reflects the strategy of holding kids hostage to win woke concessions.

"COVID-19 has exacerbated the deep inequalities in our society and underscored the need for additional public investments to combat this inequity," the document states. "As we face growing recessionary forces, we can't simply limp out of this crisis or revert to a status quo. We need a renewed sense of national urgency to reimagine a better America and a pathway to a better life for all." It also calls for wide-ranging federal spending in the economy and "a progressive economic agenda," ignoring deficits. "We are trying to both save lives and ensure the quality and dignity of those lives. It is completely appropriate to ask our future selves to help pay for that."

---

32 *In Search of Scapegoats: The GOP's Failed Scheme to Blame the American Federation of Teachers for School Closures During the Pandemic.* American Federation of Teachers. October 10, 2023. https://www.aft.org/sites/default/files/media/documents/2023/AFT_Report_on_Scapegoats_and_School_Closures.pdf Accessed March 22, 2024.

Finally, the document frames its recommendations in an extremely hostile manner toward the then-president. It urges Trump to "cease using the power of the presidency, his public press conferences and his Twitter account to endanger the lives of working people." This "recommendation" suggests it is less a roadmap to reopening than an attempt to set a political agenda.[33]

Weingarten claimed that AFT "always advocated for safe reopening of schools." Yet X (the social media platform formerly known as Twitter) added a "community note" to her post, noting that Weingarten had condemned the Trump administration's guidelines for reopening schools by the fall of 2020 as "reckless," "callous," and "cruel."[34]

"Randi Weingarten *desperately* wants to rewrite history," Neily, the Parents Defending Education president, posted in response to Weingarten's claim. "I would too if I was responsible for locking kids out of the classroom after I forced the federal government to delay the full reopening of schools."

THE STUDENT LOAN BAILOUT

The American Federation of Teachers has long championed various forms of student loan bailouts. In a May 2023 report, AFT took credit for President Biden's attempt to zero out a great deal of student debt.[35] The report explains how AFT sued former Education Secretary Betsy DeVos for allegedly mismanaging the Public Student

---

33 "A Plan to Safely Reopen America's Schools and Communities." American Federation of Teachers. https://www.aft.org/sites/default/files/media/2020/covid19_reopen-america-schools.pdf Accessed April 15, 2024.

34 Tietz, Kendall. "Randi Weingarten gets slapped with another fact check for claiming she 'always' supported reopening schools." Fox News. October 19, 2023. https://www.foxnews.com/media/randi-weingarten-gets-slapped-fact-check-claiming-supported-reopening-schools Accessed April 15, 2024.

35 *AFT's Fight For Student Loan Debt Forgiveness.* American Federation of Teachers. May 2023. https://www.aft.org/sites/default/files/media/documents/2023/pslf_report_may2023.pdf Accessed April 12, 2024.

Loan Forgiveness (PSLF) program that President George W. Bush signed into law in 2007. The Biden administration settled the lawsuit, granting a student loan bailout that the AFT report estimates will expunge about $19 billion overall for more than 260,000 government and nonprofit workers. This seems an echo of the "sue-and-settle" strategy I will discuss in Chapter 4.

The report also boasts about AFT assembling another coalition "to persuade President Biden to deliver on a different campaign promise." hailing Biden's August 2022 student loan forgiveness plan. In that month, Biden promised to cancel up to $20,000 in student loan debt for borrowers who qualified for Pell Grants when they were college students, up to $10,000 for every borrower with an income under $125,000 ($250,000 for households). AFT's report notes that the student loan bailout scheme faced court challenges, which AFT attributed to "right-wing politicians and dark-money groups" making "common cause with Trump-appointed judges to shut down this effort."

In order to justify the bailout, the Department of Education cited the post-9/11 HEROES Act of 2003, which enables the Education secretary to allow military troops to delay their student debt obligations during national emergencies. The Supreme Court disagreed. Writing for a 6–3 majority, Chief Justice John Roberts wrote that "the HEROES Act provides no authorization for the [Education] secretary's plan even when examined using the ordinary tools of statutory interpretation—let alone 'clear congressional authorization' for such a program."[36]

The AFT report concludes with a promise that "the national union led by AFT President Randi Weingarten will continue to fiercely advocate on behalf of all student borrowers, not just those eligible for PSLF" (the program AFT sued DeVos over).

---

36 Aschieris, Samantha. "BREAKING: Supreme Court Strikes Down Biden's Student Loan 'Forgiveness' Plan." *The Daily Signal.* June 30, 2023. https://www.dailysignal.com/2023/06/30/breaking-supreme-court-strikes-down-bidens-student-loan-forgiveness-plan/ Accessed April 12, 2024.

In April 2024, Biden announced that his administration would cancel $7.4 billion in student loans for 277,000 borrowers, claiming that the latest move helps borrowers enrolled in the Saving on a Valuable Education (SAVE) repayment plan, as well as those in Income-Driven Repayment or Public Service Loan Forgiveness plans. The program brings the total amount of loan "forgiveness" under Biden to $153 billion, impacting 4.3 million Americans, according to the White House.[37]

Republican attorneys general, representing eighteen states, filed two lawsuits to block the latest bailout attempt.[38]

Despite this, on May 23, the White House announced it had approved $7.7 billion in more bailouts for 160,500 borrowers. This brought the total to $167 billion in student loans for 4.75 million people, representing one in ten student loan borrowers.[39]

It seems the administration is intent on finding new ways to give borrowers handouts, even though many Americans have already paid off their loans or never took out loans in the first place. Critics have suggested Biden is merely using student loan "forgiveness" as an election tool to appeal to young voters, though the AFT clearly has a role in this effort, as well.

---

37 "President Joe Biden Announces $7.4 Billion in Student Debt Cancellation for 277,000 More Americans, Pursuing Every Path Available to Cancel Student Debt." White House Briefing Room. April 12, 2024. https://www.whitehouse.gov/briefing-room/statements-releases/2024/04/12/president-joe-biden-announces-7-4-billion-in-student-debt-cancellation-for-277000-more-americans-pursuing-every-path-available-to-cancel-student-debt/ Accessed April 12, 2024.

38 Binkley, Collin. "More Republican states sue to block Biden's student loan repayment plan." *The Associated Press.* April 9, 2024. https://apnews.com/article/student-debt-cancellation-college-forgiveness-f94b9706bd-395b32e44d4d1b3f6ff051 Accessed May 20, 2024.

39 Picchi, Aimee. "Biden administration cancels $7.7 billion in student debt for 160,500 people. Here's who qualifies." CBS News. May 23, 2024. https://www.cbsnews.com/news/student-loan-forgiveness-7-7-billion-heres-who-qualifies-biden/ Accessed May 28, 2024.

The Vices of 'Forgiveness'

It sounds noble to forgive student loan debt. After all, many Americans borrow tremendous amounts of money to pursue a college degree in the hope of a better career, but then either drop out or realize that their career did not require the degree they pursued. Some Americans must pay off thousands in debt, without even getting a degree, and even those who find a good job after college often spend years getting out of the hole—college tuition has increased faster than inflation, and students struggle to keep up.

Yet "forgiving" student loan debt will only lead colleges to increase tuition further. Since the 1991–92 academic year, total federal aid (including student loans and grants) increased 295 percent, and colleges and universities have more than doubled their tuition and fees in inflation-adjusted terms.[40]

Ultimately, the forgiveness of student loans amounts to a bailout for a select few of those who went to college, that comes at the expense of the entire economy. Forgiving student loans enables colleges and universities to charge more for tuition, due to the prospect of later bailouts. The one-time bailout helps people who have loans at the moment, but it does not help those who have already paid off their loans or those who are about to take out new loans. It encourages recklessly taking out loans that the borrower does not plan to pay back.

Ultimately, student loan forgiveness amounts to a bailout helping some borrowers at the expense of others, but fundamentally helping to prop up a system that Americans increasingly distrust.

As recently as 2015, more than half (57 percent) of Americans told Gallup they had "a great deal of" confidence or "quite a lot" of confidence in higher education. By 2018, that number dropped to 48 percent, and it plummeted to 36 percent in 2023. Respondents

---

40 "Trends in Student Aid 2021." The College Board. October 2021. https:// research.collegeboard.org/media/pdf/trends-student-aid-presentation-2021. pdf Accessed April 16, 2024. p. 2. "Trends in College Pricing 2021." The College Board. October 2021. https://research.collegeboard.org/media/pdf/ trends-college-pricing-presentation-2021.pdf Accessed April 16, 2024. p. 6.

who identified as Republican shifted the fastest, from 56 percent in 2015 to 19 percent in 2023. Self-described Independents also lost faith in higher ed, decreasing from 48 percent expressing high confidence to only 32 percent doing so. Self-described Democrats have proven steadier, with 59 percent of them still expressing faith in higher education in 2023.[41]

The leftward tilt of universities helps explain why Republicans—previously more likely to express faith in higher education than Independents—have quickly grown disillusioned with colleges and universities.

The student loan bailout, by propping up the higher education system amid strong political headwinds, insulates the increasingly radical university bureaucracy. It alleviates the pressure for colleges and universities to change.

A LASTING IMPACT

These unions have impacted concrete federal policy under Biden, but their funding for other left-wing groups and their influence in the administrative state make them a long-term asset for the Woketopus. The way they funnel teachers' paychecks into propping up woke causes is perverse, and it helps explain how the Left's influence campaign operates.

Expect more such advocacy from the AFT and the NEA, regardless of the White House's occupant.

---

41   Brenan, Megan. "Americans' Confidence in Higher Education Down Sharply." Gallup. July 11, 2023. https://news.gallup.com/poll/508352/americans-confidence-higher-education-down-sharply.aspx Accessed May 20, 2024.

3

BIG LABOR'S FUNDING RACKET

While most Americans work a traditional nine-to-five job, more and more of us are finding ways to work more flexibly. Some of us need to keep our own hours to care for family, or we want to work for multiple clients, or we just need extra income for a season, so taking a "contractor" role makes the most sense.

The Woketopus doesn't want us to have that option. You see, when Americans work for themselves, only contracting with employers, a jealous middleman—organized labor—is cut out of the action. The Woketopus wants to insert unions—or quasi-union equivalents like the National Domestic Workers Alliance—into every workplace, and if you work for yourself, you can't unionize.

As soon as these unions get a foothold, they'll put down roots, and they'll send a portion of your union dues to their cronies in the Democratic Party and the other parts of the Woketopus. That's why bureaucrats in California and Washington, D.C., have developed new rules to limit independent contracting, and the Woketopus has its fingerprints all over this policy.

The Woketopus has also subverted the Department of Labor to promote union-funded propaganda, so Americans don't think to ask too many inconvenient questions. Meanwhile, the Department of Labor engages in a form of election denial by rejecting the results of worker votes when they choose not to unionize.

President Biden has abetted these efforts, but the Woketopus' pro-union tentacles in the administrative state are unlikely to be severed even when he ultimately leaves office.

BIDEN'S PRO-UNION BIAS

On the eve of the 2020 presidential election, Biden promised "to be the most pro-union president you've ever seen."[1] The president has indeed promoted the interests of organized labor in government policy, arguably beyond the purview of his office and in a way that strengthens Big Labor's ties to the administrative state. He has even framed the U.S. government's role as not simply applying the law evenly, to ensure that workers who want to join unions may do so, but as *actively promoting* unions.

"Since 1935, when the National Labor Relations Act was enacted, the policy of the federal government has been to *encourage* worker organizing and collective bargaining, not to merely allow or tolerate them," he stated about his executive order creating the White House Task Force on Worker Organizing and Empowerment (emphasis original).[2]

In this statement, Biden twisted history and the law. The National Labor Relations Act actually states:

> It is hereby declared to be the policy of the United States to eliminate the causes of certain substantial obstructions to the free flow of commerce and to mit-

---

1   Associated Press 2020 presidential election live blog. November 3, 2020. https://apnews.com/article/election-2020-donald-trump-virus-outbreak-district-of-columbia-elections-3f42f2ddb730a8dff916b54be74672a0 Accessed April 2, 2024.

2   "FACT SHEET: Executive Order Establishing the White House Task Force on Worker Organizing and Empowerment." White House Briefing Room. April 26, 2021. https://www.whitehouse.gov/briefing-room/statements-releases/2021/04/26/fact-sheet-executive-order-establishing-the-white-house-task-force-on-worker-organizing-and-empowerment/ Accessed April 17, 2024.

igate and eliminate these obstructions when they have occurred by encouraging the practice and procedure of collective bargaining and by protecting the exercise by workers of full freedom of association, self-organization, and designation of representatives of their own choosing.[3]

These "obstructions" to commerce refer to strikes, protests, riots, or other things that prevent business from taking place. In other words, the National Labor Relations Act aimed to protect workers' freedom of association *and* to prevent disruptive strikes by safeguarding a process by which workers can organize and engage with management—not to entrench unions with or without worker support.[4]

Senator Robert F. Wagner (D-NY), the primary author of the act, declared that the government would be neutral on unions. He said in a 1935 radio address, "The malicious falsehood has been widely circulated that the measure was designed to force men into unions, although the text provides in simple English prose that workers shall be absolutely free to belong to or refrain from belonging to any organization."

DARK MONEY FUNDING

The perverse system of directing union dues to prop up the Left and the Democratic Party is not unique to teachers' unions like the AFT and NEA. Established labor unions also prop up the Left's dark money network, using their members' dues to bankroll causes those members may or may not support.

---

3   29 U.S. Code Section 151. https://www.law.cornell.edu/uscode/text/29/151 Accessed via Cornell Law School's Legal Information Institute, May 20, 2024.

4   Higgins, Sean. "When Joe Biden Talks About Worker Choice, He Means Only 1 Choice." *Reason.* April 27, 2021. https://reason.com/2021/04/27/when-joe-biden-talks-about-worker-choice-he-means-only-1-choice/ Accessed April 17, 2024.

The American Federation of Labor-Congress of Industrial Organizations, better known as the AFL-CIO, has contributed:

- $410,000 to Sixteen Thirty Fund from 2014 to 2017 (Arabella)
- $250,000 to New Venture Fund from 2010 to 2017 (Arabella)
- $468,000 to Tides Advocacy from 2021 to 2023
- $200,000 to the Tides Center in 2011
- $100,000 to the Tides Foundation in 2015

It has also contributed to the Center for American Progress, Demos, the Economic Policy Institute ($750,000 from 2014 to 2023), and the Lawyers' Committee for Civil Rights Under Law.[5]

Like the NEA and AFT, the AFL-CIO must file a form LM-2 with the Department of Labor. That form, which is public, shows how much money the union has spent on various expenses. Between July 1, 2022, and June 30, 2023, the AFL-CIO spent only 13.9 percent of its members' dues on "representational activities"—the typical employer-employee bargaining that forms the main purpose of a union—while spending 30.5 percent of its funds on overhead, administration, and benefits.

The AFL-CIO directed $33.6 million to "political activities and lobbying," representing 22.5 percent of the national union's proportion of members' dues, and another $1.4 million to "contributions, gifts, and grants"—just under 1 percent of its cut of members' dues. This may represent a small fraction of its spending, but the AFL-CIO's "charitable giving" supports efforts to restrict oil and gas and the campaign to turn the federal government into a get-out-the-vote machine (see Chapters 4 and 8).

Funneling money through Tides and Arabella allows the AFL-CIO to cloak exactly which woke projects its members' dues are supporting—but those dues could be propping up any of the major efforts I'll expose in this book.

---

5   OLMS search results, accessed May 20, 2024.

Similarly, the Service Employees International Union, better known as SEIU, has sent:

- $100,000 to Hopewell Fund in 2023 (Arabella)
- $1.6 million to New Venture Fund from 2013 to 2022 (Arabella)
- $5.2 million to Sixteen Thirty Fund from 2013 to 2023 (Arabella)
- $105,500 to the Tides Center in 2021
- $1.1 million to the Tides Advocacy Fund from 2011 to 2019
- $1.8 million to the Tides Foundation from 2012 to 2016

It has also funded the Center for American Progress and its action fund ($2.6 million to the action fund from 2016 to 2023), Demos, failed Georgia gubernatorial Democratic candidate Stacey Abrams's Fair Fight PAC (sending it $615,000 in 2020 and 2021), and Planned Parenthood Federation and its advocacy fund.[6]

This means SEIU members are unwittingly funding efforts to oppose reliable sources of energy, efforts to undermine election integrity, and whichever additional Arabella and Tides projects that SEIU leaders support (but may not want to reveal to their members).

The SEIU owns Amalgamated Bank, a financial institution dedicated to unions and other woke causes. Amalgamated Bank launched a donor-advised fund called the Amalgamated Charitable Foundation in 2017.

Amalgamated Charitable has directed funds to the Left's dark money network. It sent:

- $2.4 million to New Venture Fund between 2020 and 2022 (Arabella)[7]
- $1.3 million to Hopewell Fund between 2020 and 2022 (Arabella)[8]

---

6   OLMS search results, accessed May 20, 2024.
7   The precise figure is $2,433,500. "Amalgamated Charitable Foundation," Form 990, Schedule I for 2020–2022 https://projects.propublica.org/nonprofits/organizations/821517696.
8   "Amalgamated Charitable Foundation," Form 990, Schedule I for 2020–2022.

- $484,000 to Windward Fund between 2020 and 2022 (Arabella)[9]
- $1.9 million to the Proteus Fund between 2020 and 2022[10]
- $2.9 million to the Tides Center between 2020 and 2022[11]
- $9.2 million to the Tides Foundation between 2020 and 2022[12]
- $194,248 to Tides Advocacy between 2020 and 2021[13]

It also contributed to the Southern Poverty Law Center, the National Domestic Workers Alliance, Demos, the Center for American Progress, Planned Parenthood, and other groups.

In 2019, Amalgamated Charitable launched a campaign pressuring philanthropic organizations to blacklist the mainstream conservative and Christian organizations that the Southern Poverty Law Center had branded "hate groups." The "Hate Is Not Charitable" campaign relies upon a discredited "hate map" that compares conservative groups to the Ku Klux Klan (more on this in Chapter 6). The foundation said it had enlisted eighty-seven organizations in its campaign, including the Tides Foundation and the Proteus Fund, among others.[14]

Thus, the SEIU-connected Amalgamated Charitable is not just helping to bankroll the Left's influence campaign, but attempting to starve conservative nonprofits of funding, as well, in the name of fighting "hate."

---

9   "Amalgamated Charitable Foundation," Form 990, Schedule I for 2020–2022.

10 The precise figure is $1,943,980. "Amalgamated Charitable Foundation," Form 990, Schedule I for 2020–2022.

11 The precise figure is $2,877,567. "Amalgamated Charitable Foundation," Form 990, Schedule I for 2020–2022.

12 The precise figure is $9,164,069. "Amalgamated Charitable Foundation," Form 990, Schedule I for 2020–2022.

13 "Amalgamated Charitable Foundation," Form 990, Schedule I for 2020–2021.

14 "Hate Is Not Charitable." Amalgamated Foundation. March 19, 2019. https://www.amalgamatedfoundation.org/insights-and-initiatives/hate-is-not-charitable Accessed May 30, 2024.

A third large union, the American Federation of State, County, and Municipal Employees, better known as AFSCME, has also contributed:

- $207,500 to New Venture Fund from 2013 to 2016 (Arabella)
- $1.4 million to Sixteen Thirty Fund from 2012 to 2022 (Arabella)
- $125,000 to the Tides Foundation between 2011 and 2020
- $100,000 to the Tides Center in 2010

It also bankrolled the Center for American Progress ($1.5 million between 2014 and 2023), Demos, the Economic Policy Institute ($729,000 between 2014 and 2023), Fair Fight PAC ($1.4 million between 2019 and 2020), and Planned Parenthood.[15]

In 1936, AFSCME received a separate charter from the AFL before it united with the CIO in 1955. AFSCME remains part of the AFL-CIO's labor federation, which means its members are also unwittingly funding many left-wing projects to influence the administrative state, some of which the AFSCME also cloaks by sending funds through Arabella and Tides.

It is no secret that these unions heavily contribute to Democrats and have done so for a long time, even though some of their members sent money to Trump's campaign in 2020—which shows that these unions do not fully represent their members.

According to Open Secrets, the AFL-CIO spent $5.5 million supporting Democrats and $1.15 million opposing Republicans in the 2020 election cycle.[16] The union spent $4.36 million supporting Biden and $540,643 opposing Trump.[17] AFL-CIO employees con-

---

15 OLMS search results accessed May 20, 2024.
16 AFL-CIO profile. "Independent Expenditures." Open Secrets. https://www.opensecrets.org/orgs/afl-cio/summary?topnumcycle=2020&toprecip-cycle=2024&contribcycle=2024&lobcycle=2024&id=D000000088&out-spendcycle=2020 Accessed April 16, 2024.
17 AFL-CIO profile. "AFL-CIO Recipients, 2020. Targeted Candidates." Open Secrets. https://www.opensecrets.org/outside-spending/detail/2020?cmte=A-FL-CIO&tab=targeted_candidates Accessed April 16, 2024.

tributed $42,985 to Biden and $558 to Trump.[18] The SEIU spent $13.4 million supporting Democrats in 2020 and $2.54 million opposing Republicans, but it also spent a paltry $207,811 against Democrats and $64 for Republicans that year.[19] SEIU employees contributed $14,429 to Biden's campaign and none to Trump's. The AFSCME spent $15.5 million against Republicans and $4.7 million for Democrats in 2020.[20] AFSCME employees contributed $52,434 to Biden and a mere $1,146 to Trump.[21]

WHITE HOUSE ACCESS

The heads of these three unions have also enjoyed close access to the Biden White House.

Elizabeth H. Shuler, the AFL-CIO president, has visited the White House at least twenty-eight times under Biden. She and her father had a personal meeting with President Biden, and she twice met one-on-one with Jason Miller, deputy director for management at the Office of Management and Budget, an influential policy hub at the White House. The AFL-CIO's secretary-treasurer, Frederick D. Redmond, has visited the White House at least three times.[22]

April D. Verrett, elected SEIU president in May 2024, has had at least twelve meetings at the White House. On November 17, 2021, she brought to the White House June Barrett, who had previously served as a Dorothy Bolden Fellow with the We Dream in Black program at the National Domestic Workers Alliance (more

---

18 Open Secrets "AFL-CIO" profile, "Recipients," all recipients.

19 Service Employees International Union profile, "Independent Expenditures." Open Secrets. https://www.opensecrets.org/orgs/service-employees-international-union/summary?topnumcycle=A&toprecipcycle=2024&contribcycle=2024&lobcycle=2024&id=D000000077&outspendcycle=2020 Accessed April 16, 2024.

20 American Federation of State, County & Municipal Employees profile. "Independent Expenditures." Open Secrets. https://www.opensecrets.org/orgs/american-federation-of-state-cnty-munic-employees/summary?topnumcycle=A&toprecipcycle=2024&contribcycle=2024&lobcycle=2024&id=D000000061&outspendcycle=2020 Accessed April 16, 2024.

21 Ibid. "Recipients" for 2020.

22 White House Visitor Logs.

about this group below).[23] Another of Verrett's White House meetings included Ai-Jen Poo, the NDWA president.[24]

Mary Kay Henry, the SEIU's immediate past president, has had at least eight meetings at the White House, including one with Neera Tanden, former president of the Center for American Progress and now Director of the U.S. Domestic Policy Council in the White House.

AFSCME President Lee A. Saunders had at least seven meetings at the White House. On July 9, 2021, he attended a meeting with bureaucrats at the Federal Trade Commission, the Federal Communications Commission, the Consumer Financial Protection Bureau, and other union leaders, including NEA President Becky Pringle.[25] That meeting seems related to a Biden executive order on trade involving those same agencies, which was issued that same day.[26]

UNION LEADERS TAKE THE REINS AT DOL

Biden has consistently picked union leaders to head the Department of Labor, and one of them launched the rule cracking down on independent contractors.

He first nominated Marty Walsh, who led the Boston Building Trades Council from 2011 to 2013 before becoming Boston's mayor in 2014. Walsh served on the leadership of the C40 Cities Climate Leadership Group and supported Boston's status as a sanctuary city, establishing his climate-alarmist and pro-open borders

---

23 "June Barrett." Dorothy Bolden Fellowship Years: 2019–2021. National Domestic Workers Alliance. https://www.domesticworkers. org/programs-and-campaigns/organizing-domestic-workers-and-developing-leaders/developing-leaders/dorothy-bolden-fellows/ june-barrett/ Accessed April 17, 2024.

24 White House Visitor Logs.

25 White House Visitor Logs.

26 "Executive Order on Promoting Competition in the American Economy." White House Briefing Room. July 9, 2021. https://www.whitehouse.gov/ briefing-room/presidential-actions/2021/07/09/executive-order-on-promoting-competition-in-the-american-economy/ Accessed April 17, 2024.

bona fides. When Biden announced the appointment, he celebrated that Walsh, if confirmed, would become "the first union member to serve in this role in nearly half a century."[27]

Walsh left his role as secretary of Labor in March 2023 to become executive director of the National Hockey League Players' Association.[28] Biden nominated him to serve as governor of the U.S. Postal Service in February 2024.[29]

A month after he announced Walsh, Biden tapped Julie Su to serve as Walsh's number two—the deputy secretary of labor.

Su launched her career as the lead attorney for the seventy-two Thai nationals who had been reduced to slavery in a makeshift garment factory in the 1990s. That El Monte Thai garment slavery case catapulted her to prominence. She later served as California Labor Commissioner from 2011 to 2018, under Democratic Governor Jerry Brown, and then led the state's Department of Labor under Democratic Governor Gavin Newsom from 2019 to 2021.

Biden nominated Su, then deputy secretary of Labor, to replace Walsh as Labor secretary on February 28, 2023.[30] The Senate Committee on Health, Education, Labor, and Pensions (HELP) advanced her nomination on a party-line vote in April, despite Su's refusal to sit for an interview with Senate Republican staff.

27 Swasey, Benjamin. "Biden Taps Boston Mayor Marty Walsh As Labor Secretary." NPR. January 7, 2021. https://www.npr.org/sections/biden-transition-updates/2021/01/07/954500709/biden-to-tap-boston-mayor-marty-walsh-as-labor-secretary Accessed April 16, 2024.

28 Whyno, Stephen. "Why Marty Walsh left the Biden administration to run the NHL players' union." *The Associated Press.* June 18, 2023. https://apnews.com/article/marty-walsh-biden-administration-nhlpa-02ada79e-2a6771991433edbbcf8fa0d1 Accessed April 2, 2024.

29 "President Biden Announces Key Nominees." White House Briefing Room. February 29, 2024. https://www.whitehouse.gov/briefing-room/statements-releases/2024/02/29/president-biden-announces-key-nominees-67/ Accessed April 16, 2024.

30 "President Biden Nominates Julie Su for Secretary of the Department of Labor." White House Briefing Room. February 28, 2023. https://www.whitehouse.gov/briefing-room/statements-releases/2023/02/28/president-biden-nominates-julie-su-for-secretary-of-the-department-of-labor/ Accessed April 2, 2024.

The Senate narrowly voted to confirm Su to her position as assistant Labor secretary in July 2021. Yet when Biden nominated her to lead the Labor Department two years later, Senator Joe Manchin (D-WV) announced he would oppose her nomination.[31] Senate Majority Leader Chuck Schumer (D-NY) has yet to bring her confirmation to a vote on the Senate floor. Nevertheless, Su has been effectively carrying out the position as *acting* secretary of Labor since March 2023.

"I believe the person leading the U.S. Department of Labor should have the experience to collaboratively lead both labor and industry to force compromises acceptable to both parties," Manchin said in a statement about his opposition to Su. "While her credentials and qualifications are impressive, I have genuine concerns that Julie Su's more progressive background prevents her from doing this and for that reason I cannot support her nomination to serve as secretary of Labor."[32]

THE SORDID HISTORY OF JULIE SU

Julie Su's history sent up at least three red flags: a woke opposition to the enforcement of immigration law, a failure to crack down on fraud and abuse, and support for policies that empower labor unions at the expense of working Americans.

Senate Republicans pointed out a memo Su sent to staff while serving as California Labor commissioner,[33] in which Su directed

---

31   Roll Call Vote 117th Congress—1st Session On the Nomination (Confirmation: Julie A. Su, of California, to be Deputy Secretary of Labor). July 13, 2021. https://www.senate.gov/legislative/LIS/roll_call_votes/vote1171/vote_117_1_00256.htm Accessed April 16, 2024.

32   "Manchin Opposes Julie Su For U.S. Secretary of Labor." News release. Joe Manchin website. July 13, 2023. https://www.manchin.senate.gov/newsroom/press-releases/manchin-opposes-julie-su-for-us-secretary-of-labor Accessed April 16, 2024.

33   Braun, Mike, Mitch McConnell, and thirty-one other senators to President Joe Biden. June 20, 2023. https://www.fischer.senate.gov/public/_cache/files/38d1dc9e-dc5b-42c9-967a-4dc2d6a1b84c/call-on-president-biden-to-withdraw-julie-su-nomination-for-labor-secretary.pdf Accessed April 2, 2024.

staff not to help U.S. Customs and Immigration Enforcement agents if they come to the California Labor Commission offices. She told staff to demand ICE agents leave or produce a warrant if they wish to search the offices, stating that it is her "general policy not to permit such interference," (that of enforcement of federal immigration law) "with our state law enforcement duties"—even though the Constitution specifies that federal law trumps state law.[34] Su proved evasive when senators asked for documentation about the ICE memo.

House Republicans also urged Biden to withdraw Su's nomination, citing a report that Su failed to prevent fraud in California's unemployment insurance system while she led the state's Labor and Workforce Development Agency. Su oversaw the Employment Development Department, presiding over the department while it paid $10.4 billion on claims it later determined may be fraudulent. A January 2021 report into the fraud blamed the department's decision to remove a basic safeguard against paying individuals with unconfirmed identities, saying this policy accounted for $1 billion of the $10.4 billion of fraudulent payments. The department later estimated the amount of the fraud to be $20 billion, and an analysis from Lexis Nexis Risk Solutions estimated a total fraud of $32.6 billion when considering other benefit programs the department administered.[35]

Su said the COVID-19 pandemic exposed flaws within California's unemployment insurance system, suggesting she was not responsible. "The U.I. system was like a house with a leaky roof," she said. "In good times, you could put a couple buckets under it and mostly ignore it. But in a storm...all of its weaknesses get revealed." [36]

34 Su, Julie. "Protocols: Responding to Federal Immigration Agents Who Attempt to Enter Labor Commissioner Offices." Staff Memorandum. California Department of Industrial Relations. July 7, 2017. https://www.help.senate.gov/imo/media/doc/julie_su_memo.pdf Accessed April 2, 2024.

35 Rep. Jason Smith, R-Mo., and twelve other representatives to President Joe Biden. April 6, 2023. https://edworkforce.house.gov/uploadedfiles/ds_su_letter_final.pdf Accessed April 2, 2024.

36 Kronenberg, Annie and Sara Cook. "Acting Labor Secretary Julie Su vows to remain in job even as confirmation prospects remain dim." *The Takeout* (podcast). CBS News. March 15, 2024. https://www.cbsnews.com/news/julie-su-labor-secretary-waits-for-confirmation-the-takeout/ Accessed April 2, 2024.

Most importantly, Republicans in both the House and the Senate faulted Su for crafting California's AB5, a law that forcibly reclassifies independent contractors in the state as W-2 employees, restricting the relationship between employers and employees. Su said she would support a similar policy as secretary of Labor, and she has carried out that threat (more on that later).[37]

"In the past three months since she was nominated to be secretary of Labor, Ms. Su has given senators no indication that her past positions and actions are not indicative of future positions and actions she would take as secretary," thirty-three Republican senators wrote in a letter to Biden, urging him to withdraw her nomination. "She has avoided answering questions whenever possible and she has refrained from providing distinct specificity to her answers when she has responded to inquiries."[38] But Biden has not rescinded Su's nomination, and she remains acting secretary of the Department of Labor, ignoring the Senate's role in confirming her.

Concerning AB5, Su declared, "I do not apologize for making sure that employees who deserve protections and the right to organize [are] covered under employee status."[39]

The Biden administration has trumpeted labor union support for Su's confirmation. "Julie Su has been a champion for labor, and labor is mobilizing in the way only we can," AFL-CIO spokesman Ray Zaccaro said.[40] "AFSCME members are behind Julie Su 100 percent," AFSCME posted on its website in February 2024. "We want the U.S. Senate to confirm Su—who has ably served as acting labor secretary since March 2023—to the position for good."[41]

---

37 Braun and McConnell.

38 Ibid.

39 Kronenberg.

40 "ICYMI: 'Unions Pour on Support' for Acting Secretary Julie Su." White House Briefing Room. April 22, 2023. https://www.whitehouse.gov/briefing-room/statements-releases/2023/04/22/icymi-unions-pour-on-support-for-acting-secretary-julie-su/ Accessed April 2, 2024.

41 "AFSCME to U.S. Senate: Confirm Julie Su as labor secretary." AFSCME website. February 28, 2024. https://www.afscme.org/blog/afscme-to-u-s-senate-confirm-julie-su-as-labor-secretary Accessed April 17, 2024.

Meanwhile, some business associations have continued to oppose her confirmation, citing policies Su had implemented. "No matter how many times she's renominated, Julie Su's record remains a huge red flag for our industry and any senator concerned about radical policies from California becoming federal law," American Trucking Associations President and CEO Chris Spear said in February 2024.

Spear highlighted a rule the Labor Department finalized under Su, which rewrites regulations about whether an employer can give someone work as a contractor without being forced to provide benefits available to employees (such as holidays, overtime pay, unemployment insurance, and more). "The independent contractor rule she just finalized as acting secretary undermines the livelihoods of 350,000 professional truck drivers across our country who choose to run their own small businesses, and she needs to answer for it," Spear stated. "A public hearing is warranted so that committee members can have the opportunity to question her on the impact of this destructive rule."[42]

THE INDEPENDENT CONTRACTOR RULE

Spear was far from the first to warn about Su's rules that restrict an employer's ability to hire independent contractors, and her policy sheds light on how government can tip the scale in favor of unions and against Americans' ability to work in innovative ways.

The Labor Department finalized an independent contractor rule on March 11, 2024. The rule created a complicated six-factor test to determine if an employee counted as an independent contractor under the Fair Labor Standards Act. "The ultimate inquiry is whether, as a matter of economic reality, the worker is economically dependent on the employer for work (and is thus an employee)

---

42 "ATA Reasserts Strong Opposition to Julie Su's Nomination." American Trucking Associations news release. February 27, 2024. https://www.truck-ing.org/news-insights/ata-reasserts-strong-opposition-julie-sus-nomination Accessed April 2, 2024.

or is in business for themselves (and is thus an independent contractor)," the rule states.[43]

The test seems not only complicated but subject to interpretation. One of the factors, for example, "opportunity for profit or loss depending on managerial skill," suggests that a contractor must be considered an employee if he or she cannot hire more people to do the work. The law firm Nixon Peabody notes that "a decision to work more hours or take more jobs when paid a fixed rate per hour or per job typically does not require the exercise of managerial skill that would be required for an independent contractor classification."[44] This interpretation excludes many contractors based on a factor many would consider irrelevant. Ultimately, this test inserts the federal government into the relationship between employer and employee, constraining Americans' ability to work more flexibly or to hire more flexible workers.

According to a December 2023 Upwork study, 64 million Americans performed freelance work in 2023, representing 38 percent of the U.S. workforce and contributing approximately $1.27 trillion in annual earnings to the U.S. economy.[45] As Rachel Greszler, a senior research fellow in workforce and public finance at The Heritage Foundation, explained, these contractors are more than just accountants and Uber drivers—they're IT consultants,

---

43 "Employee or Independent Contractor Classification Under Fair Labor Standards Act." Wage and Hour Division of the Department of Labor. January 10, 2024. https://www.federalregister.gov/documents/2024/01/10/2024-00067/employee-or-independent-contractor-classification-under-the-fair-labor-standards-act Accessed April 2, 2024.

44 Michaud, Shelagh and Jeffrey Gilbreth. "DOL narrows definition of 'independent contractor' under FLSA." Nixon Peabody. January 16, 2024. https://www.nixonpeabody.com/insights/alerts/2024/01/16/dol-narrows-definition-of-independent-contractor Accessed April 16, 2024.

45 "Upwork Study Finds 64 Million Americans Freelanced in 2023, Adding $1.27 Trillion to U.S. Economy." Upwork news release. December 12, 2023. https://investors.upwork.com/news-releases/news-release-details/upwork-study-finds-64-million-americans-freelanced-2023-adding Accessed April 3, 2024.

makeup artists, musicians, interpreters, fitness instructors, copy editors, and truck drivers.[46]

Currently, when workers are classified as employees, rather than contractors, they become entitled to a minimum wage, overtime pay, unemployment insurance, workers' compensation, and more. Su claims that "misclassifying employees and independent contractors is a serious issue that deprives workers of basic rights and protections. This rule will help protect workers, especially those facing the greatest risk of exploitation, by making sure they are classified properly and that they receive the wages they've earned."[47] Greszler notes, however, that rules restricting workers' ability to contract independently don't actually help their employment prospects. Employers seek to hire contractors in part because these jobs *don't* require benefits like health insurance. In turn, contractors seek out this work in part because they value the flexibility of having multiple clients and being able to find new work easily.

Americans can take a sneak peek at how this rule will impact the labor force by examining AB5's impacts in California. The prognosis is not good. California enacted AB5 in January 2020, but by August 2020 lawmakers had to pass a "cleanup bill" exempting many professions from the rules. Then, in November 2020, California voters passed Proposition 22, which exempted rideshare drivers with Uber and Lift from the onerous regulations.

Kim Kavin, a freelance writer, wrote about her experience with the law. "Freelancers never asked for relief from the ills that AB5 purports to cure—because we like our independence and the sys-

46   Greszler, Rachel. "64 Million Americans Risk Losing Work Under Biden Admin." *The Daily Signal.* February 1, 2024. https://www.dailysignal.com/2024/02/01/64-million-americans-risk-losing-work-under-biden-admin/ Accessed April 3, 2024

47   "US Department of Labor Announces Final Rule on Classifying Workers as Employees or Independent Contractors Under the Fair Labor Standards Act." Department of Labor news release. January 9, 2024. https://www.dol.gov/newsroom/releases/whd/whd20240109-1 Accessed April 2, 2024.

tem that has allowed us to live such creative and flexible lives," she wrote. "Many of us have family, schooling, health or other reasons for preferring to have total control of our schedules." She also noted that "the largest group of independent contractors in America is in the top quartile of earners," so "[m]ost of us aren't being exploited, and most of us aren't ride-share drivers. We are hardworking people who are trying to live the American Dream."[48]

The group Freelancers Against AB5 claims that the law has negatively impacted more than six hundred professions, and Americans for Tax Reform documents more than six hundred personal testimonials from workers hurt by the law. The Mercatus Center at George Mason University found in January 2024 that AB5 reduced self-employment by 10.5 percent on average for affected occupations, and overall employment in the Golden State dropped by 4.4 percent on average for affected occupations, without leading to a corresponding increase in traditional employment.[49]

If the Labor Department rule has a similar impact nationally, then it would cost 6.7 million U.S. workers their jobs.

Labor's Role in Passing AB5

If AB5 doesn't help contractors, why did the California Legislature pass it? Labor unions appear to be the culprits. The California Labor Federation, the Golden State's arm of the AFL-CIO, supported AB5 from the beginning. Art Pulaski, the federation's executive secretary-treasurer, explained why to *The Los Angeles Times* in September

---

48 Kavin, Kim. "California voters saved Uber and Lyft—and writers, artists and other independent workers." NBC News Opinion. November 5, 2020. https://www.nbcnews.com/think/opinion/california-voters-saved-uber-lyft-gig-economy-backing-prop-22-ncna1246680 Accessed April 2, 2024.

49 Palagashvili, Liya, Paola Suarez, Christopher M. Kaiser, and Vitor Melo. "Assessing the Impact of Worker Reclassification: Employment Outcomes Post-California AB5." The Mercatus Center at George Mason University. January 31, 2024. https://www.mercatus.org/research/working-papers/assessing-impact-worker-reclassification-employment-outcomes-post   Accessed April 2, 2024.

2019, as Governor Newsom signed the bill:[50] "We won't rest until all misclassified workers in California receive the basic protections they deserve, including the right to form or join a union."

Carmel Foster, a woman who testified in favor of AB5, later revealed that she was having an affair with Democratic Assemblyman Phil Ting at the time. Homeless at the time, she claimed Ting exploited her, connecting her with the California Labor Federation and the National Domestic Workers Alliance, which had supported the bill since February 2019.[51]. She stayed with a director of the California Domestic Workers Coalition, part of the National Domestic Workers Alliance,[52] which then compelled her to testify in favor of AB5. "These unions controlled my testimonies, got stories out of me, and then tossed me out," Foster told the (now defunct) news outlet *Communities Digital News*. "It was a payday for them, not to help domestic workers."[53]

"Assemblymember Ting never had any knowledge of or involvement in Ms. Foster's legislative activities," Miranda Nannette, communications director for assemblyman Ting, told me in remarks for this book. "He also did not sponsor AB 5, although he supported the legislation when it reached the Assembly Floor." Ting did not contradict reports of the affair.

---

50   Myers, John and Johana Bhuiyan and Margot Roosevelt. "Newsom signs bill rewriting California employment law, limiting use of independent contractors." *Los Angeles Times.* September 18, 2019. https://www.latimes.com/california/story/2019-09-18/gavin-newsom-signs-ab5-employees0independent-contractors-california Accessed April 3, 2024.

51   "FACT SHEET—AB 5 (Gonzalez)." California Labor Federation. February 2019. https://calaborfed.org/wp-content/uploads/2019/02/Factsheet-AB-5-Dynamex-LOBBY-DAY.final_-1.pdf Accessed April 3, 2024.

52   O'Connell, Jennifer Oliver. "Carmel Foster, the political pawn of Phil Ting, L. Gonzalez and the AB5 bill." *Communities Digital News.* June 24, 2020. Accessed via Internet Archive. https://web.archive.org/web/20200726215224/https://www.commdiginews.com/politics-2/carmel-foster-the-political-pawn-of-phil-ting-l-gonzalez-and-the-ab5-bill-130336/ Accessed April 3, 2024.

53   O'Connell, Jennifer Oliver. "Did CA Budget Chair Phil Ting use an extramarital affair to craft legislation?" *Communities Digital News.* June 19, 2020. Accessed via Internet Archive. https://web.archive.org/web/20200728195430/https://www.commdiginews.com/politics-2/did-ca-budget-chair-phil-ting-uses-extramarital-affair-to-craft-legislation-130185/ Accessed April 3, 2024.

The bill's lead sponsor admitted that beefing up unions was the main reason to support AB5. In September 2019, after California Democratic Assemblywoman Lorena Gonzalez introduced AB5, she wrote about the bill on X (then known as Twitter). "We won't accept employee misclassification or a third classification of employment," she wrote. "No sub-standard workers in CA," she added with the hashtag "#AB5ForAUnion." When a Twitter user asked, "What does your hashtag mean?" she replied, "It means we get AB5—then we organize workers into a union."[54]

In January 2022, Gonzalez announced she would resign her role in the California Assembly and join the California Labor Federation. She cashed in on her success in implementing the union's agenda, taking the reins as its executive secretary-treasurer in July 2022.[55]

Su Lets the Cat Out of the Bag

Su, the acting Labor secretary, likely revealed her true motivation behind the independent contractor rule when she celebrated the growth of union membership under Biden. "The Bureau of Labor Statistics reported an increase in union membership, with 139,000 more union members in 2023 than in 2022, meaning this country has 400,000 more union workers than we had in 2021," she said in a January 2024 statement. "The gains under the Biden-Harris administration underscore President Biden's commitment to being the most pro-worker, pro-union president in history."[56] She added:

---

54 X (formerly Twitter) thread between Lorena Gonzales (@LorenaSGonzalez) and (@mclanea). September 6, 2019. https://twitter.com/LorenaSGonzalez/status/1170162731137130496 Accessed April 3, 2024.

55 "Assemblywoman Lorena Gonzalez to Resign, Assume Union Leadership Role." NBC San Diego. January 3, 2022. https://www.nbcsandiego.com/news/politics/politically-speaking/assemblywoman-lorena-gonzalez-to-resign-assume-union-leadership-role/2830200/ Accessed April 3, 2024.

56 "Acting U.S. Secretary of Labor Julie Su Issues Statement on Annual Union Membership Data." U. S. Department of Labor news release. January 23, 2024. https://www.dol.gov/newsroom/releases/osec/osec20240123 Accessed April 17, 2024.

Unions have been under attack for decades, with unionbusting laws being passed in states across the country. But multiple states in recent years have rolled back some of these so-called "right-to-work" laws, recognizing the damage they can do to worker organizing. We also know that current federal law allows unionbusting to stifle workers exercising their rights, which is why the Biden-Harris administration continues to support passage of the Protecting the Right to Organize Act.

The Protecting the Right to Organize Act (also referred to as the "PRO Act")—a piece of Democratic legislation aimed at empowering unions—would not only overturn right-to-work laws in twenty-six states, but would also overturn the gig economy. It would eviscerate the franchising business model, which would impact roughly 750,000 franchise establishments across the country. More than three hundred types of businesses across the U.S. use a franchise model, where investors can run a small business using a format or system developed by a company and employ that company's name. The model extends far beyond fast-food restaurants to enterprises like car dealerships, gas stations, hotels, and gyms. Franchise businesses employ nearly 8 million workers.[57]

Right to work, the policy Su condemned, allows employees to opt out of joining a union or paying dues to a union as a condition of employment. Union advocates claim that such laws allow employees to be "freeloaders," gaining the benefits of collective bargaining without joining a union. Yet, as we've seen earlier in this chapter, unions often adopt divisive political stances that have nothing to do with the specifics of employee contracts. Considering the political slant of unions like the AFL-CIO, the SEIU, and the AFSCME, it seems workers might want another option.

---

57   Greszler, Rachel. "6 Ways a Union-Backed Bill Will Upend the Job Market." *The Daily Signal.* February 5, 2020. https://www.dailysignal.com/2020/02/05/6-ways-a-union-backed-bill-will-upend-the-jobs-market/ Accessed April 17, 2024.

In the pivotal case *Janus v. AFSCME* (2018), the Supreme Court ruled that government employees cannot lose their jobs for refusing to financially support a union. This decision struck down mandatory "agency fees" that unions required from workers who refused to become dues-paying members. The unions imposed these fees in part because they ostensibly went to support only "non-political" activities of the unions. Yet the supposedly non-political agency fees at AFSCME—the union the plaintiff Mark Janus was forced to financially support—went to promote Hillary Clinton, the Democratic nominee for president, at the union's 2016 convention. Janus's local union, AFSCME Council 31, spent $268,855 for "convention expense," taking this money from the funds gathered through "non-political" agency fees. The convention featured a lengthy "AFSCME FOR HILLARY" program, culminating with a speech from the candidate herself.

As Thomas Jefferson wrote in the Virginia Statute for Religious Freedom, "To compel a man to furnish contributions of money for the propagation of opinions which he disbelieves and *abhors*, is sinful and tyrannical."[58]

A WOKE AB5 UNION'S TIES IN THE BIDEN ADMINISTRATION

The National Domestic Workers Alliance (NDWA), one of the prominent quasi-unions behind AB5 in California, also carries sway among congressional Democrats and in the Biden administration. NDWA represents part of the "alt-labor" movement, where union-like groups organize workers in industries that fall outside the scope of traditional unions.[59] NDWA organizes domestic workers for

---

58 Jefferson, Thomas. "Virginia Statute for Religious Freedom." Monticello website. https://www.monticello.org/research-education/thomas-jefferson-encyclopedia/virginia-statute-religious-freedom/ Accessed April 17, 2024.

59 Eidelson, Josh. "Alt-Labor." *The American Prospect.* January 29, 2013. https://prospect.org/notebook/alt-labor/ Accessed May 21, 2024.

the purposes of a traditional union, without technically being a union itself.

NDWA has powerful allies in the Democratic Party and the administrative state, and has achieved many of its policy goals by working with Su, who has spoken at NDWA events. NDWA played a large role in AB5 in California, and its ties to Su suggest it may have had a hand in the Labor Department rule, as well.

On March 30, 2023, the Congressional Progressive Caucus released an executive action agenda for the Biden administration. A section urging the administration to "Raise Wages and Empower Workers" asked the president to "issue a presidential proclamation recognizing care workers that includes specific guidance to federal agencies that will better address the needs of the care economy and identify gaps in America's care sector following a summit of care workers."[60]

On April 18, 2023, as the National Domestic Workers Alliance, SEIU, AFL-CIO, American Federation of Teachers, and AFSCME gathered for a summit on care workers, Biden issued an executive order on "increasing access to high-quality care and supporting caregivers," with more than 50 directives to federal agencies.[61]

The National Domestic Workers Alliance rushed to praise the executive order as "a tremendous milestone for families and workers across the country," an "unprecedented" order that represents "the most comprehensive set of actions any president has ever taken to improve the care infrastructure and support families and care work-

60 "Congressional Progressive Caucus Executive Action Proposals for the 118th Congress." Congressional Progressive Caucus. March 30, 2023. https://progressives.house.gov/_cache/files/1/d/1d9cdfa4-8438-444b-b9be-022a3577f-5ca/854CC6D4FB4BF446CAEDBCED8D28513A.cpc-executive-action-slate-for-the-118th-congress.pdf Accessed April 3, 2024.

61 "Executive Order on Increasing Access to High-Quality Care and Supporting Caregivers." White House Briefing Room. April 18, 2023. https://www.whitehouse.gov/briefing-room/presidential-actions/2023/04/18/executive-order-on-increasing-access-to-high-quality-care-and-supporting-caregivers/ Accessed April 3, 2024.

ers." Ai-Jen Poo, the alliance's president, said that "the magnitude of these investments cannot be overstated."[62]

NDWA worked for this access, loudly hailing Julie Su's nomination to lead the Department of Labor, and praising her after she announced the Department of Labor's sample employment agreement for domestic workers such as nannies, cleaners, and home care workers.[63] Poo said that Su's "track record has shown her commitment to protecting workers' core workplace rights to ensure that all workers—including those who work in the margins of our economy—have dignity and earn fair wages for working families to achieve economic security."[64] Su joined a virtual event with NDWA on "Care in the Home: Supporting Positive Domestic Work Environments," in 2023.[65]

The Left's dark money network has also propped up NDWA, which received:

62 "National Domestic Workers Alliance Statement on the Biden-Harris Administration's Historic Executive Actions to Improve Care Affordability and Care Jobs." National Domestic Workers Alliance news release. April 18, 2023. https://www.domesticworkers.org/press-releases/national-domestic-workers-alliance-statement-on-the-biden-harris-administrations-historic-executive-actions-to-improve-care-affordability-and-care-jobs/ Accessed April 3, 2024.

63 "Joint Statement on the Department of Labor's Sample Employment Agreement for Domestic and Care Workers." National Domestic Workers Alliance news release. November 2, 2023. https://www.domesticworkers.org/press-releases/joint-statement-dol-sample-agreement/ Accessed April 3, 2024.

64 "Statement from the National Domestic Workers Alliance Supporting Julie Su as Secretary of Labor." National Domestic Workers Alliance news release. February 21, 2023. https://www.domesticworkers.org/press-releases/statement-from-the-national-domestic-workers-alliance-supporting-julie-su-as-secretary-of-labor/ Accessed April 3, 2024.

65 "ICYMI: Department of Labor Joins Virtual Event with National Domestic Workers Alliance and Hand-in-Hand." National Domestic Workers Alliance news release. December 12, 2023. https://www.domesticworkers.org/press-releases/care-in-the-home-supporting-healthy-domestic-work-environments/ Accessed April 3, 2024.

- $7 million in grants from the Open Society Foundations from 2016 to 2020.[66]
- $30,000 from Hopewell Fund in 2021 (Arabella)[67]
- $1 million from New Venture Fund from 2016 to 2021 (Arabella)[68]
- $58,500 from Proteus Fund from 2017 to 2020[69]
- $2.3 million from The Tides Foundation from 2018 to 2022[70]
- Just under $400,000 from the SEIU from 2016 to 2023[71]
- $2.7 million from Amalgamated Charitable Foundation from 2018 to 2022[72]
- $20,000 from the Rockefeller Family Fund in 2020[73]
- $6.5 million from Rockefeller Philanthropy Advisors from 2018 to 2022[74]
- $25,000 from Demos in 2019[75]

NDWA employs Alicia Garza, a self-described "trained Marxist" who co-founded the Black Lives Matter movement, as special proj-

---

66 "Awarded Grants" page search results for "National Domestic Workers Alliance." Open Society Foundations. https://www.opensocietyfoundations.org/grants/past?filter_keyword=National+Domestic+Workers+Alliance&grant_id=OR2020-72194 Accessed April 3, 2024.
67 "Hopewell Fund." Form 990, Schedule I for 2021.
68 The New Venture figure is $1,084,495. "New Venture Fund." Form 990, Schedule I for 2016, 2017, 2021.
69 "Proteus Fund." Form 990, Schedule I for 2017, 2018, 2020.
70 The precise figure is $2,334,027. "Tides Foundation." Form 990, Schedule I for 2018–2022.
71 OLMS search results accessed May 21, 2024.
72 The precise figure is $2,688,350. "Amalgamated Charitable Foundation." Form 990, Schedule I for 2018, 2020, 2021, 2022.
73 "Rockefeller Family Fund." Form 990, Schedule I for 2010.
74 The precise figure is $6,451,500. "Rockefeller Philanthropy Advisors." Form 990, Schedule I for 2018–2022.
75 "Demos A Network For Ideas And Action Ltd." Form 990, Schedule I for 2019.

ects director.[76][77] Ai-Jen Poo, the alliance's president, has visited the White House at least thirty-two times. She also joined actor Seth Rogen and his wife, Lauren Miller Rogen, in White House meetings for their Alzheimer's charity, Hilarity for Charity, on September 14, 2022. She twice met with Vice President Kamala Harris one-on-one.[78]

GOVERNMENT RESOURCE PAGE POSTS UNION PROPAGANDA

The administrative state has also promoted union-funded pro-union propaganda, which helps entrench the unions that bankroll the Democratic Party and the Woketopus.

Under Su, the Department of Labor launched the Worker Organizing Resource and Knowledge (WORK) Center, which bills itself as the "premiere online resource" for information on labor unions. The center, which launched in August 2023, cites data from organizations that receive their funding from labor unions. It posts graphics that cite the Economic Policy Institute, the Center for Economic and Policy Research, the Institute for Women's Policy Research, and the Center for American Progress.[79]

The WORK Center makes hyperbolic claims about the positive impact of unions, straining to tie unions to woke priorities like weaker election integrity laws, closing racial wealth gaps, and a $15/hour minimum wage.[80]

Each of the WORK Center's sources has received hefty union funding:

76   Steinbuch, Yaron. "Black Lives Matter co-founder describes herself as 'trained Marxist.'" *The New York Post.* June 25, 2020. https://nypost.com/2020/06/25/blm-co-founder-describes-herself-as-trained-marxist/ Accessed April 3, 2024.

77   "Alicia Garza." *LinkedIn* Profile. https://www.linkedin.com/in/buildthemovement/ Accessed April 3, 2024.

78   White House Visitor Logs, analyzed by Tyler O'Neil, downloaded from https://www.whitehouse.gov/disclosures/visitor-logs/ on March 21, 2024.

79   "Data Center." Worker Organizing Resource and Knowledge Center. https://www.workcenter.gov/data-center/ Accessed April 3, 2024.

80   "Resource Library." Worker Organizing Resource and Knowledge Center. https://www.workcenter.gov/resource-library/ Accessed April 2, 2024.

o   14 percent of The Economic Policy Institute's funding came from unions in 2021[81]

o   The Center for American Progress received $1.5 million from the SEIU between 2014 and 2023 (see above)

o   The SEIU sent $100,000 to the Center for Economic and Policy Research from 2013 to 2017, while the AFL-CIO and AFSCME sent similar sums in a comparable time period[82]

o   The American Federation of Teachers has contributed to the Institute for Women's Policy Research[83]

The WORK Center includes a disclaimer stating:

> Any links to non-federal websites on this page provide additional information that is consistent with the intended purpose of this federal site, but linking to such sites does not constitute an endorsement by the U.S. Department of Labor of the information or organization providing such information.

Yet the WORK Center does not disclose that unions may be funding the information it cites in order to demonstrate the positive impact of unions.

"Workers should know they're only getting half the story from the Department of Labor," Charlyce Bozzello, communications director at the Center for Union Facts, told *The Washington Free Beacon*. "Instead of pushing union-funded studies, the Department of Labor should be making it easier for union members and the public to access information on how unions spend members' dues."[84]

81   "Who Supports Us" section on "About" Page. Economic Policy Institute. https://www.epi.org/about/ Accessed April 3, 2024.

82   OLMS search results accessed May 21, 2024.

83   OLMS search results accessed May 21, 2024.

84   Ross, Chuck. "Biden Labor Department Relies on Union-Funded Think Tanks To Push Pro-Union Message." *The Washington Free Beacon*. March 18, 2024. https://freebeacon.com/biden-administration/biden-labor-department-relies-on-union-funded-think-tanks-to-push-pro-union-message/ Accessed April 3, 2024.

UNION DECERTIFICATION BATTLES

The federal government hasn't just kowtowed to unions through the independent contractor rule and the promotion of union-funded propaganda, however. The National Labor Relations Board (NLRB) has put its thumb on the scale for unions even when most workers voted against joining one.

So much for defending "democracy" and "representation."

Workers at an Amazon fulfillment center in Bessemer, Alabama, a suburb of Birmingham, have twice voted against joining the Retail, Wholesale and Department Store Union (RWDSU). In an April 2021 election, 1,798 (or 59 percent of those who cast a ballot) voted against joining the union, while only 738 (or 24 percent) voted for it (the remaining 505 ballots were challenged).[85]

RWDSU officials objected, however, claiming that Amazon interfered with the election by installing its own mailbox to collect ballots, and—because Amazon security guards had access to the mailbox—giving workers the impression that Amazon controlled the results. The National Labor Relations Board ordered Amazon to hold another election.

"Our employees have always had the choice of whether or not to join a union, and they overwhelmingly chose not to join the RWDSU earlier this year," Amazon representative Kelly Nantel told *The Verge*. "It's disappointing that the NLRB has now decided that those votes shouldn't count."[86]

The Amazon employees again voted against the union on March 31, 2022, although the results were closer: 993 to 875 or

---

85   "NLRB Announces Results in Amazon Election." National Labor Relations Board news release. April 9, 2021. https://www.nlrb.gov/news-outreach/news-story/nlrb-announces-results-in-amazon-election Accessed April 17, 2024.

86   Brandom, Russell. "Amazon must redo Bessemer union election, orders labor board official." *The Verge*. November 29, 2021. https://www.theverge.com/2021/11/29/22565851/amazon-bessemer-union-vote-nlrb-appeal-overturned-second-election Accessed April 17, 2024.

43.4 percent against the union and 38.3 percent for it.[87] An NLRB administrative law judge will review this second election to determine whether Amazon engaged in unfair labor practices, necessitating a third election.[88]

This refusal to admit that workers may not want to join the union echoes the sentiments of Richard Trumka, then president of the AFL-CIO. Trumka, who passed away in August 2021, condemned the Bessemer union vote in August 2021 as systematic of a broader "societal failure," writing on X (formerly Twitter): "We can't allow this societal failure to deprive one more worker of the freedom to organize.... This is the fight of our time, and it starts with passing the #PROAct."[89]

In another case, an NLRB judge ruled in September 2023 that Starbucks broke the law by providing raises and additional benefits to non-union workers without offering the same increases to union staff.

Starbucks denounced the ruling, announcing its intention to appeal. "We continue to contend that Starbucks adhered to established organizing and collective bargaining rules," the company stated. Starbucks argued that the judge's conclusion "creates an untenable situation...where employers violate the law if they unilaterally include organizing or unionized employees when making changes in wages and benefits and violate the law if they do not do so."[90]

---

87 "Region 10-Atlanta Announces Results of Bessemer Amazon Ballot Count." National Labor Relations Board news release. March 31, 2022. https://www.nlrb.gov/news-outreach/region-10-atlanta/region-10-atlanta-announces-results-of-bessemer-amazon-ballot-count Accessed April 17, 2024.

88 Thornton, William. "Will Bessemer Amazon workers have a third union election? Decision could come soon." AL.com. January 31, 2024. https://www.al.com/business/2024/01/will-bessemer-amazon-workers-have-a-third-union-election-decision-could-come-soon.html Accessed April 17, 2024.

89 Trumka, Richard. Post on X. April 9, 2021. 11:35 a.m. https://twitter.com/RichardTrumka/status/1380544905890652160 Accessed April 17, 2024.

90 Robertson, Nick. "NLRB judge: Starbucks violated labor law in offering pay raises, benefits to nonunion workers." The Hill. September 30, 2023. https://thehill.com/business/4231618-nlrb-judge-starbucks-violated-labor-law-in-offering-pay-raises-benefits-to-nonunion-workers/ Accessed April 17, 2024.

Aggressive pro-union actions extend beyond Amazon and Starbucks. In February 2024, the Federal Trade Commission sued to block the Kroger Company's $24.6 billion acquisition of the Albertsons Companies, in part because "the combined Kroger and Albertsons would have more leverage to impose subpar terms on union grocery workers that slow improvements to wages, worsen benefits, and potentially degrade working conditions."[91]

The Federal Trade Commission Act states that the agency's mission is to prevent "unfair methods of competition in or affecting commerce," with no mention of union activity. Other federal agencies, such as the Labor Department and the NLRB, exist to oversee labor practices. The FTC's move arguably represents bureaucratic overreach, with the purpose of telegraphing the importance of unions across the federal government. Not only do unions have Julie Su, the Department of Labor, and the NLRB on their side, but they can now count on the FTC to stretch its legal bounds to leap to their defense, as well.[92]

Not to be outdone, in May 2024 Su claimed credit for helping to secure a labor contract for more than 1,500 unionized workers at Blue Bird Corporation, a ninety-seven-year-old publicly traded company which manufactures school buses in Georgia. She told *Axios* that she brought workers from Blue Bird to the White House last year for a meeting with union organizers, and visited Georgia in March to meet with Blue Bird CEO Phil Horlock, urging him to bargain in good faith for a first contract.

Blue Bird employees voted to unionize with the United Steelworkers in May 2023. Ahead of the vote, the United Steelworkers filed more than ten unfair labor practice charges against

---

91 "FTC Challenges Kroger's Acquisition of Albertsons." Federal Trade Commission news release. February 26, 2024. https://www.ftc.gov/news-events/news/press-releases/2024/02/ftc-challenges-krogers-acquisition-albertsons Accessed April 17, 2024.

92 Higgins, Sean. "FTC declares mergers to be union-busting." Competitive Enterprise Institute. March 1, 2024. https://cei.org/blog/ftc-declares-mergers-to-be-union-busting/ Accessed April 17, 2024.

Blue Bird, including claims that the company threatened to close the plant or freeze pay if workers approved the union. The claims appeared baseless, the union later withdrew the charges, and CEO Horlock touted the deal. It seems the United Steelworkers were preparing to call their friends in the federal government if those workers dared to vote the wrong way.[93]

Blue Bird currently focuses on electric vehicles—which are less reliable than gas vehicles—after President Biden's infrastructure law directed funds to EVs.

If Su is so happy to take credit for this union activity, what other union contracts is she working to secure? Did she know United Steelworkers was planning to pre-emptively declare the election results tainted and does she support such practices?

It seems Biden has been keeping his pledge to be "the most pro-union president you've ever seen," but the labor unions' ties to the administrative state make it unlikely that this influence campaign will end when Biden leaves office in 2025 or 2029. Biden did not sign an executive order directing the FTC to block the Kroger acquisition, and he did not direct NLRB judges to refuse workers' stated intention *not* to join unions. The administrative state seems more than capable—and willing—enough to pull the strings for unions with or without him.

The administrative state's preference for unions helps entrench a key funding apparatus for the Democratic Party and the Woketopus. If the independent contractor rule forces more Americans to give up contracting and enter traditional employment that can be unionized, that system will further bolster the Woketopus' funding stream.

93   Peck, Emily. "Biden's dealmaker: How Julie Su helped broker a union contract in hostile South." *Axios.* May 30, 2024. https://www.axios.com/2024/05/30/julie-su-blue-bird-labor-contract Accessed May 30, 2024.

4

THE GREEN REVOLVING DOOR

While the Woketopus fights to force American workers into unions, it also hamstrings the U.S. energy economy by manipulating the federal government. So-called green interests oppose U.S. drilling for oil—even though America drills for oil in a far less emissions-intensive way than other countries—and support less reliable wind and solar energy, even though these methods rely on rare earth minerals—a market dominated by America's top adversary, China.

The Woketopus' impact on energy and environment issues began before Biden and will continue after him, and it reaches throughout the administrative state.

Most Americans support conserving the natural environment, and respect organizations that teach wildfire prevention, oppose littering, and preserve the outdoors. Organizations like the Sierra Club and the National Wildlife Federation launched for these reasons, but in the past few decades, they appear to have minimized conservation programs to devote most of their energy to "climate change," or to the latest craze, "climate justice" (a fancy term for climate change with a healthy dose of Critical Race Theory).

No one disputes that the climate changes, but the alarmists claim that human activity—particularly the burning of fossil fuels—will cause irreparable harm to the global climate and usher in natural disaster.

Which natural disaster, exactly? That remains unclear. In the 1970s, climate scientists noted that global temperatures were cooling, and some feared a coming ice age.[1] By the 1980s, the trend toward increased temperatures had become clear, and alarmists started warning about "global warming." Yet the statistical models these alarmists developed to predict future temperatures failed: temperature increases proved smaller than predicted, and warnings about the flooding of Florida and the disappearance of snow on Mount Kilimanjaro failed to materialize.[2]

Now, alarmists have crafted a far more cunning strategy. They use the phrase "climate change" to predict a more generic doom, so that they can attribute whatever disasters may come to human activity.

The alarmists claim that Science—with a capital "S"—has delivered a "climate change consensus" from above. In 2021, people who looked at any Facebook post mentioning climate started seeing a note to check out a "Climate Science Information Center," a feature Facebook launched to dispel "misinformation" on climate. However, that center itself promoted a shocking piece of climate misinformation: the oft-repeated claim that "at least 97 percent of published climate experts agree that global warming is real and caused by humans."

But where does that claim come from? It traces back to a study led by John Cook titled "Quantifying the consensus on anthropogenic global warming in the scientific literature," published in the journal *Environmental Research Letters* in 2013. The study's authors analyzed all published peer-reviewed academic research papers from 1991 to 2011 that used the terms "global warming" or

1   Struck, Doug. "How the 'Global Cooling' Story Came to Be." *Scientific American.* January 10, 2014. https://www.scientificamerican.com/article/how-the-global-cooling-story-came-to-be/ Accessed May 7, 2024.

2   O'Neil, Tyler. "Egg on Their Faces: 10 Climate Alarmist Predictions for 2020 That Went Horribly Wrong." *PJ Media.* December 28, 2020. https://pjmedia.com/tyler-o-neil/2020/12/28/egg-on-their-faces-10-climate-alarmist-predictions-for-2020-that-went-horribly-wrong-n1289371 Accessed May 7, 2024.

"global climate change." The full tally came to 11,944 papers, but the authors did not closely analyze all those papers. Instead, they discounted 7,930 of them (66.4 percent) as not making relevant claims, and then broke up the remaining papers into seven categories. The authors combined three of those categories to come up with 3,896 papers, and contrasted that number with the 118 papers the scholars had placed in other categories. Only by excluding the vast majority of the papers in the sample did the authors come up with a 97 percent figure.

Even then, many of the scientists who wrote the original papers Cook's team analyzed complained that this study mischaracterized their research. The survey "included 10 of my 122 eligible papers. 5/10 were rated incorrectly. 4/5 were rated as endors[ing climate change] rather than neutral," complained Dr. Richard Tol, professor of the economics of climate change at Vrije Universiteit.[3]

Facebook's willingness to bombard users with its biased climate orthodoxy illustrates just how certain many of America's elites are about the truth of climate change—and the utter contempt they have for anyone who dares question their dogma.

Acting on this apparently unshakeable faith, alarmists oppose U.S. drilling of fossil fuels in the name of fighting "climate change," even though American oil extraction involves far fewer emissions than oil producer competitors such as Russia, China, Brazil, Iran, Iraq, and Nigeria.[4] Restricting U.S. drilling means that other countries will extract more oil to meet demand, yielding more global emissions.

Alarmists also tend to prioritize renewable energy sources such as solar and wind, even though these energy sources are notoriously

3   O'Neil, Tyler. "Facebook slammed for stifling 'wrong-think' on climate change." Fox Business. November 4, 2021. https://www.foxbusiness.com/politics/facebook-slammed-for-stifling-wrong-think-on-climate-change Accessed May 7, 2024.

4   Acosta, Joel. "Report: U.S. Beats Competitors With Low Carbon Intensity Oil." Energy In Depth. June 2, 2023. https://www.energyindepth.org/report-u-s-beats-competitors-with-low-carbon-intensity-oil/ Accessed May 7, 2024.

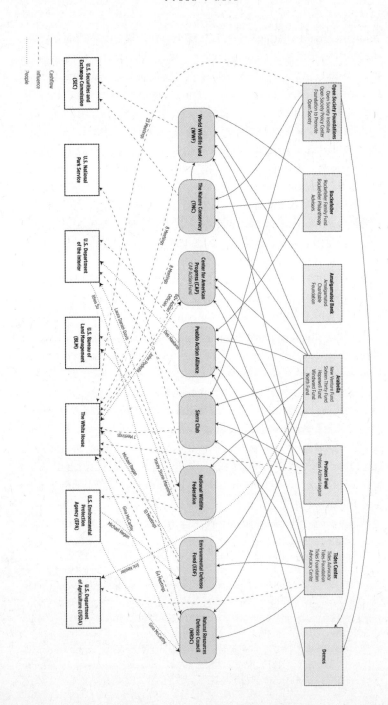

unreliable compared to fossil fuels. Solar and wind also rely on rare earth minerals. China, America's greatest foreign adversary, reportedly produces about 60 percent of the world's rare earth elements and processes 85 percent of them. To make matters worse, the mining and refinement of these metals damages the environment.[5]

A Heritage Foundation study found that the U.S. environmental agenda "has harmed natural U.S. energy advantages—and U.S. energy consumers—in the name of combating climate change," and that transitioning to the green activists' preferred energy sources would make the U.S. "heavily increase its dependence on Chinese materials." Climate alarmists may not intend to empower China at America's expense, but their agenda will arguably do just that.

GREEN REVOLVING DOOR EXHIBIT A: JOHN PODESTA

The administrative state has become the enforcer of the green activist agenda, turning fringe extremism into federal regulation. A revolving door enables activist-minded bureaucrats to find homes in pressure groups, only to then move back to positions of government power where they have massive grant-making capacity as well as the ability to make sweeping rule changes. Green groups have colluded with administrative agencies to change policy through both backroom lobbying and clever legal strategies, including a nefarious "sue and settle" scheme that leaves the American people's interests out in the cold.

Completing the picture, the Left's dark money network keeps the activists in business, providing the oxygen for them to demonize CO2.

One man helps illustrate the green revolving door perhaps more than any other, and he forms a hinge around which Biden's green agenda turns.

---

5   Ezrati, Milton. "How Much Control Does China Have Over Rare Earth Elements?" *Forbes*. December 11, 2023. https://www.forbes.com/sites/miltonezrati/2023/12/11/how-much-control-does-china-have-over-rare-earth-elements/?sh=48a4d9765b21 Accessed May 7, 2024.

John Podesta has gone in and out of the White House for decades. He and his brother Tony founded a lobbying firm called The Podesta Group in 1988, and its fortunes rose with John Podesta's prominence. The firm would develop close ties with the Democratic Party, raking in $29.3 million in 2010[6] and earning Tony Podesta the rank of third most influential lobbyist in 2007. [7] The firm dissolved in 2017, but by then John Podesta had been firmly established. [8]

John Podesta worked for the Justice Department as a lawyer, and then spent years on Capitol Hill before becoming President Bill Clinton's chief of staff in 1998, after helping the Clinton White House manage the Monica Lewinsky scandal. After Clinton's term ended, Podesta founded the Center for American Progress in 2003, which he envisioned as a Democratic alternative to conservative think tanks such as the Heritage Foundation and the American Enterprise Institute.[9] *Politico* has described the Center for American Progress as "the most influential think tank of the Biden era." Leaders at the Center for American Progress have visited the White House at least thirty-five times.[10]

While leading CAP, Podesta also joined corporate boards and consulted for left-leaning nonprofits. Between 2010 and 2014, he served on the board of the green energy company Joule Unlimited,

6   Bogardus, Kevin and Rachel Leven. "On K Street, 2011 was year to forget." *The Hill.* January 20, 2012. https://thehill.com/business-a-lobbying/103439-on-k-street-2011-was-year-to-forget/ Accessed April 22, 2024.

7   Eisler, Kim. "Hired Guns: The city's 50 top lobbyists." *The Washingtonian.* June 1, 2007. https://web.archive.org/web/20071124105158/https://www.washingtonian.com/articles/mediapolitics/4264.html Accessed via Internet Archive on April 22, 2024.

8   Palmer, Anna. "Tony Podesta stepping down from lobbying giant amid Mueller probe." *Politico.* October 30, 2017. https://www.politico.com/story/2017/10/30/tony-podesta-stepping-down-from-lobbying-giant-amid-mueller-probe-244314 Accessed March 21, 2024.

9   Dreyfuss, Bob. "An Idea Factory for the Democrats." *The Nation.* March 1, 2004. https://www.thenation.com/article/archive/idea-factory-democrats/ Accessed May 24, 2024.

10   White House Visitor Logs.

which later collapsed.[11] In 2013, he earned $90,000 as a consultant to the HJW Foundation of West Chester, Pennsylvania, a nonprofit group run by Hansjörg Wyss; the major Swiss donor who contributes to the Left's dark money network has also been a major CAP donor.[12]

In 2012, the United Nations secretary-general appointed Podesta to the panel on a post-2015 development agenda, which led to the UN's climate change program Sustainable Development Goals in 2016.[13]

Podesta served as co-chair of the Obama-Biden transition to the White House in 2008 and 2009. He left CAP in 2014 to become senior adviser to President Obama and oversee the Obama administration's climate change and energy policies. He then served as chairman of Hillary Clinton's 2016 presidential campaign.

Biden tapped John Podesta to serve as Senior Advisor to the President for Clean Energy Innovation and Implementation in 2022, tasking him with directing the "clean energy and climate provisions" in the bill Democrats termed the Inflation Reduction Act.[14] He directs hundreds of billions of dollars approved under the bill.[15]

In 2021, Patrick Gaspard, who had served as president of the Open Society Foundations, took the reins as CAP's president,

11   Kirsner, Scott. "How a biofuel dream turned into a nightmare." *The Boston Globe.* September 1, 2017. https://www.bostonglobe.com/business/2017/09/01/how-biofuel-dream-turned-into-nightmare/rt5ve7mE4Y-UZUOrqdaTqWK/story.html Accessed May 24, 2024.

12   Lipton, Eric. "New Obama Adviser Brings Corporate Ties." *The New York Times.* December 13, 2013. https://www.nytimes.com/2013/12/13/us/politics/new-obama-adviser-brings-corporate-ties.html Accessed May 24, 2024.

13   "UN Secretary-General appoints high-level panel on post-2015 development agenda." United Nations Development Programme news release. July 31, 2012. Archived January 27, 2014. https://web.archive.org/web/20140127034259/http://www.undp.org/content/undp/en/home/presscenter/pressreleases/2012/07/31/un-secretary-general-appoints-high-level-panel-on-post-2015-development-agenda.html Accessed May 24, 2024.

14   "President Biden Announces Senior Clean Energy and Climate Team." White House Briefing Room. September 2, 2022. https://www.whitehouse.gov/briefing-room/statements-releases/2022/09/02/president-biden-announces-senior-clean-energy-and-climate-team/ Accessed March 21, 2024.

15   "Inflation Reduction Act Guidebook." The White House. https://www.whitehouse.gov/cleanenergy/inflation-reduction-act-guidebook/ Accessed March 21, 2024.

replacing Neera Tanden, who left the post to become a senior adviser to President Biden. CAP has fed more than sixty officials into the Biden administration and helped shape Biden's legislative initiatives and executive actions.[16]

What Does CAP Say About Climate Change?

CAP describes climate change as "the greatest challenge facing the United States—and the world—over the next decade and beyond." It claims that "the burning of fossil fuels, deforestation, and other human activities raise global temperatures with costly and deadly impacts, including extreme heat, droughts, storms, wildfires, sea-level rise, and more." The group also claims that these disasters disproportionately harm "disadvantaged communities and low-income areas, exacerbating existing social and economic inequalities."[17]

CAP has long supported electric vehicles and urged the Biden administration to spend more on green technologies. In October 2021, the Center for American Progress Action urged Congress to pass the "Build Back Better Act's Clean Energy Tax Credits RIGHT NOW."[18] In March 2023, it celebrated funds set aside in the "Infrastructure Investment and Jobs Act" and the "Inflation Reduction Act." Those bills directed billions of dollars to fund electric vehicle charging infrastructure.[19]

---

16   Stein, Sam, and Natasha Korecki. "The most influential think tank of the Biden era has a new leader." *Politico*. June 30, 2021. https://www.politico.com/news/2021/06/30/center-for-american-progress-new-leader-497167 Accessed May 31, 2024.

17   "Climate Change" page. Center for American Progress. https://www.americanprogress.org/topic/climate-change/ Accessed March 21, 2024.

18   Advocacy Team. "Congress Must Pass the Build Back Better Act's Clean Energy Tax Credits RIGHT NOW." Center for American Progress Action. October 21, 2021. https://www.americanprogressaction.org/article/congress-must-pass-the-build-back-better-acts-clean-energy-tax-credits-right-now/ Accessed March 21, 2024.

19   "Biden's EV Charging Infrastructure Improvements Are Powering the Economy and Speeding Up the Adoption of Clean Energy Technology." Center for American Progress Action. March 30, 2023. https://www.americanprogressaction.org/article/bidens-ev-charging-infrastructure-improvements-are-powering-the-economy-and-speeding-up-the-adoption-of-clean-energy-technology/ Accessed March 21, 2024.

Lobbying Podesta: The LNG Pause

In January 2024, the Biden White House announced a temporary pause on pending approvals of liquefied natural gas (LNG) exports.[20] The pause raised eyebrows because liquefied natural gas is one of the cleanest fossil fuels, and Europe relied on U.S. LNG exports during the early days of the Ukraine war, when NATO countries refused to import Russian LNG.

In November 2023, two months before the Biden administration paused them, the Center for American Progress published an article condemning the increase in LNG exports.[21] It warned that exporting American LNG would allow natural gas prices to fluctuate with the global market and undermine "climate objectives by directing investments away from clean energy initiatives and perpetuating dependency on fossil fuel markets that remain exposed to the decisions of petrostate dictators." The Rockefeller family and other billionaire donors then launched an influence campaign in favor of the LNG export pause.

According to *The Wall Street Journal*, Senator Jeff Merkley (D-OR) personally pressured John Podesta on the issue.[22] Trevor Higgins, senior vice president for energy and environment at the Center for American Progress, praised the LNG pause on the day

---

20 "FACT-SHEET: Biden-Harris Administration Announces Temporary Pause on Pending Approvals of Liquefied Natural Gas Exports." White House Briefing Room. January 26, 2024. https://www.whitehouse.gov/briefing-room/statements-releases/2024/01/26/fact-sheet-biden-harris-administration-announces-temporary-pause-on-pending-approvals-of-liquefied-natural-gas-exports/ Accessed March 21, 2024.

21 Martinez, Chris. "LNG Exports Raise Natural Gas Prices for Americans." Center for American Progress. November 6, 2023. https://www.americanprogress.org/article/lng-exports-raise-natural-gas-prices-for-americans/ Accessed March 21, 2024.

22 Morenne, Benoit and Andrew Restuccia. "How the Rockefellers and Billionaire Donors Pressured Biden on LNG Exports." *The Wall Street Journal.* February 8, 2024. https://www.wsj.com/us-news/climate-environment/how-the-rockefellers-and-billionaire-donors-pressured-biden-on-lng-exports-c1bf0ff8 Accessed March 21, 2024.

Biden announced it. "This is a welcome move that signals a new, fairer standard for determining whether additional LNG exports are really in our national interest," Higgins said. "Exporting LNG to other countries increases fuel prices for Americans, contributes to climate change, and threatens the health and safety of the—predominantly Black [*sic*]—communities living near LNG processing facilities."[23]

On July 1, Judge James Cain of the U.S. District Court for the Western District of Louisiana (a Trump appointee) issued a stay blocking the LNG export pause. Cain ruled that the pause contradicted the language of the Natural Gas Act and subverted "Congress's determination that LNG exports are presumptively in the public interest." His order does not require the Department of Energy to approve new LNG applications, but it does require the department to restart the process of considering them.[24] Even if the pause gets fully reversed, this policy has negatively impacted LNG exports through the first half of 2024.

Ford's Green Payday

It remains unclear how much money Podesta has directed toward CAP donors, but his role allows him to reward his friends and allies in the movement.

Podesta likely played a major role in securing the largest government loan for an automaker since the 2009 auto bailouts that followed the 2007–2008 financial crisis. In June 2023, the U.S. Department of Energy awarded a $9.2 billion loan to Ford Motor Company and the South Korean battery manufacturer SK On Co.,

23 "STATEMENT: CAP's Trevor Higgins Praises Move To Consider Climate Impact of LNG Terminal." Center for American Progress press release. January 24, 2024. https://www.americanprogress.org/press/statement-caps-trevor-higgins-praises-move-to-consider-climate-impact-of-lng-terminal/ Accessed March 21, 2024.

24 Farah, Niinah. "Judge overturns Biden's LNG export pause." *E&E News by Politico.* July 2, 2024. https://www.eenews.net/articles/judge-overturns-bidens-lng-export-pause/ Accessed July 10, 2024.

Ltd. for the BlueOval SK joint venture. The companies plan to build three electric vehicle battery plants, two in Kentucky and one in Tennessee.

This loan comes through the Department of Energy's Loan Programs Office, or LPO, which has disbursed nearly $33 billion over the past fourteen years. In 2009, the LPO offered $535 million in loans to the notorious solar startup Solyndra, which filed for bankruptcy in 2011. It also lent $465 million to Tesla in 2010, which helped the company ramp up its first factory in Fremont, California. Tesla has since become the world's most valuable carmaker.[25]

It remains unclear exactly how Ford secured the deal, but key Ford employees who had previously worked in the Obama administration frequented the White House and met with Podesta. Christopher A. Smith, Ford's chief government affairs officer, served in the Department of Energy under Obama, rising to the position of assistant secretary for fossil energy.[26] Smith has gone to the White House at least three times. Stephen P. Croley, now chief policy officer and general counsel at Ford, spent three years in the Obama White House, rising to deputy White House counsel, before he became general counsel at the Department of Energy under Obama,[27] who also appointed Croley to another federal agency, the Council of the Administrative Conference of the United States.[28]

25 Rathi, Akshat, Ari Natter, and Keith Naughton. "Ford Gets $9.2 Billion to Help US Catch Up With China's EV Dominance." Bloomberg. June 22, 2023. https://www.bloomberg.com/graphics/2023-ford-ev-battery-plant-funding-biden-green-technology/ Accessed April 22, 2024.

26 "Christopher Smith." Ford employee profile. https://media.ford.com/content/fordmedia/fna/us/en/people/christopher-smith.html Accessed April 22, 2024.

27 "Steven Croley." LinkedIn profile. https://www.linkedin.com/in/steven-croley/ Accessed April 22, 2024.

28 "President Obama Announces More Key Administration Posts." White House news release. May 22, 2014. https://obamawhitehouse.archives.gov/the-press-office/2014/05/22/president-obama-announces-more-key-administration-posts Accessed via Obama White House archive on April 22, 2024.

He joined Ford in July 2021. He has visited the White House at least four times, once meeting with Podesta one-on-one in 2023.[29]

Podesta's Green Revolving Door Network

Podesta has cultivated relationships with a large network of former Obama and Biden administration officials who now work in climate change funding and nonprofits. These organizations appear to be vehicles for climate bureaucrats to move from government into the philanthropic sector, using their governmental expertise and donor funds to advocate for green initiatives and to direct government funds to pet projects. Some of them also return to government after stints in these roles.

For instance, Podesta has met frequently with leaders at What Works Plus, which describes itself as a "funder collaborative" and "coordination hub across philanthropy, non-profits, and different levels of government to advance equity and climate resilience by addressing gaps in the implementation of…funding" from the laws President Biden has signed, including the American Rescue Plan Act and the Inflation Reduction Act.[30] The Biden White House mentioned What Works Plus as the force behind "The Catalyze Registry," a philanthropic registry and matchmaking service that "enables philanthropy to scale needed support for initiatives that build a diverse talent pool for quality infrastructure careers."[31] Podesta has met frequently with leaders at What Works Plus and its parent company, Freedman Consulting. The Democratic-leaning

29   White House Visitor Logs, analyzed by Tyler O'Neil.
30   "What Works Plus Collaborative." Home page. https://whatworksplus.com/ Accessed April 22, 2024.
31   "FACT SHEET: White House Releases New Technical Assistance Resources to Help Communities Unlock Opportunities from President Biden's Investing in America Agenda." White House Briefing Room. September 13, 2023. https://www.whitehouse.gov/briefing-room/statements-releases/2023/09/13/fact-sheet-white-house-releases-new-technical-assistance-resources-to-help-communities-unlock-opportunities-from-president-bidens-investing-in-america-agenda/ Accessed April 22, 2024.

THE WOKETOPUS

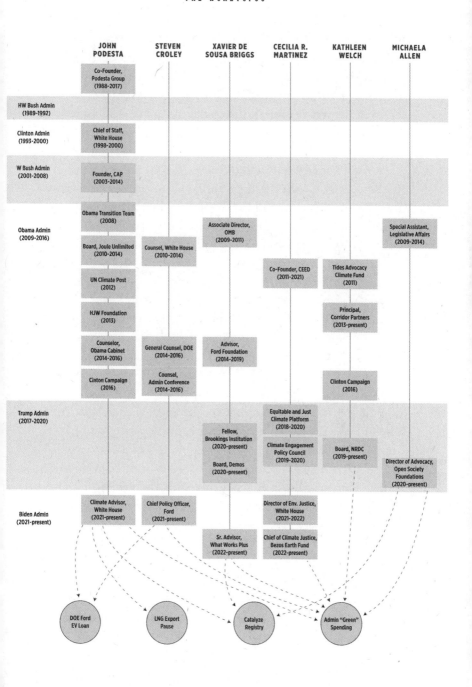

123

firm acts as a go-between for donors and government, working with the Ford Foundation, the Hewlett Foundation, the Open Society Foundations, the Rockefeller Foundation, and others.[32]

Podesta has frequently met with Xavier de Souza Briggs, who served as a program associate director at the Office of Management and Budget under Obama, as an adviser at the Ford Foundation, and as a senior fellow at the Brookings Institution. He now serves as a senior advisor at What Works Plus.

Ramoncita Cecilia Martinez, former director of environmental justice at the White House Council on Environmental Quality in the Biden administration, now serves as chief of environmental and climate justice at the Bezos Earth Fund. [33] She has met with Podesta multiple times.

Kathleen Welch, principal and founder at Corridor Partners, has also repeatedly met with Podesta at the White House. Welch directed the Environment and Climate Action Fund, a project of Tides Advocacy that supports climate policy. She advised Hillary Clinton's 2016 campaign on climate and energy issues.[34] According to the Huffington Post, Welch "advises wealthy donors and is a highly influential figure in Democratic fundraising circles, playing a central role in steering money to environmental and climate coalitions."[35] She sits on the board of the National Resources Defense Council, one of America's largest environmentalist groups.

Michaela Allen, director of U.S. advocacy at the Open Society Foundations, has also met repeatedly with Podesta. Before joining Open Society, she served as a special assistant to President

32 "Our Work." Freedman Consulting, LLC. https://tfreedmanconsulting.com/our-work/ Accessed April 22, 2024.

33 "Cecilia Martinez." LinkedIn Profile. https://www.linkedin.com/in/cecilia-martinez-3268346/ Accessed April 22, 2024.

34 "Kathleen Welch." Influence Watch profile. The Capital Research Center. https://www.influencewatch.org/person/kathleen-welch/ Accessed April 22, 2024.

35 Grim, Ryan and Lucia Graves. "OFA Refuses To Push On Keystone." *HuffPost.* May 16, 2013. https://www.huffpost.com/entry/ofas-keystone-grassroots_n_3276622 Accessed April 22, 2023.

Obama in the Office of Legislative Affairs from February 2009 to January 2014.

WHERE DOES THE HEAD OF EPA GO?

Gina McCarthy, who headed up the Environmental Protection Agency under Obama from 2013 to 2017, found a home in the Woketopus until she could return to the administrative state under Biden.

McCarthy became notorious for a 2015 rule applying the Clean Water Act of 1972 to streams and wetlands, in addition to larger bodies of water. The rule expanded the definition of "Waters of the United States," extending the EPA's authority to regulate more of America's land. This would have restricted the use of a great deal of land, as the EPA could claim that by filling small streams and "wetlands" with dirt, citizens were sending pollutants into the waters of the U.S. The EPA under Trump formally repealed the rule in 2019, but the Biden EPA essentially revived it in 2023. The Supreme Court unanimously rejected McCarthy's rule in *Sackett v. EPA* (2023), ruling that the Clean Water Act only allows EPA to regulate "navigable waters" involved in interstate commerce.[36]

McCarthy's rule made her more popular among climate advocates, however, and she took the reins as president of the Natural Resources Defense Council in 2020, where she remained until she rejoined the administration as Biden's White House national climate advisor. She stepped down from that role in September 2022.[37]

NRDC is one of America's largest environmentalist groups. According to its website, the council

---

36   Davis Jr., J. Kennerly. "Supreme Court's 'Waters of US' Ruling a Milestone in Curbing EPA's Unlawful Overreach." *The Daily Signal.* June 2, 2023. https://www.dailysignal.com/2023/06/02/supreme-courts-waters-us-ruling-milestone-curbing-epas-unlawful-overreach Accessed May 24, 2024.

37   Friedman, Lisa. "Gina McCarthy, Biden's Top Climate Adviser, to Step Down September 16." *The New York Times.* September 2, 2022. https://www.nytimes.com/2022/09/02/climate/gina-mccarthy-resignation.html Accessed May 7, 2024.

combines the power of more than 3 million members and online activists with the expertise of some seven hundred scientists, lawyers, and other environmental specialists to confront the climate crisis, protect the planet's wildlife and wild places, and to ensure the rights of all people to clean air, clean water, and healthy communities.

The group also advocates for "long-overdue justice for communities of color that are already the hardest hit by climate change."[38]

Senator Ted Cruz (R-TX) and Representative James Comer (R-KY) have raised concerns about NRDC's apparent ties with China, writing a letter to Attorney General Merrick Garland claiming that "both the NRDC China Program directors are former CCP [Chinese Communist Party] officials."

The NRDC claims it has "been carrying out environmental protection work in China since the 1990s" and "actively cooperates and communicates" with many Chinese government agencies. It has praised China as a world leader in "clean power development," while failing to mention—Cruz and Comer charged—that China is responsible for emitting over one-fourth of global carbon dioxide and a third of the world's greenhouse gases. While NRDC told *The Daily Signal* that it "receives no funding from the Chinese government and does the bidding of no government everywhere," Cruz and Comer wrote that "NRDC acts as a mouthpiece for Chinese propaganda, signaling that it either takes direction from the CCP or that it is willing to self-censor to maintain a positive relationship with the communist regime."[39]

---

38 Natural Resources Defense Council, "About Us" page https://www.nrdc.org/about and "Climate Crisis" page https://www.nrdc.org/climate-crisis Accessed May 24, 2024.

39 Mooney, Kevin. "EXCLUSIVE: Ted Cruz Wants Answers on Left-Wing Actors Who May Violate Foreign Agent Registration Act." *The Daily Signal.* November 17, 2023. https://www.dailysignal.com/2023/11/17/exclusive-sen-ted-cruz-pushes-attorney-general-to-probe-green-activists-ties-to-china-other-nations/ Accessed May 24, 2024.

NRDC has also vocally opposed nuclear energy, even though nuclear represents the most reliable form of energy production that does not involve the burning of fossil fuels.[40] (Between 1990 and 2021, nuclear power accounted for 19 to 20 percent of U.S. energy production, the largest non-carbon source of energy.[41])

Before McCarthy took the reins at NRDC, another Obama administration official led the organization. Rhea Su, who worked at the Department of the Interior under Obama from 2009 to 2015, became NRDC president in January 2015.[42]

Unsurprisingly, NRDC still has strong ties to the administrative state. Manish Bapna, NRDC's current president and CEO, has attended at least three White House meetings, including one with John Podesta. Christy Goldfuss, NRDC's executive director, has attended at least twenty-three meetings at the White House, including a one-on-one meeting with Gina McCarthy in March 2022, and four meetings with John Podesta. Kathleen Welch, chair of NRDC's board of trustees, has had at least thirty-eight White House meetings, eight with John Podesta.[43]

When approached for comment about its role in the green revolving door, the NRDC dismissed concerns about its influence on the administrative state as "partisan scaremongering." NRDC Senior Press Officer Mark Drajem said his group focuses on "core areas like addressing the climate crisis, getting lead out of drinking water, and protecting endangered species, lands, and waters. These are goals that every American can get behind, and no amount of partisan scaremongering will distract us from pursuing them."

It seems ironic to hear warnings about "partisan scaremongering" from a group that claims the continued burning of fossil fuels is "an existential threat to our planet and people."

40   "NRDC." Environmental Progress. Updated April 4, 2018. https://environmentalprogress.org/nrdc Accessed May 24, 2024.

41   "Nuclear Explained." U.S. Energy Information Administration. https://www.eia.gov/energyexplained/nuclear/us-nuclear-industry.php Accessed May 24, 2024.

42   "Rhea Suh." LinkedIn Profile. https://www.linkedin.com/in/rheasuh/ Accessed May 7, 2024.

43   White House Visitor Logs.

WHERE DOES THE NEW EPA HEAD COME FROM?

In another example of the green revolving door, President Biden nominated Michael Regan, North Carolina's environmental regulator, to head the EPA in December 2020.[44] After working nine years at the EPA under Presidents Bill Clinton and George W. Bush, Regan spent eight years at the Environmental Defense Fund, rising from the organization's Southeast climate and energy program director to its associate vice president for U.S. climate and energy and Southeast regional director.[45]

The Environmental Defense Fund has other ties with the Biden administration. EDF leaders have had at least ten White House meetings. President Frederic D. Krupp has met with John Podesta.[46] The organization launched in 1967, focusing its early efforts on banning the pesticide DDT, which caused bird eggshells to thin and break, threatening the osprey, the bald eagle, and the peregrine falcon. The fund has since teamed up with economists to design "market-based solutions" and foster corporate partnerships to protect the environment.[47]

While it still focuses on some concrete threats to the environment, the Environmental Defense Fund has also adopted an alarmist narrative and embraced a DEI agenda. "By leveraging our deep expertise in science and economics, EDF delivers bold, game-changing solutions to address the biggest challenge of our lifetime—climate change," the website's "Mission and Values" page states.[48]

44   Puko, Timothy and Eliza Collins. "Biden Picks Regan for EPA, Haaland for Interior." *The Wall Street Journal.* December 17, 2020. https://www.wsj.com/articles/biden-picks-north-carolina-regulator-michael-regan-to-lead-epa-11608229080 Accessed April 22, 2024.

45   "Michael S. Regan." LinkedIn Profile https://www.linkedin.com/in/michael-reg/ Accessed March 21, 2024.

46   White House Visitor Logs.

47   Environmental Defense Fund. "Our Story: How EDF got started." https://www.edf.org/about/our-history Accessed March 21, 2024.

48   Environmental Defense Fund. "Our Mission and values." https://www.edf.org/our-mission-and-values Accessed March 21, 2024.

EDF also touts a dedication to "Climate Justice."[49] "As climate change builds upon historic injustices and inequities, our climate solutions must center justice," its website states. "Communities of color, low-income areas and those who live next to power plants and other polluters face the greatest risk, are hit first and worst by climate change, and suffer real environmental injustices."

DISDAIN FOR THE SENATE

Most Americans may not have heard of the Department of the Interior, but this massive federal agency manages roughly 600 million acres of federal land, along with vast reserves of oil and natural gas. The department oversees most of the land in states like Alaska, Idaho, Nevada, and Utah.[50] A 2023 report noted that Interior is directing $2 billion in funds through the Bipartisan Infrastructure Law and the Inflation Reduction Act.[51]

President Biden has nominated green radicals to help lead this agency and the agencies beneath it. As with Acting Labor Secretary Julie Su (see Chapter 3), the president has continued to put radicals in positions of power even when the Senate—which has a small Democratic majority—refuses to confirm them. Between stints in the administrative state, some of these radicals found a temporary home at the anti-fossil-fuel pressure group, the National Wildlife Federation (NWF).

Laura Daniel-Davis, who served as the chief of staff at the Department of the Interior under Obama, worked at the federation for three years, as a vice president for conservation strategy and chief of policy and advocacy. In late 2020 and into 2021, she worked on

49   Environmental Defense Fund. "Climate Justice." https://www.edf.org/climate-environmental-justice Accessed March 21, 2024.

50   "Federal land ownership by state." Ballotpedia. https://ballotpedia.org/Federal_land_ownership_by_state Accessed April 26, 2024.

51   *America the Beautiful 2023 Annual Report.* Department of the Interior. January 2024. https://www.doi.gov/sites/default/files/documents/2024-01/jan-2024america-beautiful-2023-annual-report508-1.pdf Accessed April 26, 2024.

climate issues on the Biden-Harris transition team, landing back at Interior in 2021.[52]

Biden nominated Daniel-Davis to serve as assistant secretary of Interior for land and minerals management in June 2021, but the Senate Energy Committee deadlocked on her nomination, which timed out, and Biden renominated her in January 2022. He ultimately appointed her acting deputy secretary at Interior in October 2023.

Senator Joe Manchin (D-WV) announced his opposition to Daniel-Davis on March 10, 2023, faulting the nominee for agreeing with Interior's decision-making on an oil and gas lease sale off the coast of Alaska.[53] Manchin claimed it involved the administration "putting their radical climate agenda ahead of the needs of the people of Alaska and the United States." He criticized Biden for re-appointing Daniel-Davis after the Senate failed to confirm her, saying, "This appointment is yet another example of this administration disregarding Congress and elevating nominees when they are unable to get the bipartisan support needed for confirmation.... Their insistence on ignoring the confirmation process to advance their agenda undermines the role of the Senate and should be troubling to everyone."[54]

ENVIRONMENTAL ACTIVIST HEADS UP BLM

Biden's pick to lead the Bureau of Land Management proved even more shocking. That nominee, Tracey Stone-Manning, faced accu-

---

52 "Laura Daniel Davis." LinkedIn profile. https://www.linkedin.com/in/laura-daniel-davis-74168859/ Accessed April 27, 2024.

53 Frazin, Rachel. "Manchin indicates opposition to Biden lands nominee over internal memo." *The Hill.* March 3, 2023. https://thehill.com/policy/energy-environment/3883311-manchin-jeopardizes-chances-for-biden-lands-nominee/ Accessed April 27, 2024.

54 "Manchin Statement on Daniel-Davis Being Named Acting Deputy Secretary at Interior." Senator Joe Manchin news release. October 31, 2023. https://www.manchin.senate.gov/newsroom/press-releases/manchin-statement-on-daniel-davis-being-named-acting-deputy-secretary-at-interior Accessed April 27, 2024.

sations that she had placed metal spikes in trees to stop loggers. A former prosecutor said he investigated her in 1989 and 1993, and he described her as "vulgar, antagonistic, and extremely anti-government." Stone-Manning confessed that she had edited, retyped, and sent a threatening letter to the U.S. Forest Service on behalf of tree-spiking eco-terrorists.[55] While she later claimed she "had no involvement in the spiking of trees" and does "not condone tree spiking or terrorism of any kind,"[56] her willingness to write a threatening letter on behalf of eco-terrorists should be disqualifying for leadership in the Bureau of Land Management.

Stone-Manning worked for four years at the environmentalist National Wildlife Federation after years in Montana politics.[57]

COORDINATION WITH THE FEDERAL GOVERNMENT

In addition to providing half of the green revolving door, environmentalist groups also influence federal policy. They do so in overt ways, sometimes by writing memos that bureaucrats then pass off as their own, and in more covert ways, such as filing lawsuits to force agencies to adopt environmentalist policies. They also use intimidation tactics such as violent riots.

---

55 "Lead Investigator: Tracy Stone-Manning Helped Plan 1989 Tree Spiking & Was a Target of the Investigation." Senate Committee on Energy & Natural Resources news release. July 15, 2021. https://www.energy.senate. gov/2021/7/lead-investigator-tracy-stone-manning-helped-plan-1989-tree-spiking-was-a-target-of-the-investigation Accessed April 27, 2024.

56 Lefebvre, Ben, Anthony Adragna, and Burgess Everett. "Biden's BLM pick hit with new allegations from former investigator in tree-spiking case." *Politico.* July 15, 2021. https://www.politico.com/news/2021/07/15/biden-blm-pick-allegations-499739 Accessed April 27, 2024.

57 "Tracey Stone-Manning." LinkedIn profile. https://www.linkedin.com/in/tracy-stone-manning-49a1542a/ Accessed July 10, 2024.

The National Wildlife Federation

The National Wildlife Federation, where both Daniel-Davis and Stone-Manning found a home between stints at Interior, enjoys a great deal of access to the federal government, including federal funding for its initiatives. For example, its website claims, "The National Wildlife Federation, working with federal agency partners, developed an innovative planning approach known as 'climate-smart conservation.'"[58] The National Park Service, part of Interior, collaborated with the National Wildlife Federation on Climate Smart Conservation and cited the federation in its materials on the project.[59]

The National Wildlife Federation's close ties to Interior should not come as a surprise. In 2009, an Interior Department investigation into the Bureau of Land Management found that BLM was consulting federation staff on budgeting, and federation staff were writing and editing official BLM materials to promote the federation's priorities. An Inspector General report concluded that National Landscape Conservation System directors had engaged in inappropriate relationships with advocacy groups, creating "the potential for conflicts of interest or violations of law."[60] The Justice Department declined to prosecute in lieu of administrative action.

In 1959, the federation developed "Ranger Rick," a cartoon character whose stories teach children about the importance of wildlife conservation. In its 2018 federal tax return, the federation

58   "Climate-Smart Conservation." National Wildlife Federation. https://www. nwf.org/Our-Work/Climate/Climate-Change/Climate-Smart-Conservation Accessed April 27, 2024.

59   "Climate Smart Conservation Planning for the National Parks." National Park Service. https://www.nps.gov/articles/000/climatesmartconservation. htm Accessed April 27, 2024.

60   Straub, Noelle. "BLM Employees Too Cozy With Advocacy Groups—IG Report Says." *The New York Times.* October 5, 2009. Archived. https:// archive.nytimes.com/www.nytimes.com/gwire/2009/10/05/05greenwire-blm-employees-too-cozy-with-advocacy-groups-ig-20341.htmlAccessedApril 27, 2024.

claimed to have spent $19.8 million and reached 11 million children through its K-12 and higher education programs.[61] Most recently it also received at least $17,000 from the EPA in grants for "Earth Tomorrow," an after-school and summer education program.[62] It describes the program as its "longest-standing environmental justice education program," which "creates opportunities for youth in frontline communities, particularly youth of color, to deepen their understanding of environmental issues and provide solutions to address environmental injustices."[63]

The federation also promoted former Vice President Al Gore's climate propaganda documentary film, *An Inconvenient Truth*, which predicted that "there will be no more snows of Kilimanjaro" by 2016. Yet it continues to snow on the mountain in Tanzania.

Its executive vice president, Mustafa Santiago Ali, demonstrates just how "woke" this group has become. Ali spent twenty-four years at the EPA, becoming a founding member of the agency's "Office of Environmental Justice." After leaving the EPA and before joining the federation, he served as senior vice president for the Hip Hop Caucus, a nonprofit organization connecting the hop-hop community to the civic process.[64]

61 "Form 990, Section 501(c), 527 oe 4947(a)(1), for 2017." National Wildlife Federation. https://www.nwf.org/-/media/Documents/PDFs/Annual-Reports/FY18_NWF-990-Tax-Form-Public-Disclosure.ashx Accessed May 7, 2024.

62 "Project Title: Earth Tomorrow: An Interdisciplinary After-School And Summer Program." EPA Grant Awards Database. https://web.archive.org/web/20210926122450/https://yosemite.epa.gov/oarm/igms_egf.nsf/9e-9c2a5934a808d585256fb6006df292/5079abae84d6366185257d6f0071ee16!OpenDocument Accessed May 7, 2024, via Internet Archive.

63 "Earth Tomorrow: An Interdisciplinary After-School And Summer Program" National Wildlife Federation website. https://www.nwf.org/Educational-Resources/Education-Programs/Earth-Tomorrow Accessed May 7, 2024.

64 "Mustafa Santiago Ali." National Wildlife Federation profile. https://www.nwf.org/About-Us/Leadership/Mustafa-Santiago-Ali Accessed May 7, 2024.

Ali moderated a Democratic presidential forum on "environmental justice," during which he declared that "environmental racism is the new Jim Crow in regards to food, housing, jobs, education," and that "many communities of color, low-income communities, and indigenous populations are literally dying for a breath of fresh air." He further argued that "communities of color, low-income communities, and indigenous lands" become "the sacrifice zones for coal-fired power plants, for certified animal feeding operations, for waste treatment facilities, for unhealthy housing where we find lead and so many other impacts that are happening." [65]

Ali has also criticized the environmental movement for promoting Swedish teen Greta Thunberg, saying it reveals a focus on white people. "I hope as much attention will be given to a number of kids of color who have been literally, not just standing on the front lines, but living in the front lines for decades now," he said.[66]

"We're honored that some of team members have served in and gone on to serve in essential state, local, and federal roles, including in Democratic and Republican administrations," National Wildlife Federation Vice President of Communications Mike Saccone told me when asked about the green revolving door. He stated that NWF "complies with all ethical, lobbying, and legal restrictions" and he touted its work on bipartisan measures such as the Great American Outdoors Act, which Trump signed in August 2020. He did not address the radicalism of Stone-Manning, his organization's woke turn, or what the Left's dark money network gets for supporting NWF.

---

65 "WATCH: 2019 Presidential Forum on Environmental Justice." Democracy Now. November 8, 2019. https://www.democracynow.org/live/watch_2019_presidential_forum_on_environmental Accessed May 7, 2024.

66 Beeler, Caroline. "How did teen climate activist Greta Thunberg rise to fame so quickly?" *The World.* October 10, 2019. https://theworld.org/stories/2019/10/10/greta-thunberg Accessed May 7, 2024.

Restricting Oil and Gas

Green pressure groups like the Sierra Club openly brag about collaborating with the administration in supporting wind energy at the expense of oil and gas.

On July 12, 2023, six environmental groups—including Earthjustice and the Sierra Club—petitioned the Bureau of Ocean Energy Management at Interior, urging the agency to "end a routine practice of fast-tracking approval for offshore oil and gas projects." They condemned Interior's "categorial exclusion" for oil and gas activities beginning in 1981, urging Interior to tighten restrictions for "oil-and-gas exploration and development in the Gulf [of Mexico]."[67]

Two months later, Interior issued a press release bragging that it announced the "fewest offshore oil and gas lease sales in history" for the Gulf of Mexico. Its plan for the 2024-2029 National Outer Continental Shelf Oil and Gas Leasing Program includes a maximum of three potential oil and gas lease sales. Interior Secretary Deb Haaland said:

> The Biden-Harris administration is committed to building a clean energy future that ensures America's energy independence. The Proposed Final Program, which represents the smallest number of oil and gas lease sales in history, sets a course for the department to support the growing offshore wind industry and protect against the potential for environmental damage and adverse impacts to coastal communities.[68]

---

67 "Gulf and Environmental Groups Call on Interior Department to End Routine Fast-Tracking of Offshore Oil Drilling Projects." EarthJustice. July 12, 2023. https://earthjustice.org/press/2023/gulf-and-environmental-groups-call-on-interior-department-to-end-routine-fast-tracking-of-offshore-oil-drilling-projects Accessed April 27, 2024.

68 "Reflecting America's Rapid and Accelerating Shift to Clean Energy, Interior Department Announces Fewest Offshore Oil and Gas Lease Sales in History in Proposed Final Program for 2024–2029." U.S. Department of the Interior news release. September 29, 2023. https://www.doi.gov/pressreleases/reflecting-americas-rapid-and-accelerating-shift-clean-energy-interior-department Accessed April 27, 2024.

A few months later, Interior announced a new wind offshore leasing plan allowing for twelve auctions in federal waters.[69]

The Sierra Club praised these new rules from Interior, which restrict oil and gas lease sales in the Gulf to three, but plans for twelve offshore wind auctions in federal waters. "We are enthusiastic about these developments and remain dedicated to *collaborating with the Biden administration* and all stakeholders to maximize the potential of offshore wind, which is crucial for enhancing energy security and meeting our climate goals," Sierra Club Deputy Legislative Director Xavier Boatright said (emphasis added). [70]

This plan proved so extreme that it inspired legal action from America's largest fossil fuel industry association, the American Petroleum Institute. API sued Interior in February 2024, arguing that the plan restricting future offshore fossil fuel lease sales puts American consumers at risk and threatens U.S. energy security. "In issuing a five-year program with the fewest lease sales in history, the administration is limiting access in a region responsible for generating among the lowest carbon-intensive barrels in the world, putting American consumers at greater risk of relying on foreign sources for our future energy needs," Ryan Meyers, API senior vice president and general counsel, told Fox News.[71]

Ben Jealous, the Sierra Club's executive director, has had at least seven White House meetings. He met one-on-one with President Biden and has repeatedly met with John Podesta.[72]

---

69 "Secretary Haaland Announces New Five-Year Offshore Wind Leasing Schedule." U.S. Department of the Interior news release. April 24, 2024. https://www.doi.gov/pressreleases/secretary-haaland-announces-new-five-year-offshore-wind-leasing-schedule Accessed July 10, 2024.

70 "Sierra Club Statement on Biden Administration Five-Year Plan for Offshore Wind." Sierra Club news release. April 24, 2024. https://www.sierraclub.org/press-releases/2024/04/sierra-club-statement-biden-administration-five-year-plan-offshore-wind Accessed April 27, 2024.

71 Catenacci, Thomas. "Biden admin hit with legal challenge over historic restrictions on offshore oil drilling." Fox News. February 12, 2024. https://www.foxnews.com/politics/biden-admin-hit-legal-challenge-historic-restrictions-offshore-oil-drilling Accessed April 27, 2024.

72 White House Visitor Logs, analyzed by Tyler O'Neil, downloaded from https://www.whitehouse.gov/disclosures/visitor-logs/ on March 21, 2024.

The Sue-and-Settle Strategy

Not all of the environmentalist efforts to change policy are so straightforward. Various arms of the Woketopus have taken advantage of a legal mechanism called "sue and settle" to circumvent the regular rulemaking process and get their policies enacted without waiting for public comment.

A brief refresher from the introduction: Congress has granted broad power to the administrative state through laws like the Clean Air Act of 1963. In that law, Congress declared that Americans should have clean air, and it tasked the Environmental Protection Agency to draft regulations to achieve the law's goals.

Another law, the Administrative Procedure Act of 1946, dictates how agencies like the EPA make such regulations. Agencies must follow certain steps, such as providing public notice and allowing the public to comment on a rule before they implement it. Yet in the 1970s, Congress passed laws with exceptions to the Administrative Procedure Act, allowing agencies to make new rules via settlement agreements in lawsuits. The Clean Air Act, the Clean Water Act, and the Endangered Species Act allow citizen lawsuits empowering activists to challenge agency policy in court.

If green activists inside the administrative state want to issue new regulations but don't want to go through the regular process, they can outsource that work to an activist organization.

The strategy works like this. A green group, such as the Sierra Club, files a lawsuit against an agency, such as the National Marine Fisheries Service. The Sierra Club's lawsuit, filed in 2020, claims that the agency violated the Endangered Species Act by issuing a regulation allowing oil and gas activities in the Gulf of Mexico.[73] Although President Biden paused federal drilling auctions shortly after taking office in 2021, the so-called Inflation Reduction Act required the government hold the Gulf of Mexico lease sale.

---

73   Sierra Club, et al. v. National Marine Fisheries Service, et al., filed October 21, 2020. U.S. District Court for the District of Maryland. https://climate-casechart.com/wp-content/uploads/case-documents/2020/20201021_docket-20-cv-3060_complaint.pdf Accessed May 7, 2024.

In August 2023, the Sierra Club announced that it had settled the lawsuit. The National Marine Fisheries Service agreed to reconsider the opinion it issued under Trump, and a completely separate agency, the Bureau of Ocean Energy Management, will remove 6 million acres in the Gulf of Mexico from oil and gas leasing, and place new restrictions on oil and gas procedures in areas near where the endangered Rice's whales live.[74] The bureau—which was not a party to the case—imposed the "voluntary" set of "recommendations" and "guidance" for vessels engaged in existing fossil fuel energy activities within the area of the Rice's whale, based on "one recent study." While the bureau may call these "recommendations" voluntary, any fossil energy operations vessels that harms a Rice's whale in the area, while not abiding by them, will likely be subject to the penalties imposed in the Endangered Species Act of 1973.

As Benjamin Zycher, a senior fellow at the American Enterprise Institute, explained, "the restrictions do not apply to the thousands of vessels engaged daily in fishing, construction of offshore wind energy facilities, or other activities not related to fossil energy operations."

Zycher highlighted the absurdity of applying these rules in the name of protecting wildlife when the true motivation is to restrict fossil fuels: "In BOEM's view, then, it is unacceptable for an oil tanker to cause the death of a Rice's whale, but if another vessel kills it then it's just the cost of doing business," he quipped.

He noted that BOEM avoided a specific finding that fossil energy ships are likely to collide with Rice's whales because "that kind of finding would have to be justified in a formal rulemaking subject to public notice and comment, an exercise in actual cost-benefit analysis that this sue-and-settle racket is designed explicitly to

---

74 "Lawsuit Spurs Agreement to Better Protect Endangered Rice's Whale From Offshore Drilling." The Sierra Club news release. August 24, 2023. https://www.sierraclub.org/press-releases/2023/12/lawsuit-spurs-agreement-better-protect-endangered-rice-s-whale-offshore Accessed May 7, 2024.

circumvent."[75] This sue-and-settle strategy allowed BOEM to issue new regulations without engaging in the normal process, in the name of bringing justice to the Sierra Club's complaint.

The American Petroleum Institute, joined by then-Louisiana Attorney General Jeff Landry and Chevron, sued to block the BOEM restrictions.[76]

When an activist group sues the federal government, the public expects the federal government to defend the people's interests against the activist group. In the sue-and-settle strategy, however, no one at the table represents the people's interests, because the agency agrees with the activist group.

The sue-and-settle strategy long predates 2023. In 2017, then-EPA Administrator Scott Pruitt attempted to block it. He sent a letter to the EPA general counsel and to regional EPA administrators with guidelines regarding consent decrees and settlement agreements:

> In the past, the U.S. Environmental Protection Agency has sought to resolve litigation through consent degrees and settlement agreements that appear to be the result of collusion with outside groups. Behind closed doors, EPA and the outside groups agreed that EPA would take an action with a certain end in mind, relinquishing some of its discretion over the agency's priorities and duties and handing them over to special interests and the courts. When negotiating these agreements, EPA excluded intervenors, interested stakeholders, and affected states from those discussions. Some of these

---

75 Zycher, Benjamin. "Biden administration continues its anti-democratic 'sue-and-settle' masquerade." *The Hill.* September 14, 2023. https://thehill.com/opinion/energy-environment/4200673-biden-administration-continues-its-anti-democratic-sue-and-settle-masquerade/ Accessed May 7, 2024.

76 "Oil companies sue U.S. over Gulf auction changes meant to protect whale." *Reuters.* August 25, 2023. https://www.reuters.com/sustainability/oil-companies-sue-us-over-gulf-auction-changes-meant-protect-whale-2023-08-25/ Accessed May 7, 2024.

agreements even reduced Congress's ability to influence policy.

"The days of this regulation through litigation are ended," Pruitt declared, directing the agency to avoid it in the future.[77]

However, in March 2022, EPA Administrator Michael Regan formally withdrew Pruitt's directive and memorandum, claiming that the documents "contained inaccurate characterizations of the agency's settlement practices as well as of EPA attorneys and staff who have for decades appropriately negotiated settlements to resolve litigation." He insisted, "Appropriate settlement of environmental claims against the EPA preserves agency resources to focus on the vital work the agency carries out under the environmental statutes," and claimed that Pruitt's directive "established procedural requirements inappropriately favoring certain stakeholders in settling environmental claims brought against the EPA."[78]

Contrary to Regan's claim, however, the U.S. Chamber of Commerce found that between 2009 and 2012, the EPA chose not to defend itself in over sixty lawsuits from special interest advocacy groups. The cases resulted in settlement agreements and EPA publishing more than one hundred new regulations, including the Clean Power Plan.[79] The Natural Resources Defense Council settled nine sue-and-settle agreements with the EPA under Obama, according

---

77 Pruitt, E. Scott. Memorandum to administrators and the Office of General Counsel. October 16, 2017. https://www.epa.gov/sites/default/files/2017-10/text_of_memo_from_epa_administrator_scott_pruitt_to_epa_managers_adhering_to_the_fundamental_principles_of_due_process_rule_of_law_and_cooperative_federalism_in_consent_decrees_and_settlement_agreements_october_16_2.txt Accessed May 7, 2024.

78 Regan, Michael S. Memorandum to administrators, General Counsel, and more. March 18, 2022. https://www.epa.gov/system/files/documents/2022-03/ogc-22-000-2698_0.pdf Accessed May 7, 2024.

79 U.S. Chamber of Commerce. "Sue and Settle: Regulating Behind Closed Doors." March 6, 2018. https://www.uschamber.com/regulations/sue-and-settle-regulating-behind-closed-doors Accessed May 7, 2024.

to a 2013 *Washington Examiner* analysis,[80] which also found that Regan's own previous employer, the Environmental Defense Fund, settled five lawsuits with the EPA under Obama's tenure.[81]

The EPA under Biden has paid $6.9 million to settle lawsuits, according to documents the federal spending watchdog Open the Books obtained through a Freedom of Information Act request. This means the EPA under Biden has paid about twice as much to settle lawsuits as it did under Trump, and more even than in the last four years of Obama, when the EPA paid $5.7 million.[82]

The Pueblo Action Alliance

Deb Haaland, who leads the Department of the Interior, has close ties with a group that helped lead a riot at the Interior Department in October 2021. Protesters swarmed the agency's headquarters, causing "multiple injuries" to security personnel. Police arrested fifty-five people.[83]

The agitators responsible, a coalition of organizations known as "Build Back Fossil Free," included the Pueblo Action Alliance, a radical left-wing group with ties to the Cuban government. (Haaland's own daughter, twenty-nine-year-old Somah Haaland, had been involved with another "Build Back Fossil Free" riot a few days earlier

---

80 The Washington Examiner Editorial Board. "EPA's back-room 'sue and settle' deals require reform." *The Washington Examiner.* May 25, 2013. https://www.washingtonexaminer.com/opinion/424083/epas-back-room-sue-and-settle-deals-require-reform/ Accessed May 7, 2024.

81 Ibid.

82 The Washington Examiner Editorial Board. "'Sue and settle' business is booming at Biden's EPA." *The Washington Examiner.* August 14, 2023. https://www.washingtonexaminer.com/news/business/1517018/sue-and-settle-business-is-booming-at-bidens-epa/ Accessed May 7, 2024.

83 Justice, Tristan. "Will Liz Cheney, House Democrats Investigate Insurrectionist Takeover Of Interior Department?" *The Federalist.* October 15, 2021. https://thefederalist.com/2021/10/15/will-liz-cheney-house-democrats-investigate-insurrectionist-takeover-of-interior-department/ Accessed May 7, 2024.

at the Government Accountability Office. Somah Haaland reportedly began working with the Pueblo Action Alliance in 2020.)

As House Republicans wrote in a letter to Deb Haaland, the alliance advocates "for the dismantling of America's economic and political system and believe America is irredeemable because there is no 'opportunity to reform a system that isn't founded on good morals or values.'"[84]

The alliance's website states that it aims to "build international solidarity with the indigenous global struggle," which "includes standing in solidarity with our Palestinian relatives by upholding their demands for 'a permanent ceasefire, an end to the siege and illegal occupation in Gaza, and no more US/CANADIAN/UK military aid to Israel."

Secretary Haaland appears in a video the alliance released. The video, narrated by her daughter, demands a moratorium on oil leases around New Mexico's Chaco Cultural National Historical Park. In June 2023, Haaland shut down oil and gas opportunities in that area. The moratorium will cost the Navajo Nation, a tribe in the region that lobbied in favor of oil and gas development, $194 million over the next two decades, according to the Western Energy Alliance.[85]

Ties between the Pueblo Action Alliance and Haaland have raised ethics concerns, which Haaland brushed off. "I have carefully assessed whether my participation would raise a question regarding my impartiality and performing my official duties," Haaland told federal ethics authorities. "In undertaking this assessment, I have considered the relevant facts about the particular matter in question

84   U.S. House of Representatives Committee on Natural Resources letter to Interior Secretary Deb Haaland. June 5, 2023. https://naturalresources.house.gov/uploadedfiles/2023.06.05_haaland_ethics_compliance.pdf Accessed May 7, 2024.

85   Justice, Tristan. "Who Is Somah Haaland, The Activist Daughter Of Biden's Interior Secretary?" *The Federalist.* October 13, 2023. https://thefederalist.com/2023/10/13/who-is-somah-haaland-the-activist-daughter-of-bidens-interior-secretary/ Accessed May 7, 2024.

and have determined that I believe that a reasonable person with knowledge of those facts would not question my impartiality."[86]

Deb Haaland's response does not dispel concerns, and her connections with the Pueblo Action Alliance are alarming. She does not appear to have condemned the alliance or the "Build Back Fossil Free" coalition, despite the violent riots at Interior and the GAO.

Subverting Capitalism

While many of the Left's donors and nonprofits walk in lockstep on a host of issues, some environmental causes actually divide them. In at least one case, half of the Woketopus advocated for a new green idea, influencing the administrative state before other groups spoke up to try to shut it down. Both sides went directly to a federal agency or the public, rather than lobbying Congress for new legislation.

The idea was rightly controversial. Green activists wanted to use the mechanisms of capitalism against the development of land, by creating "natural asset companies" (NACs), which would assign value to specific parcels of undeveloped land and then use that value to trade on the New York Stock Exchange.

The idea is inherently problematic from a free market perspective. In a free market, consumers choose to buy or not buy goods and services at certain prices. This activity sends a message to producers that a certain item is more or less desirable, and worth a certain price. This arrangement helps producers learn how much money they can make for each good or service, and it works through the natural give-and-take of the market. If McDonald's wants to sell a McChicken at $15, consumers will buy something else, so McDonald's will decrease the price.

Natural Asset Companies would have none of that feedback mechanism. Instead, they would arbitrarily assign value to land that would remain undeveloped, then use that arbitrary value to

---

86   Haaland, Deb. Email to Ann M. Bledsoe Downes, May 2, 2023. 3:32 p.m. https://protectpublicstrust.org/wp-content/uploads/2024/01/SOL-2024-000061-Records.pdf Accessed May 7, 2024.

compete on the stock exchange with companies that get their value by selling goods and services to consumers. This would artificially increase the amount of money in the stock exchange, but it would devalue the companies that actually provide wealth for everyone, in order to prevent land from being developed in a way that would arguably add more wealth for everyone. In other words, it would use the engine of capitalism against the economic flourishing that free markets provide, unleashing a vicious cycle of false wealth that would actually impoverish people.

"The fundamental problem is that there's no way to assign a fair market value to an NAC," Chris Nicholson, head of research at Strive Asset Management, tells me in remarks for this book. "Normal companies are worth the present value of all their future earnings, but an NAC doesn't seek earnings, it seeks to maximize 'ecological performance.'" He adds:

> NAC supporters have designed an entire alternative accounting system to assign financial value to the clean air trees produce and so on, but when the market crashes, only monetary earnings can help a company climb out of the dip—in a crash, Google can keep making profits and even use them to buy back its own shares cheaply, but an NAC can't suddenly monetize clean air. NACs don't try to make actual money; therefore, they aren't worth any actual money.

Yet this idea nearly made it into practice, due to the Woketopus.

The story starts with The Nature Conservancy, the world's largest nongovernmental conservation organization and the seventeenth largest charity in the U.S., according to Forbes.[87] TNC reports holding 3.1 million acres of U.S. land under conservation easements, land agreements that limit landowners' rights in order to conserve the land.

---

87 "The 100 Largest U.S. Charities." *Forbes.* https://www.forbes.com/top-charities/list/#tab:rank Accessed May 17, 2024.

The Nature Conservancy describes climate change as "an extinction-level threat."[88] It supports tax incentives to use less carbon, a softer version of a "carbon tax."[89]

TNC has pioneered "green" financial schemes in ways that make its environmentalist allies uncomfortable, however. NACs are a natural match for TNC's advocacy, so it came as no surprise when TNC backed the proposal to add NACs to the New York Stock Exchange.

The conservancy's relationship with America's energy producers, such as Chevron and Duke Energy, has drawn criticism from other environmental groups.[90] TNC has hired former fossil fuel industry leaders and maintains a Business Council with many companies, including oil and gas firms. Green activists have criticized it for having any ties to these companies whatsoever.

The Nature Conservancy has faced scandals for abusing its financial practices. The IRS audited The Nature Conservancy in 2003, after the group had given a $1.5 million home loan to its then-president, Steven J. McCormick. The conservancy had also given employees free housing and the use of TNC-paid automobiles, and reportedly failed to disclose these benefits to the IRS.

TNC also faced accusations that it abused its conservation easements. According to *The Washington Post*, the conservancy purchased a New York property for $2.1 million, applied conservation easement restrictions—which excluded most of the land from development while allowing one single residential home—and then resold it to a donor and TNC trustee for $500,000, who then made

88   "A Natural Solution to Climate Change." Video. "Tackling Climate Change" page of The Nature Conservancy website. https://www.nature.org/en-us/what-we-do/our-priorities/tackle-climate-change/ Accessed May 17, 2024.

89   "Tax Policy for Nature." The Nature Conservancy. April 7, 2020, updated July 28, 2023. https://www.nature.org/en-us/about-us/who-we-are/how-we-work/policy/tax-policy/ Accessed May 17, 2024.

90   Gillis, Justin. "Group Earns Oil Income Despite Pledge on Drilling." *The New York Times*. August 3, 2014. https://www.nytimes.com/2014/08/04/science/group-earns-oil-income-despite-pledge-on-drilling.html   Accessed May 17, 2024.

a $1.6 million tax-deductible contribution to TNC.[91] Facing scrutiny from both the IRS and Congress, TNC announced several changes to its business practices, vowing not to engage in land deals with employees and officers, among other things.[92]

TNC focuses on transforming finance to achieve its goals. It launched a program called "Blue Bonds," by which it helps the governments of island nations restructure their debt to finance conservation activities, particularly in the ocean. As part of the deal, governments agree to restrict the use of approximately 30 percent of their ocean areas, while TNC purchases the country's debt at a discount, refinancing it with better interest rates and setting up structures to fund efforts to preserve the oceans.[93]

In September 2021, The New York Stock Exchange announced that it was developing natural asset companies in partnership with the Intrinsic Exchange Group, a company that launches NACs. The NYSE claimed that "natural assets produce an estimated $125 trillion annually in ecosystem services," and this "formidable output underscores the financial potential of an asset class that is wholly based on environmental investment."[94]

---

91 Stephens, Joe, and David B. Ottaway. "Nonprofit Sells Scenic Acreage to Allies at a Loss." *The Washington Post.* May 6, 2003. https://www.washingtonpost.com/archive/politics/2003/05/06/nonprofit-sells-scenic-acreage-to-allies-at-a-loss/905ef074-56ad-4034-8690-d2d8910d8e4b/ Accessed May 17, 2024.

92 "In Wake of Criticism, Nature Conservancy Changes Policies." *The New York Times.* June 14, 2003. https://www.nytimes.com/2003/06/14/national/in-wake-of-criticism-nature-conservancy-changes-policies.html Accessed May 17, 2024.

93 "Blue Bonds: An Audacious Plan to Save the World's Ocean." The Nature Conservancy. July 27, 2023. https://www.nature.org/en-us/what-we-do/our-insights/perspectives/an-audacious-plan-to-save-the-worlds-oceans/ Accessed May 17, 2024.

94 "NYSE And Intrinsic Exchange Group Partner to Launch A New Asset Class to Power a Sustainable Future." The Rockefeller Foundation news release. September 14, 2021. https://www.rockefellerfoundation.org/news/nyse-and-intrinsic-exchange-group-partner-to-launch-a-new-asset-class-to-power-a-sustainable-future/ Accessed May 17, 2024.

The Rockefeller Foundation supported the move. Its president, Rajiv J. Shah, commented:

> Climate change is an existential threat, one that demands all of us to urgently consider every opportunity to mobilize resources to protect vulnerable ecosystems and communities and fight for the future of billions of people around the world. This is why we are proud to have been an early supporter of IEG's approach to identifying new and sustainable ways for countries to safeguard their lands and waterways while creating a market to preserve natural assets.

In October 2023, the Securities and Exchange Commission filed a proposed rule change to amend the NYSE listed company manual to adopt standards for natural asset companies, paving the way for allowing them to trade on the New York Stock Exchange. The SEC notice cited The Nature Conservancy in claiming that it will cost between $598 billion and $824 billion annually "to reverse the biodiversity crisis by 2030."[95]

Jeffrey Schutes, director of capital markets and tax strategy at The Nature Conservancy, wrote a public comment in favor of the rule change:

> The Nature Conservancy supports the development and scaling up of innovative instruments to unlock finance to deliver investment in nature at scale. This is why we believe Natural Asset Companies (NACs) have potential as a new tool for countries and landowners

---

95 "Self-Regulatory Organizations; New York Stock Exchange LLC; Notice of Filing of Proposed Rule Change To Amend the NYSE Listed Company Manual To Adopt Listing Standards for Natural Asset Companies." Securities and Exchange Commission. October 4, 2023. https://www.federalregister.gov/documents/2023/10/04/2023-22041/self-regulatory-organizations-new-york-stock-exchange-llc-notice-of-filing-of-proposed-rule-change Accessed May 17, 2024.

to finance the protection and restoration of ecosystems around the world.[96]

Schutes himself went to the White House in December 2023. Matthew C. Arnold, global head of impact finance and markets at TNC, had three White House meetings in 2022. TNC CEO Jennifer L. Morris went to the White House four times in 2022 and 2023.

The World Wildlife Fund also supported the FEC proposal. Its president, Carter S. Roberts, wrote in a comment on the proposed rulemaking:

> We believe that a financial mechanism to define, measure, and disclose the value of natural capital is necessary to create incentives for the financial system to protect natural capital.... WWF-US is excited to see NACs develop as a new tool to protect nature and to see them successfully deployed to protect critical habitats and ecosystems that can benefit from the support that this new market may offer.[97]

WWF leaders have visited the White House at least eight times since Biden took office.[98]

Despite strong support from TNC and WWF, the SEC's proposed rule for natural asset companies faced headwinds from other groups in the Woketopus. Ben Cushing, director of the Sierra Club's fossil-free finance campaign, condemned the idea of monetizing natural resources. "If investors want to pay a landowner to improve

96   Schutes, Jefferey J. Nature Conservancy to Securities and Exchange Commission. Comment on proposed rulemaking. https://www.sec.gov/comments/sr-nyse-2023-09/srnyse202309-296179-719782.htm   Accessed May 17, 2024.

97   Roberts, Carter S. World Wildlife Fund to Securities and Exchange Commission. Comment on proposed rulemaking. October 24, 2023. https://www.sec.gov/comments/sr-nyse-2023-09/srnyse202309-280239-684122.pdf Accessed May 17, 2024.

98   White House Visitor Logs.

their soil or protect a wetland, that's great," he told *The New York Times*. "I think we've seen that when that is turned into a financial asset that has a whole secondary market attached to it, it creates a lot of distortions."[99]

Republicans also opposed the move. Twenty-three state financial officers, all Republicans, warned that making nature's value "a private commodity from which people can profit at the expense of others," is "a terribly dangerous idea."[100]

The House Committee on Natural Resources, chaired by Arkansas Republican Representative Bruce Westerman, sent the SEC a letter demanding information about the rulemaking.[101]

"The proposal designates 'unsustainable activities' as activities that cause any 'material adverse impact,' without defining what classifies as a 'material adverse impact,'" Westerman wrote. The proposal appears to outsource the rule to the Intrinsic Exchange Group, "a private company with its own interests and shareholders to answer to." He warned that "approved activity on federal land controlled by NACs will be determined by the whims of eco-activists rather than government scientists or Congress."

In January 2024, the New York Stock Exchange withdrew the proposed rule, without giving an explanation.[102]

This particular rule's failure won't stop similar efforts in the federal government, however. In January 2023, the Biden administration released a fifteen-year-plan aimed at incorporating the value

---

99   DePillis, Lydia. "Nature Has Value. Could We Literally Invest in It?" *The New York Times*. March 10, 2024. https://www.nytimes.com/2024/02/18/business/economy/natural-assets.html Accessed May 17, 2024.

100 Alaska State Financial Officers to Vanessa A. Countryman at the Securities and Exchange Commission. January 17, 2024. https://treasurer.utah.gov/wp-content/uploads/NAC-Financial-Officer-Comment-Letter-January-2024.pdf Accessed May 17, 2024.

101 Westerman, Bruce, et al. to Gary Gensler, Securities and Exchange Commission Chair. January 11, 2024. https://naturalresources.house.gov/uploadedfiles/hnr_letter_to_sec_on_nacs.pdf Accessed May 17, 2024.

102 Securities and Exchange Commission release. January 17, 2024. https://www.sec.gov/files/rules/sro/nyse/2024/34-99355.pdf Accessed May 17, 2024.

of the natural world alongside traditional economic statistics such as gross national product. The Office of Science and Technology Policy, the Office of Management and Budget, and the Department of Commerce released a joint report creating a system of "natural accounting and associated environmental-economic statistics."[103]

"The nation's economy and environment are deeply intertwined," the report states. It presents a system to "help us understand and consistently track changes in the condition and economic value of land, water, air, and other natural assets." This analysis of "natural capital" will "provide data to guide the federal government and the economy through the transition we need for sustainable growth and development, a stable climate, and a healthy planet."

The Nature Conservancy and the World Wildlife Fund may not have gotten NACs, but they may still work with the administrative state to tweak capitalism to serve their interests.

THE MONEY BEHIND THE MOVEMENT

The green revolving door and the environmentalists' influence campaign enjoy heavy infusions of cash from the Left's dark money network.

The Center for American Progress has received:

- ◆ $315,000 from Hopewell Fund between 2020 and 2022 (Arabella) [104]
- ◆ $2.97 million from New Venture Fund between 2012 and 2021 (Arabella)[105]

---

103 Prabhakar, PhD, Arati., Shalanda D. Young, and Gina M. Raimondo. "National Strategy to Develop Statistics for Environmental-Economic Decisions." Office of Science and Technology, Office of Management and Budget, Department of Commerce. January 2023. https://www.whitehouse. gov/wp-content/uploads/2023/01/Natural-Capital-Accounting-Strategy-final.pdf Accessed May 17, 2024.

104 "The Hopewell Fund." Form 990 Schedule I for 2020, 2021, and 2022, accessed on April 22, 2024.

105 "New Venture Fund." Form 990 Schedule I for 2012–2021, accessed on April 22, 2024.

- $300,000 from Sixteen Thirty Fund between 2014 and 2021, with $250,000 of that sum earmarked for "environmental (climate, conservation & energy) programs (Arabella)[106]
- $155,000 from The Proteus Fund between 2016 and 2019[107]
- $65,000 from The Tides Foundation in 2020[108]
- $50,000 from the AFL-CIO between 2010 and 2018[109]
- $2.05 million from the AFSCME between 2010 and 2022[110]
- $860,000 from the National Education Association between 2011 and 2021[111]

The Natural Resources Defense Fund received:

- $1.1 million from New Venture Fund between 2010 and 2018 (Arabella)[112]
- $851,000 from Sixteen Thirty Fund between 2018 and 2022 (Arabella)[113]

---

106 "Sixteen Thirty Fund." Form 990 Schedule I for 2014 and 2021, accessed on April 22, 2024.

107 "Proteus Fund Inc." Form 990 Schedule I for 2016 and 2019, accessed on April 22, 2024.

108 "Tides Foundation." Form 990 Schedule I for 2020, accessed on April 22, 2024.

109 "American Federation Of Labor & Congress Of Industrial Orgs." Form 990 Schedule I for 2010, 2011, 2012, and 2018, accessed on April 22, 2024.

110 "American Federation Of State County & Municipal Employees." Form 990 Schedule I for 2010–2022, accessed April 22, 2024.

111 The true figure may be larger. NEA labeled one contribution to CAP "Action Fund" using the EIN number of CAP in 2012. If that figure went to the center, rather than its action fund, the overall figure would be $895,000. "National Education Association of the United States." Form 990 Schedule I for 2011–2021, accessed April 22, 2024.

112 "New Venture Fund." Form 990 Schedule I for 2010–2018, accessed on April 23, 2024.

113 "Sixteen Thirty Fund." Form 990 Schedule I for 2018, 2022, accessed on April 23, 2024.

- $1.6 million from Windward Fund in 2022 (Arabella)[114]
- $7 million from The Tides Foundation between 2018 and 2022[115]

The Environmental Defense Fund received:

- $3.5 million from between 2018 and 2021 (Arabella)[116]
- $1.6 million from New Venture Fund between 2013 and 2022 (Arabella)[117]
- $675,000 from Sixteen Thirty Fund in 2015 (Arabella)[118]
- $3.96 million from Windward Fund between 2018 and 2022 (Arabella)[119]
- $37,600 from The Tides Foundation between 2019 and 2021[120]

The National Wildlife Federation netted:

- $800,000 from New Venture Fund between 2010 and 2016 (Arabella)[121]
- $100,000 from Windward Fund in 2020 (Arabella)[122]

The Sierra Club received:

114 "Windward Fund." Form 990 Schedule I for 2022, accessed on April 23, 2024.

115 The precise figure is $6,984,600. "Tides Foundation." Form 990 Schedule I for 2018–2022, accessed on April 23, 2024.

116 "Hopewell Fund." Form 990 Schedule I for 2018–2021, accessed on April 22, 2024.

117 "New Venture Fund." Form 990 Schedule I for 2013–2022, accessed on April 22, 2024.

118 "Sixteen Thirty Fund." Form 990 Schedule I for 2015, accessed on April 22, 2024.

119 "Windward Fund." Form 990 Schedule I for 2018, 2019, and 2022, accessed on April 22, 2024.

120 "Tides Foundation." Form 990 Schedule I for 2019 and 2021, accessed on April 22, 2024.

121 "New Venture Fund." Form 990, Schedule I, for 2010–2016, accessed April 27, 2024.

122 "Windward Fund." Form 990, Schedule I for 2020, accessed on April 27, 2024.

- $50,000 from New Venture Fund in 2015 (Arabella)[123]
- $3.6 million from Sixteen Thirty Fund between 2014 and 2022 (Arabella)[124]
- $150,000 from the Wyss Foundation in 2022[125]
- $12,500 from Proteus Action League in 2020[126]
- $950,000 from Tides Advocacy between 2018 and 2021[127]
- $415,000 from The Open Society Policy Center between 2020 and 2022[128]

The Southwest Organizing Project, Pueblo Action Alliance's parent organization, received:

- $1.5 million from New Venture Fund between 2014 and 2022 (Arabella)[129]
- $356,500 from Windward Fund between 2020 and 2022 (Arabella)[130]
- $17,500 from The Proteus Fund between 2019 and 2020[131]
- $200,000 from The Tides Center between 2021 and 2022[132]

---

123 "New Venture Fund." Form 990, Schedule I for 2015, accessed May 6, 2024.

124 The exact figure is $3,623,333. "Sixteen Thirty Fund." Form 990, Schedule I for 2014, 2016, and 2022, accessed May 6, 2024.

125 Wyss Foundation 2022 grants page. https://www.wyssfoundation.org/grants Accessed May 20, 2024.

126 "Proteus Action League." Form 990, Schedule I for 2020, accessed May 6, 2024.

127 "Tides Advocacy." Form 990, Schedule I for 2018-2021, accessed May 6, 2024.

128 "Open Society Policy Center." Form 990, Schedule I for 2020-2022, accessed May 6, 2024.

129 The exact figure is $1,554,050. "New Venture Fund." Form 990, Schedule I for 2014–2022, accessed May 7, 2024.

130 "Windward Fund." Form 990, Schedule I for 2020–2022, accessed May 7, 2024.

131 "Proteus Fund." Form 990, Schedule I for 2019, 2020, accessed May 7, 2024.

132 "Tides Center." Form 990, Schedule I for 2021, 2022, accessed May 7, 2024.

- $105,000 from The Tides Foundation between 2020 and 2022[133]
- $72,500 from Demos (more on this in Chapter 8) between 2014 and 2015[134]
- $200,000 from Rockefeller Philanthropy Advisors between 2020 and 2022[135]

The Nature Conservancy has received:

- $6 million from Hopewell Fund in 2019 (Arabella)[136]
- $8.3 million from New Venture Fund between 2010 and 2022[137]
- $5.6 million from the Wyss Foundation in 2022[138]
- $160,000 from The Foundation to Promote Open Society in 2020 and 2021[139]
- $2.3 million from The Rockefeller Foundation between 2015 and 2022[140]

---

133 "Tides Foundation." Form 990, Schedule I for 2020–2022, accessed May 7, 2024.

134 "Demos A Network For Ideas and Action." Form 990, Schedule I for June 2014–June 2016, accessed May 7, 2024.

135 "Rockefeller Philanthropy Advisors." Form 990, Schedule I for 2020–2022, accessed May 7, 2024.

136 The precise figure is $6,378,340. "Hopewell Fund." Form 990, Schedule I, for 2019.

137 The precise figure is $8,300,240. "New Venture Fund." Form 990, Schedule I, for 2010–2022.

138 Wyss Foundation 2022 grants page. https://www.wyssfoundation.org/grants Accessed May 20, 2024.

139 "Awarded Grants" page search results for "Nature Conservancy." Open Society Foundations, https://www.opensocietyfoundations.org/grants/past?-filter_keyword=Nature+conservancy Accessed May 17, 2024.

140 "Our Grants" search results for "Nature Conservancy." The Rockefeller Foundation. https://www.rockefellerfoundation.org/grants/?post_type=grant&grant_active_status=&keyword=Nature+Conservancy&from_month=1&from_year=2015&to_month=12&to_year=2024&submit=Submit Accessed May 17, 2024.

- ◆ $3.9 million from Rockefeller Philanthropy Advisors between 2012 and 2022[141]
- ◆ $20,000 from the Rockefeller Family Fund in 2022[142]
- ◆ $100,000 from the Rockefeller Brothers Fund in 2023[143]

The World Wildlife Fund received:

- ◆ $20 million from New Venture Fund between 2014 and 2021 (Arabella)[144]
- ◆ $1 million from Windward Fund in 2022 (Arabella)[145]
- ◆ $12 million from The Tides Foundation between 2018 and 2022[146]
- ◆ $10.8 million from Rockefeller Philanthropy Advisors between 2011 and 2022[147]
- ◆ $400,000 from The Rockefeller Brothers Fund (marked for energy initiatives in China) in 2019[148]
- ◆ $4 million from The Rockefeller Foundation between 2017 and 2023[149]

---

141 The precise figure is $3,888,837. "Rockefeller Philanthropy Advisors." Form 990, Schedule I, for 2012–2022.

142 "Rockefeller Family Fund." Form 990, Schedule I, for 2022.

143 Rockefeller Brothers Fund grant recipient: Nature Conservancy. https://www.rbf.org/grantees/nature-conservancy Accessed May 17, 2024.

144 The precise figure is $20,869,312. "New Venture Fund." Form 990, Schedule I, for 2014–2021.

145 "Windward Fund." Form 990, Schedule I, for 2022.

146 The precise figure is $12,035,483. "Tides Foundation." Form 990, Schedule I, for 2018–2022.

147 The precise figure is $10,803,463. "Rockefeller Philanthropy Advisors." Form 990, Schedule I for 2011–2022.

148 Rockefeller Brothers Fund grant recipient: World Wildlife Fund. https://www.rbf.org/grantees/world-wildlife-fund-inc Accessed May 17, 2024.

149 The precise figure is $4,048,000. The Rockefeller Foundation grants search results for "World Wildlife Fund." https://www.rockefellerfoundation.org/grants/?post_type=grant&grant_active_status=&keyword=World+Wildlife+fund&from_month=1&from_year=2015&to_month=12&to_year=2024&submit=Submit Accessed May 17, 2024.

- $28,000 from Amalgamated Charitable between 2019 and 2021[150]
- $1.4 million from The Nature Conservancy between 2014 and 2021[151]

Windward Fund, which bankrolled many of the groups above, told me in remarks for this book that it follows all nonprofit regulations in working "to safeguard the environment using a variety of innovative strategies, including advocating for legislative change regardless of which party is in power." The group also stated that "climate change is the defining challenge of our lifetime."

This money helps prop up a green revolving door, through which green activists move from the administrative state to activist groups and back again, all while pressuring the government to adopt radical policies that constrain reliable sources of energy in exchange for less reliable energy sources that also empower America's greatest geopolitical rival. Commonsense Americans should demand an end to perverse mechanisms like sue and settle, and advocate for ways to prevent these incestuous relationships.

While the Woketopus explains the federal government's absurd bias on climate change, it also makes sense of another absurdity— how the administrative state adopted radical gender ideology seemingly overnight, turning common sense and biology on their heads.

---

150 "Amalgamated Charitable Foundation." Form 990, Schedule I for 2019–2021.
151 The precise figure is $1,430,309. "Nature Conservancy." Form 990, Schedule I for 2014–2021.

5

THE TRANSGENDER ADMINISTRATIVE STATE

The concept of the Woketopus helps make sense of how the federal government moved to embrace a radical ideology on gender seemingly overnight. Perhaps the most shocking revelation of just how far this ideology has seeped into the administration came on Good Friday, 2024.

On Friday, March 29, 2024, the day Western Christians—including the Roman Catholic Church to which the president belongs—commemorate Good Friday, the White House released a statement declaring that the coming Sunday would be the "Transgender Day of Visibility."

"I am proud that my administration has stood for justice from the start, working to ensure that the LGBTQI+ community can live openly, in safety, with dignity and respect," Biden stated in the proclamation.

Yes, America's second Catholic president dedicated Easter, the day when Christians commemorate the most important event of their faith, the Resurrection of Jesus, to the transgender movement, a movement Biden's own church considers to be at odds with the reality of men and women made in the image of God.

The president went on to warn that "extremists are proposing hundreds of hateful laws that target and terrify transgender kids and their families—silencing teachers; banning books; and even threatening parents, doctors, and nurses with prison for helping parents get care for their children." He suggested that this trend connects to "bullying and discrimination" that led "half of transgender youth to consider suicide in the past year," and mentioned what he called an "epidemic of violence against transgender women and girls, especially women and girls of color."

"Let me be clear: All of these attacks are un-American and must end," Biden emphasized. "Today, we send a message to all transgender Americans: You are loved. You are heard. You are understood. You belong. You are America, and my entire administration and I have your back."[1]

Biden made no such declaration to the millions of Catholics and Protestants who remembered Good Friday that day. On Easter Sunday, he gave a much shorter statement with no proclamation.[2]

Biden's decision to mark Transgender Day of Visibility on Easter drew loud condemnation.

"This is what Biden cares about and who he caters to," Senator Ted Cruz (R-TX), wrote on X. "He is devaluing Easter and elevating trans recognition. Downright shameful and despicable."[3]

On Saturday, March 30, former President Donald Trump's campaign called it "appalling and insulting that Joe Biden's White House…formally proclaimed Easter Sunday as 'Trans Day of Visibility.' We call on Joe Biden's failing campaign and White House to issue an apology to the millions of Catholics and Christians across America who believe tomorrow is for one celebration only— the resurrection of Jesus Christ."[4]

1   "A Proclamation on Transgender Day of Visibility, 2024." White House Briefing Room. March 29, 2024. https://www.whitehouse.gov/briefing-room/presidential-actions/2024/03/29/a-proclamation-on-transgender-day-of-visibility-2024/ Accessed April 24, 2024.

2   "Statement from President Joe Biden on Easter." White House Briefing Room. March 31, 2024. https://www.whitehouse.gov/briefing-room/statements-releases/2024/03/31/statement-from-president-joe-biden-on-easter-2/ Accessed April 24, 2024.

3   Cruz, Ted (@TedCruz). X post. March 30, 2024. 4:19 p.m. https://twitter.com/tedcruz/status/1774169625208500494 Accessed April 24, 2024.

4   Valencia, Jamel. "Biden's 'Transgender Day of Visibility' falling on Easter Sunday sparks reaction." *The National Desk.* March 30, 2024. https://thenationaldesk.com/news/connect-to-congress/president-joe-bidens-transgender-day-of-visibility-falling-on-easter-sunday-sparks-reaction-donald-trump-demands-apology-fury-slammed-on-social-media-on-saturday-march-30-2024 Accessed April 24, 2024.

Republicans were far from alone in condemning Biden's message. "I was so extremely, extremely disappointed that our local officials and our president would use the most important religious observance of the Christian calendar to proclaim a message that is political, it is, and a source of division," Michael Burbidge, the Roman Catholic bishop of the Diocese of Arlington, Virginia, said on his April 4 podcast. "It was offensive to many people, and unnecessary."[5]

The White House defended Biden's proclamation. Press Secretary Karine Jean-Pierre said she aimed to dispel "misinformation" about it, noting that Easter Sunday (the date of which varies, according to a lunar calendar) "happened to coincide with Transgender Visibility Day," which Biden has commemorated on March 31 since 2021.[6]

Burbidge addressed this claim, however: "I know you're going to say, 'well it goes back to March 31, 2009.... But we transfer holidays all of the time. We haven't really talked about this day until it was on Easter, so I would tend to think that it was calculated and that is really, really sad, and it was offensive as Christians."[7]

Albert Mohler, president of The Southern Baptist Theological Seminary, called the proclamation "incredibly revealing."

"So President Biden, in declaring through the White House a Transgender Day of Visibility—and, yes, the main controversy was the fact that it happened on Easter Sunday—but Christians need to step back and say, as offensive as that was—and frankly, [it was] inexcusably offensive—it also was incredibly revealing,"

5   Lavenburg, John. "Bishop calls Easter observance of Transgender Day 'offensive and unnecessary.'" *Crux.* April 5, 2024. https://cruxnow.com/church-in-the-usa/2024/04/bishop-calls-easter-observance-of-transgender-day-offensive-and-unnecessary Accessed April 24, 2024.

6   Reese, Reagan. "JKP Says She's 'Surprised' By 'Misinformation' About Transgender Day, Implies Critics Don't Get How Calendars Work." *The Daily Caller.* April 1, 2024. https://dailycaller.com/2024/04/01/karine-jean-pierre-transgender-day-calendar-misinformatio-eastern/ Accessed April 24, 2024.

7   Lavenburg. "Bishop calls Easter observance."

Mohler said on his podcast, *The Briefing*, on April 1. "What was made visible is the agenda of this administration and, honestly, its war on reality."[8]

Roman Catholic doctrine has consistently opposed gender ideology, teaching that God made humans male and female and people cannot change their sex. On April 8, the Vatican released a declaration titled "Dignitas Infinita" (which translates from Latin to "Infinite Dignity"). That document emphatically condemns "gender theory" as a form of trying to "make oneself God, entering into competition with the true God of love revealed to us in the gospel."[9]

The Woketopus helps explain how a self-described Catholic president who goes to mass somehow managed to support an ideology so at odds with Catholic teaching.

WHAT'S THE BIG DEAL WITH GENDER IDEOLOGY?

Gender ideology is the idea that a person's inner sense of gender overrides his or her biological sex, such that it becomes healthy for him or her to seek medical interventions to appear like the opposite sex, and such that society must change its basic rules to accommodate males who claim to be women and females who claim to be men. Advocates claim that people who identify with the gender opposite their biological sex—referred to as "transgender"—face social stigma that worsens their mental health problems, leading them to consider suicide. In order to keep them safe from self-harm, society must affirm their "gender identities."

8   Mohler, Albert. "Transgender Day of Visibility Proclamation on Resurrection Sunday? President Joe Biden, We Get Your Message—But Visibility is Not Working." *The Briefing* (podcast transcript). April 1, 2024. https://albert-mohler.com/2024/04/01/briefing-4-1-24/ Accessed April 24, 2024.

9   "Declaration of the Dicastery for the Doctrine of the Faith 'Dignitas Infinita' on Human Dignity." The Holy See Press Office. April 8, 2024. https://press.vatican.va/content/salastampa/en/bollettino/pubblico/2024/04/08/240408c.html Accessed April 24, 2024.

While it may seem laughable to insist that a man can be a woman if he just tries hard enough, this ideology opens a Pandora's Box of very serious harms.

First, it represents a philosophical approach at odds with not only historic Christianity, Judaism, Islam, and other world religions, but also with basic biology. Contrary to the view that humans are created male and female, it presents biological sex as either mutable or rooted in a non-physical identity. This makes gender identity similar to the ancient Christian heresy of Gnosticism, which taught that the physical world was evil and the spiritual world was good, so salvation lay in escaping the physical world. Gender ideology teaches that the solution isn't to escape the physical world, but to force it to conform to an internal sense of gender that overrides biology.

Mandating this philosophy arguably undermines Americans' free speech and religious freedom. Advocates insist that Americans must use a person's preferred pronouns, for example, referring to a male who identifies as female as "she," rather than "he." Federal courts have ruled that mandating such pronouns violates free speech, however, by forcing someone to express ideas about gender with which they disagree.[10]

Furthermore, it allows biological males who have gone through puberty—and therefore have more muscle and larger hearts than women—to compete in women's sports, often pushing top-tier women to the sidelines.

Allowing males in women's private spaces, such as restrooms, locker rooms, shelters, and prisons, makes women vulnerable to predation. Many men who struggle with gender identity issues may not pose a threat to women, but a policy allowing men into these spaces based on self-declared gender identity opens the door to predators who may claim a transgender identity to gain access.

10　Meriwether, Nicholas. "The 6th Circuit Was Right: My University Can't Force Me to Endorse Ideas I Disagree With." *The Daily Signal.* June 1, 2021. https://www.dailysignal.com/2021/06/01/the-6th-circuit-was-right-my-university-cant-force-me-to-endorse-ideas-i-disagree-with/ Accessed April 24, 2024.

More than half of the men housed in Wisconsin Department of Corrections facilities who identify as transgender women have been convicted of at least one count of sexual assault or abuse.[11]

Perhaps most perniciously, this ideology encourages experimental medical interventions in the name of "gender-affirming care." Doctors have prescribed to minors so-called puberty blockers—in an attempt to stop the natural process of puberty—and cross-sex hormones—to make males appear female, or vice versa. Some hospitals have offered "gender-affirming mastectomies" to remove perfectly healthy breast tissue because a woman claims she identifies as a man. Some people ask surgeons to remove their healthy sex organs and replace them with facsimiles of those of the opposite sex. These "bottom surgeries" leave patients completely sterile, and they often make any future sexual activity painful.

Much of the U.S. medical establishment embraces these interventions, even for minors (except for surgery to remove gonads, which they support only for adults). Medical groups follow the advice of the World Professional Association for Transgender Health (WPATH), which presents itself as the arbiter of "gender-affirming care."

Yet many government agencies in Europe have reconsidered these medical interventions. England's National Health Service has stopped prescribing "puberty blockers" for children with gender dysphoria (the painful and persistent condition of identifying with the gender opposite one's biological sex) under fifteen, "because there is not enough evidence of safety and clinical effectiveness." However, the NHS also rules, "From the age of 16, teenagers who've been on hormone blockers for at least 12 months may be given cross-sex hormones, also known as gender-affirming hormones." The agency states that these hormones can cause irreversible changes, such as

---

11   Olohan, Mary Margaret. "Just How Many Imprisoned Men Who Identify as Transgender Are Guilty of Sexual Assault? More Than Half, New Data Shows." *The Daily Signal.* August 24, 2023. https://www.dailysignal.com/2023/08/24/exclusive-half-imprisoned-men-identify-transgender-women-convicted-least-one-sexual-assault/ Accessed April 24, 2024.

males developing breasts, the breaking or deepening of a female's voice, and temporary or even permanent infertility.[12]

In April, the pediatrician Hilary Cass released an in-depth report commissioned by the NHS. She found that most studies on transgender medical interventions were low quality.

> This is an area of remarkably weak evidence, and yet results of studies are exaggerated or misrepresented by people on all sides of the debate to support their viewpoint. The reality is that we have no good evidence on the long-term outcomes of interventions to manage gender-related distress.... The option to provide masculinizing/feminizing hormones from age 16 is available, but the review would recommend extreme caution.

"For the majority of young people, a medical pathway will not be the best way to manage their gender-related distress," Cass concluded in the report's summary online.[13]

Many doctors in the U.S. are also sounding the alarm.

Dr. Stephen B. Levine, a psychiatrist and early proponent of transgender medical interventions, joined and briefly helped lead the Harry Benjamin International Gender Dysphoria Association, which later became WPATH. He resigned his membership in 2002, however, due to "my regretful conclusion that the organization and its recommendations had become dominated by politics and ideology, rather than by scientific process, as it was years earlier." In a legal affidavit, he condemned the WPATH Standards of Care for gender dysphoria as "not an impartial or evidence-based document."

---

12   "Treatment for Gender dysphoria." National Health Service. https://www. nhs.uk/conditions/gender-dysphoria/treatment/ Accessed April 24, 2024.

13   Cass, Hilary. *The Cass Review: Independent Review of Gender Identity Services for Children and Young People, Final Report.* https://cass.independent-review. uk/home/publications/final-report/ Downloaded April 24, 2024. Quotes appear in the full report, which can be downloaded at the link.

Levine called transgender medical interventions "experimental therapies that have not been shown to improve mental or physical health outcomes by young adulthood." He warned that these therapies "do not decrease, and may increase, the risk of suicide." The psychologist also stated that social transition—the practice of socially recognizing a child's claimed transgender identity—"is a powerful psychotherapeutic intervention that radically changes outcomes," making it far less likely that young children will "desist" from a transgender identity.

Endocrinologists Paul Hruz, Michael Laidlaw, and Quentin Van Meter joined Levine in testifying against hormone therapies as "experimental." Hruz noted that "there are no long-term, peer-reviewed published, reliable and valid research studies" documenting the percentage of patients helped or harmed by transgender interventions. He also noted that attempts to block puberty followed by cross-sex hormones not only impact fertility, but pose risks such as low bone density, "disfiguring acne, high blood pressure, weight gain, abnormal glucose tolerance, breast cancer, liver disease, thrombosis, and cardiovascular disease."

Neurologist Sophie Scott warned that since "puberty is associated with very marked changes in the structure of the brain… the use of puberty blockers may have serious consequences for the development of the human brain."[14]

THROWING CAUTION TO THE WIND

Despite these and other concerns, Biden's administration has done as the president claimed in his declaration: it has wholeheartedly embraced gender ideology and implemented it throughout the federal bureaucracy.

---

14 O'Neil, Tyler. "EXCLUSIVE: Doctors Expose Just How Experimental 'Gender-Affirming Care' Truly Is in Florida Medicaid Case." *The Daily Signal.* April 11, 2023. https://www.dailysignal.com/2023/04/11/exclusive-doctors-expose-experimental-gender-affirming-care-truly-florida-medicaid-case/ Accessed April 24, 2024.

On his very first day in office, President Biden signed an executive order making gender ideology a kind of state-sponsored religion for the federal government (more on this later). Various federal agencies have implemented this order by rewriting laws to entrench transgenderism.

The Heritage Foundation's Oversight Project has unearthed documents showing just how far this ideology has permeated the federal bureaucracy.

The Office of Personnel Management, which oversees how federal agencies operate, issued a document titled "Guidance Regarding Gender Identity and Inclusion in the Federal Workplace" in March 2023. The document states that federal employees who refuse to use preferred pronouns may face discipline for contributing to "an unlawful hostile work environment." It directs agencies to support "transitioning" by setting up transgender points of contact and offering support for "workplace transitions," such as name and pronoun changes in employee profiles. OPM also directs agencies not to limit employees to using facilities that "are inconsistent with the employee's gender identity."

Meanwhile, U.S. Customs and Border Protection directed Border Patrol agents to use the "preferred pronouns" of illegal aliens as they unlawfully enter the United States. "DO NOT use 'he, him, she, her' pronouns until you have more information about, or provided by, the individual," the agency advises. Border Patrol agents are attempting to address an immigration crisis of epic proportions, yet their supervisors are ordering them to be proactive not in arresting illegals or preventing them from entering the country, but in determining their gender identities.

In June 2023, the Federal Bureau of Prisons issued guidance about how federal prisons should provide taxpayer-funded transgender operations for inmates. Prisoners may request procedures to remove, create, enlarge, or reshape sex organs. A Transgender Utilization Review Advisory Group then assesses whether the requested procedure is "medically needed." A list of "gender confirming procedures" includes: "enlarging the breasts using breast implants," "surgical creation of a clitoris," "removal of one or both testicles," "removal of the uterus," "construction of a penis which may involve multiple surgeries," and "an erectile prosthetic device is placed to allow for an erection."[15]

The Treasury Department created an internal policy mandating that when requiring a person to select male or female gender markers, the department must also allow the letter "X" as a gender marker, "so an individual is not required to choose between the binary male ('M') or female ('F')."[16]

In December 2021, the Antitrust Division of the Justice Department released a "Manager's Diversity Tip Sheet," urging managers to play an active role in mandating "gender identity inclusion." The document urges managers to correct employees who "misgender" coworkers and facilitate introductions by sharing their own preferred pronouns.

These documents give a taste of how gender ideology is seeping into the federal bureaucracy, without a single vote in Congress.[17]

A MAJOR DRIVING FORCE

Gender ideology has grown to dominate the Democratic Party, but one organization arguably has more impact than any other when it comes to enforcing this philosophy on American culture.

The Human Rights Campaign, an LGBTQ group founded in 1980, holds tremendous sway in corporate America through its Corporate Equality Index. HRC touts its index as "a primary driving force for LGBTQ+ workplace inclusion," and "the national bench-

---

15   Oversight Project (@OversightPR). X Post. November 20, 2023. 1:45 p.m. https://twitter.com/OversightPR/status/1726673230587662708   Accessed April 24, 2024.

16   Oversight Project (@OversightPR). X Post. December 12, 2023. 4:37 p.m. https://twitter.com/OversightPR/status/1734689072147533894   Accessed April 24, 2024.

17   Howell, Mike. "The Transgender Administrative State." *The Daily Signal.* January 26, 2024. https://www.dailysignal.com/2024/01/26/the-transgender-administrative-state/ Accessed April 24, 2024.

marking tool on corporate policies, practices and benefits pertinent to lesbian, gay, bisexual, transgender and queer employees." The index includes four key pillars: nondiscrimination policies, "equitable benefits for LGBTQ+ workers and their families;" "supporting an inclusive culture," and "corporate social responsibility." That last criterion involves "efforts in outreach and engagement to [the] broader LGBTQ+ community" and "philanthropic giving guidelines."[18]

Companies strive to receive high ratings on the index, and it seems the index may be responsible for two of the most notorious transgender controversies of 2023.

Companies that attain the maximum one hundred points earn the title "Equality 100 Award: Leaders in LGBTQ+ Inclusion." A total of 545 businesses earned one hundred points in the 2023–2024 index, but they can't sit on their laurels. James Lindsay, a podcaster best known for exposing the bias of academic journals by getting hoax articles published, told *The New York Post* that HRC uses the index ranking "like an extortion racket, like the Mafia."[19]

"HRC sends representatives to corporations every year telling them what kind of stuff they have to make visible at the company," Lindsay explained. "They give them a list of demands and if they don't follow through there's a threat that you won't keep your CEI score."

The HRC index factors into some investors' preferences for investing in companies with environmental, social, and corporate governance (ESG) standards. ESG standards weaponize leftist causes such as climate change, unionization, and Critical Race Theory, applying an ideological test to investing.

The great Bud Light kerfuffle of 2023 traces back to this index. On April 1, 2023, Bud Light released a video in which transgen-

---

18 *Corporate Equality Index 2023–2024. Workplace Reports.* Human Rights Campaign Foundation. https://www.hrc.org/resources/corporate-equality-index Accessed April 24, 2024.

19 Kennedy, Dana. "Inside the CEI system pushing brands to endorse celebs like Dylan Mulvaney." *The New York Post.* April 8, 2023. https://nypost.com/2023/04/07/inside-the-woke-scoring-system-guiding-american-companies/ Accessed April 24, 2024.

der influencer Dylan Mulvaney endorsed the beer. Transgenderism seems an odd match for Bud Light's traditional audience. Consumers responded with a boycott, and the backlash cost Bud Light its pride of place as America's top-selling beer.[20]

Bud Light first responded with an explanation of its relationship with social media influencers like Mulvaney. Then on April 14, Brendan Whitworth, CEO of Bud Light's parent company, Anheuser-Busch InBev, gave a statement that pleased neither side: "We never intended to be part of a discussion that divides people. We are in the business of bringing people together over a beer."

Jay Brown, senior vice president of programs, research, and training at HRC, said the company's reaction "really disturbed" HRC. "In this moment, it is absolutely critical for Anheuser-Busch to stand in solidarity with Dylan and the trans community," Brown wrote in an April 2023 letter to the company. "However, when faced with anti-LGBTQ+ and transphobic criticism, Anheuser-Busch's actions demonstrate a profound lack of fortitude in upholding its values of diversity, equity, and inclusion."

Two weeks after sending that letter, Brown sent another letter telling Anheuser-Busch that HRC was suspending its 100 percent index rating.[21]

Around the same time, Target rolled out new products ahead of June, which LGBTQ activists celebrate as "Pride Month." Heavily advertised in stores, the products included LGBTQ-themed gingerbread houses, onesies, and female swimsuits designed to discreetly hide male genitalia. (The company responsible for the products also makes products with satanic symbols, including a shirt reading, "Satan respects pronouns.")

---

20 Valinsky, Jordan. "Bud Light loses its title as America's top-selling beer." CNN Business. June 14, 2023. https://www.cnn.com/2023/06/14/business/bud-light-modelo-top-selling-may-sales/index.html Accessed April 24, 2024.

21 Wiener-Bronner, Danielle. "Anheuser-Busch loses top LGBTQ+ rating over its Bud Light response." CNN Business. May 19, 2023. https://www.cnn.com/2023/05/19/business/hrc-rating-bud-light/index.html Accessed April 24, 2024.

Amid backlash, Target announced that it would move the products away from the front of its stores, and Democrats responded in anger. California Democratic Governor Gavin Newsom accused Target CEO Brian Cornell of "selling out the LGBTQ+ community to extremists." HRC President Kelley Robinson demanded Target "put the products back on the shelves and ensure their Pride displays are visible on the floors," suggesting that Target was bowing to "extremist groups." HRC gathered more than two hundred LGBTQ groups to urge Target "to reject and speak out against anti-LGBTQ+ extremism going into Pride Month."[22]

Target's second-quarter sales fell for the first time in six years amid the backlash,[23] and it lost its 100 percent score on the Corporate Equality Index, getting five points deducted for "Responsible Citizenship."[24]

HRC runs other indexes, rating city governments,[25] and even hospitals and medical institutions, to push gender ideology across the country. Both Pfizer and PhRMA fund the "Healthcare Equality Index."[26]

---

22 "BREAKING: Over 200 LGBTQ+ and Allied Organizations Call on Target, Business Community to Speak Out Against Extremist Anti-LGBTQ+ Attacks." Human Rights Campaign news release. June 5, 2023. https://www.hrc.org/press-releases/breaking-over-200-lgbtq-and-allied-organizations-call-on-target-business-community-to-speak-out-against-extremist-anti-lgbtq-attacks Accessed April 24, 2024.

23 O'Neil, Tyler. "GO WOKE, GO BROKE: Target Feels the Pain Amid 'Pride Month' Backlash." *The Daily Signal.* August 16, 2023. https://www.dailysignal.com/2023/08/16/go-woke-go-broke-target-feels-pain-pride-month-backlash/ Accessed April 24, 2024.

24 "Target Corp." Human Rights Campaign employer search. https://www.hrc.org/resources/buyers-guide/target-corp.-2 Accessed April 24, 2024.

25 "Municipal Equality Index 2023." Human Rights Campaign. https://www.hrc.org/resources/municipal-equality-index Accessed April 24, 2024.

26 Olohan, Mary Margaret. "PhRMA, Pfizer Funded LGBT Index Scoring Hospitals for Promoting Gender Ideology." *The Daily Signal.* May 24, 2023. https://www.dailysignal.com/2023/05/24/phrma-pfizer-funded-lgbt-index-scoring-hospitals-promoting-gender-ideology/ Accessed April 24, 2024.

THE BIDEN EQUALITY INDEX

It seems President Biden may be just as concerned about his HRC score as brands like Target and Bud Light. The president may not have a perfect score, but he implemented the vast majority of recommendations HRC released shortly after news outlets projected that Biden had won the 2020 presidential election.

On November 11, 2020, the Human Rights Campaign released its *Blueprint for Positive Change 2020*. HRC President Alphonso David said at the time:

> The momentous election of pro-equality champions Joe Biden and Kamala Harris puts us on a path to move equality forward by advancing policies to improve the lives of millions of LGBTQ people. Over the last four years, the Trump-Pence administration has systematically attacked LGBTQ people and our nation's most sacred institutions—our courts, our Constitution, and our fundamental civil rights. The Biden-Harris administration has the opportunity to not only put our democracy back on track but deliver real positive change for LGBTQ people's daily lives.[27]

Lucas Acosta, the former deputy director of communications at HRC who published the *Blueprint*, went on to work for the Democratic National Committee before joining the White House as director of broadcast media between April 2022 and November 2023.[28]

---

27   "The HRC Blueprint for LGBTQ Equality Under Biden." Human Rights Campaign news release. November 11, 2020. https://www.hrc.org/press-releases/human-rights-campaign-charts-bold-path-for-equality-under-biden-administration Accessed April 9, 2024.

28   "Lucas Acosta." LinkedIn Profile. https://www.linkedin.com/in/lucasacosta1/ Accessed April 25, 2024.

The HRC *Blueprint* included eighty-six policy recommendations. According to my analysis, the Biden administration has implemented at least sixty-five of them, or 75.6 percent.

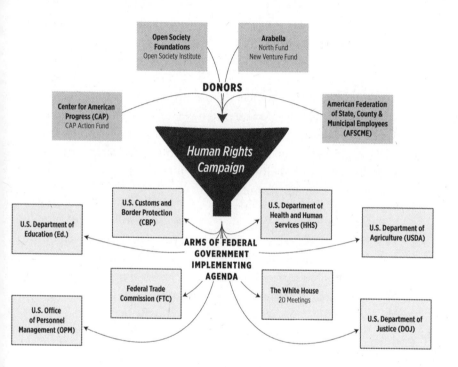

TWISTING A SUPREME COURT RULING

The White House implemented HRC's first recommendation with flying colors, twisting a Supreme Court ruling to change the law in exactly the way the Court said it was *not* trying to do.

In *Bostock v. Clayton County* (2020), the Supreme Court ruled that Title VII of the Civil Rights Act of 1964 barred employers from discriminating against potential or current employees by refusing to hire them or by firing them due to their sexual orientation or gender identity. Justice Neil Gorsuch, writing for the Court's 6–3 majority, ruled that discrimination on the basis of sex included discrimination on the basis of sexual orientation and gender identity. He claimed that an employer "discriminates" against a man on the basis of his sex when firing him for dressing as a woman, for example, because the employer would not have fired him for that action if he were a woman. This convoluted logic allowed Gorsuch to claim that a law passed in 1964 should be interpreted in a way that its authors would have abhorred and would have stridently opposed had they lived to see it.

Critics like Justice Samuel Alito noted that sexual orientation and gender identity are separate from sex, and Congress has failed to pass the Equality Act, which would explicitly bar discrimination on these grounds. Gorsuch replied to critics who feared that his ruling would extend to other issues by explicitly stating that *Bostock* only applied to employment law:

> The employers worry that our decision will sweep beyond Title VII to other federal or state laws that prohibit sex discrimination. And, under Title VII itself, they say sex-segregated bathrooms, locker rooms, and dress codes will prove unsustainable after our decision today. But none of these other laws are before us; we have not had the benefit of adversarial testing about the meaning of their terms, and we do not prejudge any such question today. Under Title VII, too, we do not purport to address bathrooms, locker rooms, or anything else of the kind. The only question before us is whether an employer who fires someone simply for being homosexual or transgender has discharged or otherwise discriminated against that individual 'because of such individual's sex.'[29]

29 Bostock v. Clayton County. 590 U.S. ____ 2020. Opinion of the Court. Justia. (p. 31.) https://supreme.justia.com/cases/federal/us/590/17-1618/#tab-opinion-4261583.

Yet throughout its recommendations, HRC applied *Bostock* to areas outside of employment law, just as Biden ultimately would do.

SO IT DOES APPLY TO BATHROOMS?

HRC's first recommendation urged Biden to "ensure consistent administrative implementation of *Bostock v. Clayton County* across all agencies enforcing civil rights statutes and provisions." Other recommendations made it abundantly clear that HRC had in mind exactly what Gorsuch said the Court was *not* doing.

While HRC accurately said that "On June 15, 2020, the Supreme Court held that Title VII of the Civil Rights Act of 1964 prohibits discrimination on the basis of sexual orientation, gender identity, and transgender status as unlawful sex discrimination," its recommendation for the Department of Justice urged the attorney general to "begin coordinating full implementation of this decision, including by publishing guidance confirming that discrimination on the basis of sexual orientation, gender identity, and transgender status is unlawful sex discrimination under all federal statutory and regulatory provisions."

When HRC urged the Department of Education to include data on bullying based on gender identity, it cited *Bostock*: "Consistent with the *Bostock* decision, ED should restore inclusion of gender identity, gender expression, and nonconformity with gender stereotypes for purposes of collecting data to bullying." HRC's recommendations for the Department of Education also referenced *Bostock* by stating that Title IX of the Education Amendments of 1972 has traditionally been interpreted in accordance with Title VII. HRC lamented that Trump-era guidance at the Department of Education, which eliminated Obama-era rules on gender identity, "encourages school officials to permit harassment of transgender students, deny access to facilities consistent with gender identity, and refuse to use correct names and pronouns—all inflicting untold emotional harm."

HRC also urged the Department of Health and Human Services to reimplement the Obama administration's regulations for Section 1557 of the Affordable Care Act (known commonly as Obamacare), which redefined "discrimination on the basis of sex" to apply to sexual orientation and gender identity in health care. HRC claimed that the Trump administration's reversal of the rule failed "to reflect the incorporation of sexual orientation and gender identity within the scope of sex discrimination protections as provided by *Bostock*."

HRC also recommended that "the Department of Homeland Security should update all nondiscrimination provisions pertaining to disaster services to protect on the basis of sexual orientation and gender identity to reflect the decision in *Bostock*."

Thus, HRC directly applied the *Bostock* ruling to "sex-segregated bathrooms, locker rooms, and dress codes," which the *Bostock* opinion claimed were beyond the scope of the Court's ruling.[30] Like good soldiers, Biden and the administrative state followed their orders.

BIDEN TOES THE LINE

Biden has issued many executive orders on transgender issues, particularly interpreting *Bostock* broadly by applying it to all federal civil rights law, contrary to the text of the decision itself. On his first day in office, he signed an executive order aimed at "preventing and combating discrimination on the basis of gender identity or sexual orientation."

> In *Bostock v. Clayton County* ... the Supreme Court held that Title VII's prohibition on discrimination 'because of ... sex' covers discrimination on the basis of gender identity and sexual orientation. ... Under *Bostock*'s rea-

---

30 *Blueprint For Positive Change 2020*. The Human Rights Campaign. https://hrc-prod-requests.s3-us-west-2.amazonaws.com/Blueprint-2020.pdf Accessed April 9, 2024. pp. 4, 13, 16

soning, laws that prohibit sex discrimination—including Title IX of the Education Amendments of 1972, … the Fair Housing Act, … and section 412 of the Immigration and Nationality Act, … along with their respective implementing regulations—prohibit discrimination on the basis of gender identity or sexual orientation, so long as the laws do not contain significant indications to the contrary.

Biden ordered each agency to "review all existing orders, regulations, guidance documents, policies, programs or other agency actions that were promulgated or are administered by the agency under Title VII or any other statute or regulation that prohibits sex discrimination" and that "are or may be inconsistent with the policy set forth in section 1 of this order."[31]

Following this order, the Department of Justice and the Department of Education adopted the HRC-Biden broad reading of *Bostock*, claiming that Title IX of the Education Amendments of 1972—which bars discrimination on the basis of sex in education—bars discrimination on the basis of sexual orientation and gender identity.

Pamela S. Karlan, the principal deputy assistant attorney general in the DOJ Civil Rights Division, wrote the order applying *Bostock* to Title IX on March 26, 2021, citing Biden's order.[32] Karlan, a voting rights and constitutional law professor at Stanford Law School who is openly lesbian, previously served in the DOJ under Obama and joined Facebook's content oversight board

---

31 "Executive Order on Preventing and Combating Discrimination on the Basis of Gender Identity or Sexual Orientation." White House Briefing Room. January 20, 2021. https://www.whitehouse.gov/briefing-room/presidential-actions/2021/01/20/executive-order-preventing-and-combating-discrimination-on-basis-of-gender-identity-or-sexual-orientation/ Accessed April 9, 2024.

32 Karlan, Pamela S. "Memorandum to Federal Agency Civil Rights Directors and General Counsels." March 26, 2021. https://www.justice.gov/crt/page/file/1383026/dl?inline Accessed April 10, 2024.

before joining the Biden DOJ.[33] Activists championed Karlan as an LGBTQ pick for President Barack Obama to select to replace retiring Supreme Court Justice David Souter in 2009.[34] Karlan has spoken at events with Chad Griffin, the former president of the Human Rights Campaign.[35]

Alphonso David, a previous HRC president, praised Karlan's memo, saying the document "will allow students, parents, and teachers to advocate for nondiscriminatory policies for LGBTQ students." He added, "Students who experience discrimination based on their sexual orientation or gender identity should feel confident filing complaints with the Department of Education."[36]

In June 2021, the Department of Education also released a rule applying *Bostock* to Title IX, citing Karlan's memo.[37]

---

33 Gilbert, Ben. "Facebook's 'Supreme Court' that has the power to overrule Mark Zuckerberg just handed down its first decisions—these are the Oversight Board's first 20 members." *Business Insider.* January 30, 2021. https://www.businessinsider.com/meet-the-first-20-members-of-facebook-supreme-court-2020-5 Accessed April 10, 2024.

34 Gerstein, Josh. "Groups push for first gay justice." *Politico.* May 5, 2009. https://www.politico.com/story/2009/05/groups-push-for-first-gay-justice-022106 Accessed April 10, 2024.

35 "Key players in groundbreaking same-sex marriage cases offer exclusive insights into Supreme Court victories at Stanford symposium." Stanford Law School news release. October 30, 2013. https://law.stanford.edu/press/key-players-in-groundbreaking-same-sex-marriage-cases-offer-exclusive-insights-into-supreme-court-victories-at-stanford-symposium/ Accessed April 10, 2024.

36 Lang, Nico. "Justice Department Affirms Title IX Protects LGBTQ+ Students From Discrimination." *Them.* April 5, 2021. https://www.them.us/story/justice-department-affirms-title-ix-protects-lgbtq-students-discrimination Accessed April 10, 2024.

37 "Enforcement of Title IX of the Education Amendments of 1972 With Respect to Discrimination Based on Sexual Orientation and Gender Identity in Light of Bostock v. Clayton County." U. S. Department of Education Office for Civil Rights. June 22, 2021. https://www.federalregister.gov/documents/2021/06/22/2021-13058/enforcement-of-title-ix-of-the-education-amendments-of-1972-with-respect-to-discrimination-based-on Accessed April 10, 2024.

Suzanne Goldberg, who wrote the Department of Education memo applying *Bostock*, previously worked as a lawyer with the LGBTQ firm Lambda Legal and founded Columbia Law School's Sexuality and Gender Law Clinic. Since September 2023, she has served as senior advisor and legal expert for Jessica Stern, the special envoy to advance the human rights of LGBTQI+ persons at the State Department.[38]

On April 19, 2024, the Department of Education finalized the rule incorporating gender identity into Title IX.[39] Under the rule, schools that receive federal funding must allow biological males to compete against females in women's sports, allow males in women's restrooms and changing rooms, and more. It remains unclear whether the rules undermine parental rights by urging schools to keep a child's stated gender identity secret from his or her parents, though an earlier draft of the rules cited a California policy to that effect.[40]

Twenty-six Republican attorneys general sued on behalf of their states to block the Title IX changes.[41] The parental rights group Moms for Liberty sued, as did the religious freedom firm Alliance Defending Freedom, which represents Carroll Independent School

38 "Suzanne Goldberg." Columbia Law School faculty page. https://www.law.columbia.edu/faculty/suzanne-goldberg Accessed April 10, 2024.

39 "U.S. Department of Education Releases Final Title IX Regulations, Providing Vital Protections Against Sex Discrimination." U.S. Department of Education news release. April 19, 2024. https://www.ed.gov/news/press-releases/us-department-education-releases-final-title-ix-regulations-providing-vital-protections-against-sex-discrimination Accessed April 25, 2024.

40 Anderson, Kate and Emilie Kao. "The Biden Administration's Proposed Changes to Title IX Threaten Parental Rights." The Federalist Society. January 5, 2023. https://fedsoc.org/commentary/fedsoc-blog/the-biden-administration-s-proposed-changes-to-title-ix-threaten-parental-rights Accessed April 25, 2024.

41 Miranda, Shauneen. "More than half of states sue to block Biden Title IX rule protecting LGBTQ+ students." *Virginia Mercury*. May 21, 2024. https://virginiamercury.com/2024/05/21/more-than-half-of-states-including-virginia-sue-to-block-biden-title-ix-rule-protecting-lgbtq-students/ Accessed May 24, 2024.

District in Texas.[42] The lawsuits raise First Amendment concerns about the rule and claim the rule violates the Administrative Procedure Act. State education officials in Florida, Louisiana, South Carolina, and Oklahoma have directed schools not to comply with the rules.[43], [44]

As of July 2, three federal judges had issued temporary injunctions preventing the Title IX rules from taking effect in fourteen states: Alaska, Idaho, Indiana, Kansas, Kentucky, Louisiana, Mississippi, Montana, Ohio, Tennessee, Utah, Virginia, West Virginia, and Wyoming.[45]

Various other agencies have also drafted new rules applying the HRC-Biden broad reading of *Bostock*.

The Food and Nutrition Service at the U.S. Department of Agriculture issued a policy update on May 5, 2022, applying *Bostock* to forbid discrimination on the basis of sexual orientation and gender identity in state agencies under Title IX and the Food and Nutrition Act.[46]

The Government Accountability Office deemed the policy update a rule, subjecting it to the Congressional Review Act's

42   Jenkins, S.E. "Texas school district sues Biden admin over Title IX changes broadening LGBTQ protections." CBS News. May 21, 2024. https://www. cbsnews.com/texas/news/texas-school-district-sues-biden-admin-over-title-ix-changes-broadening-lgbtq-protections/ Accessed May 24, 2024.

43   McCaughey, Caroline. "A Red State Revolt to Biden's Title IX Rule Changes is Brewing." *New York Sun*. April 25, 2024. https://www.nysun.com/article/a-red-state-revolt-to-bidens-title-ix-rule-changes-is-brewing   Accessed April 25, 2024.

44   Martinez-Keel, Nuria. "Walters urges Oklahoma schools to ignore new Biden administration Title IX rules." *Oklahoma Voice*. April 24, 2024. https://oklahomavoice.com/2024/04/24/walters-urges-oklahoma-schools-to-ignore-new-biden-administration-title-ix-rules/ Accessed April 25, 2024.

45   Stanford, Libby. "Biden's Title IX Rule Is Now Blocked in 14 States." *Education Week*. July 3, 2024. https://www.edweek.org/policy-politics/bidens-title-ix-rule-is-now-blocked-in-14-states/2024/07 Accessed July 10, 2024.

46   "Application of Bostock v. Clayton County to Program Discrimination Complaint Processing—Policy Update." U.S. Department of Agriculture Food and Nutrition Service. May 5, 2022. https://www.fns.usda.gov/cr/crd-01-2022 Accessed April 10, 2024.

requirement that a rule must be submitted to Congress and the GAO before it takes effect. The act also permits Congress to review and disapprove rules. U.S. Senator Roger Marshall (R-KS), sponsored a resolution to nullify the rule, and President Biden issued a statement threatening to veto it: "This legislation would mean that needy people—including children who may go hungry—could be denied food and food assistance simply because of who they are or who they love.[47] Were any transgender individuals actually in danger of losing access to food due to discrimination? Almost certainly not.

The HRC *Blueprint* had only one recommendation for the Department of Agriculture—that it would prohibit discrimination against LGBTQ participants in nutrition support programs.[48] HRC asked the agency to do one thing, and the bureaucrats did it.

THE 'QUEERING' OF THE CIVIL SERVICE

The HRC *Blueprint* also urged Biden to "Appoint Openly-LGBTQ Justices, Judges, Executive Officials, and Ambassadors." Specifically, it urged Biden to "appoint the first-ever openly-LGBTQ cabinet secretary and the first openly lesbian, bisexual, or transgender ambassador."[49] The ink was barely dry on HRC's recommendation before President-elect Biden started carrying it out. The White House has touted the fact that 14 percent of Biden's appointees identify as LGBTQ.[50] News outlets like *The Hill* have compiled

---

47 "Statement of Administration Policy" on Senate Joint Resolution 42. Executive Office of the President, Office of Management and Budget. October 26, 2023. https://www.whitehouse.gov/wp-content/uploads/2023/10/SAP-SJ-Res-42.pdf Accessed April 10, 2024.

48 HRC. *Blueprint*. p. 7.

49 HRC. *Blueprint*. p. 4.

50 "FACT SHEET: The Biden-Harris Administration Champions LGBTQ+ Equality and Marks Pride Month." White House Briefing Room. June 1, 2021. https://www.whitehouse.gov/briefing-room/statements-releases/2021/06/01/fact-sheet-the-biden-harris-administration-champions-lgbtq-equality-and-marks-pride-month/ Accessed May 25, 2024.

lists of the "history-making" LGBTQ appointments, noting at least seven high profile appointees. [51]

Many of these "history-making" appointments have gone awry.

Biden selected Pete Buttigieg, former mayor of South Bend, Indiana, and former Democratic presidential candidate, to lead the Department of Transportation in December 2020,[52] and the Senate confirmed him in February 2021.[53] To call Buttigieg unqualified would be an understatement. Even *Slate*'s Henry Grabar, no conservative, emphasized Buttigieg's lack of qualifications while noting that Buttigieg once wrote for *Slate*. "Is Pete Buttigieg the most *deserving* person for this job? Emphatically not. Does he know the most about transit? I'm not even sure he knows the most about transit among former *Slate* bloggers."[54]

Yet Buttigieg, as a former presidential candidate who had endorsed Biden during the 2020 Democratic primary, and as a man legally married to another man, seemed to meet Biden's qualifications in spades. He became the first openly gay Cabinet secretary confirmed by the Senate, edging out Ric Grennell, whom Trump appointed as director of national intelligence in 2020, because the Senate never confirmed Grennell.

51   Samuels, Brett. "Here are the history-making LGBTQ officials in the Biden administration." *The Hill*. June 2, 2023. https://thehill.com/home-news/administration/4030255-here-are-the-history-making-lgbtq-officials-in-the-biden-administration/ Accessed April 10, 2024.

52   Edelman, Adam and Rebecca Shabad. "Biden introduces Buttigieg as his nominee to lead the Department of Transportation." NBC News. December 16, 2020. https://www.nbcnews.com/politics/white-house/biden-introduce-buttigieg-his-nominee-lead-department-transportation-n1251356 Accessed April 10, 2024.

53   Roll Call Vote 117th Congress on the Nomination of Peter Paul Montgomery Buttigieg, of Indiana, to be Secretary of Transportation. February 2, 2021. https://www.senate.gov/legislative/LIS/roll_call_votes/vote1171/vote_117_1_00011.htm Accessed April 10, 2024.

54   Grabar, Henry. "Planes, Trains, and Relentless Ambition." *Slate*. December 16, 2020. https://slate.com/business/2020/12/pete-buttigieg-transportation-secretary-itll-be-fine.html Accessed May 24, 2024.

This "history-making" appointment hasn't inspired a great deal of confidence.

Buttigieg caused a stir when he effectively declared that America's roads were racist in 2021:

> I'm still surprised that some people were surprised when I pointed to the fact that if a highway was built for the purpose of dividing a White and a Black neighborhood or if an underpass was constructed such that a bus carrying mostly Black and Puerto Rican kids to a beach—or that would've been—in New York was—was designed too low for it to pass by, that that obviously reflects racism that went into those design choices.[55]

As it turns out, historians dispute the claim Buttigieg was making—that a specific overpass bridge in New York had been built too low for buses to carry poor minorities there. Glenn Kessler, the fact-checker for *The Washington Post*, (not known for his conservative bias) spoke with historians who emphasized that cost, not racism, explains the construction.[56] The overarching claim that city planners used the interstate highway system to devastate black communities in the 1960s, also fails to hold water. Cities building the highway system did damage their communities—but the changes appear due to overzealous development, not racial animus.[57]

Buttigieg doubled down, however. In 2022, he launched a $1 billion pilot program to undo the supposedly racist efforts of former city planners. While the money may end up funding benefi-

55 Bauens, Janae and John Seward. "Fact Check Team: Is racism built into some of America's infrastructure?" *The National Desk*. November 12, 2021. https://thenationaldesk.com/news/fact-check-team/fact-check-team-is-racism-built-into-some-of-americas-infrastructure Accessed July 10, 2024.

56 Cannato, Vincent J. "A Bridge Too Far." *City Journal*. November 12, 2021. https://www.city-journal.org/article/a-bridge-too-far-2 Accessed May 24, 2024.

57 Malanga, Steven. "Racist Interstates?" *City Journal*. Autumn 2020. https://www.city-journal.org/article/racist-interstates Accessed May 24, 2024.

cial projects, it seems this DEI hire is prioritizing efforts based on Critical Race Theory, rather than addressing concrete needs.[58]

In February 2023, a failing wheel bearing caught fire on a Norfolk Southern train carrying hazardous materials. Dozens of train cars derailed in the heart of East Palestine, Ohio, releasing chemicals and sending a fireball and black smoke into the sky. Republicans like Senator J.D. Vance visited the scene a few days later.[59] Buttigieg, however, did not publicly address the accident until ten days after it happened, and he did not visit the scene until nearly three weeks after the accident.[60]

Buttigieg's questionable competence proved the first of a long list of staffers whose main qualification appears to be fulfilling HRC's recommendation.

Karine Jean-Pierre became the first black, lesbian, immigrant woman to serve as White House press secretary, starting in May 2022. Unlike her immediate predecessor, Jen Psaki, or former Trump Press Secretaries Sarah Huckabee Sanders and Kayleigh McEnany, Jean-Pierre seems utterly unable to do the basic job of a press secretary.

As *Politico* noted early in her tenure, Jean-Pierre has seemed utterly clueless at times. She acted surprised when hearing that Interior Secretary Deb Haaland had tested positive for COVID-19 and had been in President Biden's presence around the same time, for instance. She seems a slave to the notes in her binder and uncomfortable answering journalists' questions. This marks a stark

58 Yen, Hope. "Buttigieg launches $1B pilot to build racial equity in roads." *The Associated Press*. June 30, 2022. https://apnews.com/article/race-and-ethnicity-racial-injustice-transportation-pete-buttigieg-48e09f-253781c89359d875f19fc70f9d Accessed May 24, 2024.

59 Vance, J.D. "After Tragedy in East Palestine, a Commonsense Solution for Railway Safety." *The Daily Signal*. May 10, 2023. https://www.dailysignal.com/2023/05/10/after-tragedy-east-palestine-commonsense-solution-railway-safety/ Accessed May 24, 2024.

60 Racker, Mini. "What to Know About Pete Buttigieg's Visit to East Palestine." *Time Magazine*. February 23, 2023. https://time.com/6257945/pete-buttigieg-east-palestine-ohio-train/ Accessed May 24, 2024.

contrast from the confident and competent engagement from Psaki, Sanders, and McEnany.

When reporters ask her questions, she repeatedly says that she just doesn't know. "While White House reporters love to complain about non-answers from communications officials, many have privately grumbled that when Jean-Pierre does have answers, they are often vague and rarely stray from the pre-written talking points prepared in the binder at the podium," *Politico*'s reporters noted.

Biden nominated Rachel Levine, a male who identifies as female, to serve as assistant secretary for health in the Department of Health and Human Services, elevating the first transgender person to such a role. Levine stands out for advocating transgender medical interventions. In May 2022, he urged the Federation of State Medical Boards to combat "misinformation about gender-affirming care for transgender and gender-diverse individuals," insisting that "the positive value of gender-affirming care for youth and adults is not in scientific or medical dispute." Quite a few detransitioners would beg to differ, not to mention the Florida Department of Public Health. He urged state medical leaders to "advocate for our tech companies to create a healthier, cleaner information environment" by suppressing this "misinformation."[61]

Levine himself has expressed gratitude that he did not undergo transition "treatments" until he had his children. "I have no regrets because if I had transitioned when I was younger then I wouldn't have my children," Levine said. "I can't imagine a life without my children."[62]

61 O'Neil, Tyler. "Rachel Levine Targets Transgender Heresy for Big Tech Suppression." *The Daily Signal.* December 29, 2022. https://www.dailysignal.com/2022/12/29/trans-inquisition-rachel-levine-enlists-state-medical-boards-pressure-big-tech-stamp-transgender-heresy/ Accessed May 24, 2024.

62 Smith, Jen. "Trans assistant health secretary Rachel Levine—who wants to 'normalize' gender affirming treatment for children—says she's happy she waited until after she had kids in resurfaced 2019 video." *The Daily Mail.* March 17, 2023. https://www.dailymail.co.uk/news/article-11872347/Trans-health-secretary-Rachel-Levine-happy-waited-kids-change-gender.html Accessed May 24, 2024

I'm glad his children exist, but perhaps he should think about that before advocating "gender-affirming care" for those who have yet to become parents, and before attempting to silence critics who want to protect kids from sterilization.

Forbidding 'Conversion Therapy'

The HRC *Blueprint* issued four recommendations opposing "conversion therapy," which HRC describes as "a range of harmful and discredited practices that seek to change a person's sexual orientation or gender identity."

Therapists who provide mainstream patient-directed talk therapy distinguish between therapy that addresses underlying issues that may affect a person's unwanted same-sex attraction or gender dysphoria, from older practices that aimed to change sexual orientation through often extreme measures like shock therapy. LGBTQ activists like HRC intentionally conflate the extreme old practices with the modern mainstream efforts by branding the latter "conversion therapy."

HRC has touted the example of Sam Brinton, a former Department of Energy staffer under Biden who left the administration after facing charges related to airport baggage thefts.[63] Brinton had claimed to have undergone conversion therapy after "coming out" as gay to his parents. He testified about this therapy in numerous settings, including urging legislators to ban "conversion therapy" due to his experience. His stories had numerous contradictions,[64] and his sister, Rachel told *The New York Post* that there was

---

63   Turner, Allison. "#AM_Equality Tipsheet: January 25, 2018." Human Rights Campaign News. January 25, 2018. https://www.hrc.org/news/am-equality-tipsheet-january-25-2018 Accessed April 10, 2024.

64   O'Neil, Tyler. "Sam Brinton Out at Department of Energy After Alleged Bag Theft, Questions About 'Conversion Therapy' Story." *The Daily Signal*. December 12, 2022. https://www.dailysignal.com/2022/12/12/breaking-department-of-energy-says-sam-brinton-is-no-longer-a-doe-employee/ Accessed April 10, 2024.

"no validity" to his claims, insisting that "the claims of conversion therapy never happened."[65]

While activist groups like HRC claim that "conversion therapy" makes LGBTQ people more likely to consider committing suicide, a new analysis of the data shows that when LGBTQ people undergo mainstream patient-directed talk therapy which aims to resolve issues underlying unwanted same-sex attraction or gender dysphoria, they are less likely to consider suicide *after* the therapy.[66] This does not prove that such therapies are correct or effective, but it does suggest that efforts to ban any therapy that doesn't bend over backwards to "affirm" LGBTQ identities are wrongheaded.

Despite all this, President Biden issued an executive order on June 15, 2022, echoing many HRC recommendations.[67]

HRC urged Biden to direct the Federal Trade Commission to prohibit "the false and misleading advertising, marketing, and other business practices of any individual or organization that provides conversion therapy," and to act "against individuals and organizations that currently offer conversion therapy in exchange for monetary compensation."

Biden's order stated, "The Federal Trade Commission is encouraged to consider whether so-called conversion therapy constitutes an unfair or deceptive act or practice, and to issue such consumer warnings or notices as may be appropriate."

65 Hernandez, Marjorie. "Non-binary ex-Biden official Sam Brinton's family slams abuse claims: 'Never happened.'" *The New York Post.* February 19, 2023. https://nypost.com/2023/02/19/family-claims-sam-brinton-lied-about-abuse-conversion-therapy/ Accessed May 25, 2024.

66 O'Neil, Tyler. "New Research on 'Conversion Therapy' Turns LGBTQ Narrative on Its Head." *The Daily Signal.* January 31, 2024. https://www.dailysignal.com/2024/01/31/new-research-conversion-therapy-turns-lgbtq-narrative-head/ Accessed May 25, 2024.

67 "Executive Order on Advancing Equality for Lesbian, Gay, Bisexual, Transgender, Queer, and Intersex Individuals." White House Briefing Room. June 15, 2022. https://www.whitehouse.gov/briefing-room/presidential-actions/2022/06/15/executive-order-on-advancing-equality-for-lesbian-gay-bisexual-transgender-queer-and-intersex-individuals/ Accessed April 25, 2024.

HRC also urged Biden to prevent the Department of Education from referring students to "conversion therapy," to prohibit mental health professionals in federally funded foster care (through the Department of Health and Human Services) from engaging in "conversion therapy," and to prohibit the Department of Justice's juvenile justice programs from engaging in "conversion therapy" or referring minors to such practices.

The Biden order directed HHS to "increase public awareness of the harms and risks associated with so-called conversion therapy for LGBTQI+ youth and their families." It also directed the Departments of Education, Health and Human Services, and Justice to "support LGBTQI+" youth and students.

PUSHING DEI

The HRC *Blueprint* urged Biden to revoke President Trump's September 2020 executive order directing that "agency diversity and inclusion efforts shall, first and foremost, encourage agency employees not to judge each other by their color, race, ethnicity, sex, or any other characteristic protected by federal law."

Trump had warned that many so-called diversity, equity, and inclusion (DEI) efforts involved race or sex stereotyping and scapegoating, assigning certain character traits to an individual based on race or sex or assigning fault or blame to members of a race or sex, in violation of federal civil rights law. Trump aimed to end DEI trainings that taught that America is systemically racist such that "white" employees are oppressors and "black" employees are oppressed.[68]

HRC characterized this order as "attacking diversity and inclusion practices of federal agencies, federal contractors, and recipients of federal grants" and prohibiting them from "engaging in diversity and inclusion training programs that address serious problems

---

68   "Executive Order on Combating Race and Sex Stereotyping." White House Executive Order (Trump administration). September 22, 2020. https://trumpwhitehouse.archives.gov/presidential-actions/executive-order-combating-race-sex-stereotyping/ Accessed April 10, 2024.

including white privilege, systemic racism, unconscious bias, and intersectionality."[69]

HRC urged Biden to revoke the order, and Biden revoked the order on his first day in office.[70]

SUPPORTING 'LGBTQ REFUGEES'

Remember the Customs and Border Protection directing Border Patrol agents not to use "he, him, she, her" pronouns to refer to illegal immigrants "unless you have more information about, or provided by" the alien?

HRC urged the Biden administration to "Improve Systems to Support LGBTQ Refugees and Asylum Seekers."

On February 4, 2021, Biden issued a memorandum for the heads of executive agencies directing the State Department and the Department of Homeland Security to "enhance their ongoing efforts to ensure that LGBTQI+ refugees and asylum seekers have equal access to protection and assistance." The memo also directed the Departments of State, Justice, and Homeland Security to "ensure appropriate training is in place so that relevant federal government personnel and key partners can effectively identify and respond to the particular needs of LGBTQI+ refugees and asylum seekers."[71]

---

69 HRC. *Blueprint.* p. 5.

70 "Executive Order On Advancing Racial Equity and Support for Underserved Communities Through the Federal Government." White House Briefing Room. January 20, 2021. https://www.whitehouse.gov/briefing-room/presidential-actions/2021/01/20/executive-order-advancing-racial-equity-and-support-for-underserved-communities-through-the-federal-government/ Accessed April 10, 2024.

71 "Memorandum on Advancing the Human Rights of Lesbian, Gay, Bisexual, Transgender, Queer, and Intersex Persons Around the World." White House Briefing Room. February 4, 2021. https://www.whitehouse.gov/briefing-room/presidential-actions/2021/02/04/memorandum-advancing-the-human-rights-of-lesbian-gay-bisexual-transgender-queer-and-intersex-persons-around-the-world/ Accessed April 10, 2024.

A WORKING GROUP ON 'ANTI-TRANSGENDER VIOLENCE'

The HRC *Blueprint* also called on Biden to "Establish an Interagency Working Group to Address Anti-Transgender Violence," citing "more than 180 cases of anti-transgender fatal violence" since 2013 (a rate of twenty-six cases per year). (However, critics have noted that HRC's own data suggest that transgender Americans suffer a homicide risk *below* the national average.[72])

On June 30, 2021, Biden announced the creation of the "Interagency Working Group on Safety, Inclusion, and Opportunity for Transgender Americans," citing "epidemic levels of violence, discrimination, and stigma" against "transgender people, especially transgender women and girls of color."[73]

HRC celebrated the working group's creation, noting on its website that "the creation of this working group aligns with recommendations outlined in HRC's *2020 Blueprint for Positive Change*."[74]

REIGNITING THE 'CAMPUS RAPE FRENZY'

The HRC *Blueprint* demanded that Biden reverse the Trump-era Department of Education policy on adjudicating sexual assault claims on college campuses.

Under Obama, the Department of Education's Office of Civil Rights released a "Dear Colleague" letter claiming that one in four

---

72   Palumbo, Brad. "No, There's No 'Epidemic' of Anti-Transgender Violence." *Quillette*. January 29, 2024. https://quillette.com/2024/01/29/no-theres-no-epidemic-of-anti-trans-violence/ Accessed April 25, 2024.

73   "FACT SHEET: Biden-Harris Administration Advances Equality for Transgender Americans." White House Briefing Room. June 30, 2021. https://www.whitehouse.gov/briefing-room/statements-releases/2021/06/30/fact-sheet-biden-harris-administration-advances-equality-for-transgender-americans/ Accessed April 10, 2024.

74   "President Biden's Pro-LGBTQ Timeline." Human Rights Campaign website. https://www.hrc.org/resources/president-bidens-pro-lgbtq-timeline Accessed April 10, 2024.

women would be sexually assaulted on college campuses and that colleges could not trust police to handle these crimes. The OCR launched investigations into colleges when female accusers claimed the colleges were too lax on the men they accused of sexual assault. This trend led colleges to establish extreme rules denying due process rights to those accused of sexual assault, in the name of "protecting" their accusers, often referred to as "survivors."

K.C. Johnson and Stuart Taylor catalogued the denial of due process in their book *The Campus Rape Frenzy: The Attack on Due Process at America's Universities*. They tell the story of Dez Wells, a black basketball star expelled from Cincinnati's Xavier University in 2012 for allegedly raping another student. A medical exam revealed no evidence of trauma. A contemporaneous criminal investigation convinced the county prosecutor that the allegation was false, and the prosecutor even considered bringing criminal charges *against Wells' accuser*. Yet the college refused to allow anyone with a law degree to represent Wells and it refused to let Wells cross-examine his accuser. The students on the conduct board who made the decision about Wells' guilt acknowledged that they did not even understand how the rape kit works.

This example illustrates how the Obama administration policy incentivized a system that dismissed due process in pursuit of a narrative that sexual assault is extremely prevalent on college campuses. A grand jury found that there was no probable cause to believe Wells had committed any crime. Hamilton County prosecuting attorney Joseph Deters publicly defended Wells, and convinced the NCAA to allow Wells to play when he moved to the University of Maryland. Yet the stigma of the rape accusation stuck with him, and fans taunted him about it, as if he had been found guilty.[75]

Under Trump, the Education Department rescinded this letter, noting that the Obama policy "led to the deprivation of rights for

---

75 Johnson, KC and Stuart Taylor Jr. *The Campus Rape Frenzy: The Attack on Due Process at America's Universities.* New York: Encounter Books, 2017.

many students—both accused students denied fair process and victims denied an adequate resolution of their complaints."[76]

Yet HRC framed the Trump administration's reversal in deceptive terms, claiming that the Trump-era rules involved "making it more difficult for student survivors of sexual harassment and assault to report their abuse and promoting policies that favor their abusers." HRC urged Biden's Education Department to issue new rules "to ensure students who have experienced sexual harassment assault are fully supported and protected by educational institutions, and that regulation should be fully inclusive of LGBTQ students." The Biden Title IX regulations substantially returned to the Obama policy.

HRC's Ties to the Administration

President Biden spoke at HRC's national dinner in October 2023 and first lady Jill Biden spoke at another HRC dinner in March 2024.[77] [78]

Kelley Robinson, HRC's president, has visited the White House at least six times since she became HRC's president in November 2022. She met one-on-one with Sofia Carratala, a policy advisor on Biden's Domestic Policy Council and a former immigration research assistant and policy staffer at the Center for American Progress.[79]

---

76   Jackson, Candice. "Dear Colleague" letter from U.S. Department of Education Office for Civil Rights. September 22, 2017. https://www2.ed.gov/about/offices/list/ocr/letters/colleague-title-ix-201709.pdf Accessed April 10, 2024.

77   "President Biden at Human Rights Campaign Dinner." C-SPAN. October 14, 2023. https://www.c-span.org/video/?531141-1/president-biden-human-rights-campaign-dinner Accessed April 25, 2024.

78   Wolf, Brandon. "ICYMI: First Lady Jill Biden Headlines Human Rights Campaign's 'Equality in Action' Event." Human Rights Campaign news release. April 12, 2024. https://www.hrc.org/press-releases/icymi-first-lady-jill-biden-headlines-human-rights-campaigns-equality-in-action-event Accessed April 25, 2024.

79   "Carratala, Sofia." LinkedIn Profile. https://www.linkedin.com/in/sofia-carratala-2a7ba4140/ Accessed April 4, 2024.

She also met with Tim Gill, the LGBTQ megadonor who has spent more than $433 million to promote LGBTQ causes through the Gill Foundation since 1994.[80]

Alphonso B. David, HRC's president from 2019 to 2021, attended two White House meetings in June 2021. (HRC fired David, who had previously worked as a lawyer for New York Democratic Governor Andrew Cuomo, after New York Attorney General Letitia James released a report claiming that Cuomo had sexually harassed eleven women and that David had helped Cuomo cover up the harassment.[81] David denied any wrongdoing and sued HRC for racial discrimination. HRC settled David's lawsuit amicably on March 15, 2023.[82]) David has since visited the White House three times since he became president and CEO of the Global Black Economic Forum in June 2022. (The forum appears to have no connection with the World Economic Forum, though David has spoken at WEF.)

Chad H. Griffin, HRC's president between 2012 and 2019, visited the White House twice.

Four other HRC leaders have visited the White House ten times.

HRC President Robinson bragged about her organization's access to Biden in July 2024. On July 2, the White House provided a statement about transgender surgery for minors to *The 19th News*. The White House said surgeries "should be limited to adults" but that the administration continues "to support gender-affirming care for minors like mental health care and respect the role of parents, families, and doctors in these decisions."

---

80   The Gill Foundation "About" page. https://gillfoundation.org/about/ Accessed April 25, 2024.

81   Chappell, Bill. "Human Rights Campaign Fires President Alphonso David Over Report That He Helped Cuomo." NPR. September 7, 2021. https://www.npr.org/2021/09/07/1034760697/human-rights-campaign-fired-alphonso-david-cuomo-harassment Accessed April 25, 2024.

82   "Joint Statement of HRC and Alphonso David." Human Rights Campaign news release. March 15, 2023. https://www.hrc.org/press-releases/joint-statement-of-hrc-and-alphonso-david Accessed April 25, 2024.

Five hours after *The 19th* published the story's initial version, however, the outlet added to the White House statement. The new version reads, "We continue to support gender-affirming care for minors, which represents a continuum of care, and respect the role of parents, families, and doctors in these decisions."[83]

Early the next morning, Robinson took credit for the change in an email titled "WH Statement Shift of Trans care." She highlighted the updated statement, saying, "This is progress, but we need to keep pushing. Pressure is working. This would not have happened without all of us."[84] With this email, Robinson revealed that HRC had spearheaded—or at least participated in—a pressure campaign on this exact statement, and she was taking credit for changing official White House statements.

DARK MONEY FUNDING

The Left's dark money network has contributed to the Human Rights Campaign, which has received:

- ◆ $1 million from the Open Society Institute between 2020 and 2021.[85]
- ◆ $37,000 from the Foundation to Promote Open Society between 2016 and 2017.[86]

---

83 Rummler, Orion. "White House says it opposes gender-affirming surgery for minors." *The 19th News*. July 2, 2024. https://19thnews.org/2024/07/white-house-statement-gender-affirming-surgery-minors/ Accessed July 10, 2024.

84 X Post. @writingblock. July 3, 2024. 1:06 p.m. https://x.com/writingblock/status/1808547774524195294?s=51&t=d9_J7hoePVMfyYzFGg0wDQ Accessed July 10, 2024.

85 The exact figure is $1,075,000. "Awarded Grants" page search results for "Human Rights Campaign." Open Society Foundations. https://www.opensocietyfoundations.org/grants/past?filter_keyword=Human+Rights+Campaign&grant_id=OR2021-79983 Accessed May 24, 2024.

86 Ibid.

- $50,000 from New Venture Fund in 2018 (Arabella)[87]
- 20,000 from North Fund in 2020 (Arabella) [88]
- $25,000 from the Center for American Progress Action Fund in 2021[89]
- $53,687 from the American Federation of State, County, and Municipal Employees in 2013. [90]

HRC gave $40,000 to New Venture Fund in 2018.[91]

In summary, the Left's dark money network helps prop up an extremely powerful LGBTQ group that aims to entrench gender ideology throughout the federal government, and it seems to have succeeded to an alarming degree.

87 "New Venture Fund." Form 990 Schedule I for 2018, accessed on April 25, 2024.

88 "North Fund." Form 990 Schedule I for 2020, accessed on April 25, 2024.

89 "Center for American Progress Action Fund." Form 990 Schedule I for 2021.

90 "American Federation Of State County & Municipal Employees." Form 990 Schedule I for 2013, accessed on April 25, 2024.

91 "Human Rights Campaign Foundation." Form 990 Schedule I for 2018, accessed on April 25, 2024.

6

THE WOKE WEAPONIZATION
OF LAW ENFORCEMENT

American history fundamentally changed on May 30, 2024, when a Manhattan jury convicted former President Donald Trump of thirty-four felony counts of falsification of business records.[1]

The case traced back to payments Trump made to Michael Cohen in 2017, reimbursing Cohen for paying Stephanie Clifford (better known by her porn stage name Stormy Daniels) to keep her from talking about an alleged affair between her and Trump during the 2016 presidential election. Prosecutors claimed that these "hush money" payments constituted a campaign expense and therefore Trump violated the law by not filing them with the Federal Election Commission. Trump's lawyers claimed Trump paid Clifford to protect his wife, Melania, from rumors and upset.

Manhattan District Attorney Alvin Bragg—who won election after touting his history of investigating Trump and pledging to

---

1   Stepman, Jarrett. "Political World Erupts After Jury Declares Trump Guilty on All 34 Counts." *The Daily Signal.* May 30, 2024. https://www.dailysignal.com/2024/05/30/guilty-jury-convicts-trump-on-all-charges/ Accessed May 31, 2024.

hold him "accountable by following the facts where they go"[2]—resurrected the "hush money" case after federal prosecutors declined to bring charges against Trump, and after Bragg's predecessor, Cyrus Vance, also declined to bring charges.[3]

Bragg fits the model of the "Rogue Prosecutors" that George Soros has funded, and the billionaire indirectly supported Bragg's campaign by contributing $1 million to Color of Change PAC. This is the political arm of Color of Change, a partner in the Black Lives Matter Global Network Foundation, the main organization of the Black Lives Matter movement. Color of Change PAC reportedly used the Soros donation to support Bragg, although the Soros donation was not earmarked for Bragg.[4]

Bragg implemented the same policies that the "reform prosecutors" have launched throughout the country. He directed his office to invest more in diversion and alternatives to incarceration, to reduce pretrial incarceration, to focus on accountability more than sentence length, and more.

It seems these soft-on-crime policies extend to everyone besides Bragg's political target—Donald Trump. For Trump, Bragg would go to extreme lengths to twist the law to secure a conviction. Neither the Federal Election Commission nor the Justice Department pursued charges against Trump, because the payment at issue was not a campaign expense under federal law, but Bragg resurrected a "zom-

2   Burman, Theo. "Did Alvin Bragg Campaign on a Promise To Prosecute Trump? What We Know." *Newsweek*. May 31, 2024. https://www.newsweek.com/did-alvin-bragg-promise-trump-prosecution-hush-money-guilty-conviction-1906705 Accessed May 31, 2024.

3   Orden, Erica. "How a hush money scandal turned into a criminal case: The whirlwind history of People v. Trump." *Politico*. April 15, 2024. https://www.politico.com/news/2024/04/15/trump-hush-money-case-history-00152172 Accessed May 31, 2024.

4   Lucas, Fred. "Soros-Backed BLM Partner Bankrolled Bragg's Election as DA, Now Praises Trump Indictment." *The Daily Signal*. April 4, 2023. https://www.dailysignal.com/2023/04/04/soros-backed-blm-partner-bankrolled-braggs-election-as-da-now-praises-trump-indictment/ Accessed May 31, 2024.

bie case" that has become Exhibit A of the political weaponization of law enforcement.

Bragg was not the first to weaponize law enforcement to target a threat to the Left's political power, however. The Woketopus has manipulated federal law enforcement to terrify its critics into silence, and the Trump conviction merely represents the logical conclusion of this horrifying trend.

This chapter will delve into three shocking aspects of the woke weaponization of law enforcement: federal agencies relying on the corrupt smear factory the Southern Poverty Law Center, an infamous letter comparing parents to domestic terrorists, and a Justice Department division prosecuting pro-life Americans who dare to protest abortion clinics.

A SHOCKING FBI MEMO

In 2023, the FBI revealed America's true enemy: traditional Catholics who say the Latin Mass.

A January 23, 2023, memo urged agents to develop "sources with access" including in "places of worship" to probe an alleged relationship between "racially or ethnically motivated, violent extremists" and "radical-traditional Catholic ideology." The document, "Interest of Racially or Ethnically Motivated Violent Extremists in Radial Traditionalist Catholic Ideology Almost Certainly Presents New Mitigation Opportunities," surfaced when FBI whistleblower Kyle Seraphin published it on UncoverDC.com in early February.[5] (He had served six years at the FBI as a special agent before the FBI indefinitely suspended him without pay in June 2022.)

The memo states that radical-traditional Catholics, to whom the document refers as "RTCs," "are typically categorized by the rejection of the Second Vatican Council (Vatican II) as a valid

---

5   Seraphin, Kyle. "The FBI Doubles Down on Christians and White Supremacy in 2023." *Uncover DC*. February 8, 2023. https://www.uncoverdc.com/2023/02/08/the-fbi-doubles-down-on-christians-and-white-supremacy-in-2023/ Accessed April 29, 2024.

church council; disdain for most of the popes elected since Vatican II, particularly Pope Francis and Pope John Paul II; and frequent adherence to anti-Semitic, anti-immigrant, anti-LGBTQ, and white supremacist ideology." It distinguishes RTCs from "'traditionalist Catholics' who prefer the Traditional Latin Mass and pre-Vatican II teachings and traditions, without the more extremist ideological beliefs and violent rhetoric."

Where did the FBI get this information? The memo did not hide its source: in a "perspective" note, the document states, "As of 2021, the Southern Poverty Law Center identified nine RTC hate groups operating in the United States." It included an appendix with a complete list of organizations the SPLC brands "radical traditional Catholic hate groups," without any acknowledgement that the SPLC's "hate" accusations have been heavily criticized as biased and inaccurate.

In 2018, then-Attorney General Jeff Sessions condemned the SPLC and promised not to rely on organizations like it. I know because I was there. "I have ordered a review at the Department of Justice to make sure that we do not partner with any groups that discriminate," he said. "We will not partner with groups that unfairly defame Americans for standing up for the Constitution or their faith."[6]

FBI leaders should have known that the Southern Poverty Law Center is not a reliable source on "hate." "We got briefings that SPLC was not legitimate when I was at Quantico," Seraphin, the FBI whistleblower who revealed the memo, told *The Daily Signal*, "A real intelligence product would quote that and say, 'unsubstantiated.'"[7]

---

6   O'Neil, Tyler. "Jeff Sessions: The DOJ 'Will Not Partner With Groups That Unfairly Defame Americans' Like the SPLC." *PJ Media*. August 8, 2018. https://pjmedia.com/tyler-o-neil/2018/08/08/jeff-sessions-the-doj-will-not-partner-with-groups-that-unfairly-defame-americans-like-the-splc-n60066 Accessed April 29, 2024.

7   O'Neil, Tyler. "WHISTLEBLOWER DOCS: FBI Cites Southern Poverty Law Center in Report on 'Radical-Traditionalist Catholic Ideology.'" *The Daily Signal*. February 8, 2023. https://www.dailysignal.com/2023/02/08/whistleblower-docs-fbi-cites-southern-poverty-law-center-in-report-on-radical-traditionalist-catholic-ideology/ Accessed April 29, 2024.

Swift Backlash

The day after Seraphin published the memo, the FBI announced that the bureau had rescinded it.

"While our standard practice is to not comment on specific intelligence products, this particular field office product—disseminated only within the FBI—regarding racially or ethnically motivated violent extremism does not meet the exacting standards of the FBI," the FBI told *The Daily Signal* in a statement.

> Upon learning of the document, FBI Headquarters quickly began taking action to remove the document from FBI systems and conduct a review of the basis for the document…. The FBI is committed to sound analytic tradecraft and to investigating and preventing acts of violence and other crimes while upholding the constitutional rights of all Americans and will never conduct investigative activities or open an investigation based solely on First Amendment protected activity.[8]

Virginia leaders, Republicans, and Catholics demanded answers, however.

"Religious freedom is a foundational tenet of our great nation, and the governor was stunned by the news reports on the FBI memo," Macaulay Porter, spokeswoman for Virginia's Republican Governor Glenn Youngkin, told *The Daily Signal*. "While he is encouraged that the FBI removed the document, he believes there must be full transparency and accountability from FBI leadership as part of the review under way."

Bishop Barry Knestout of the Diocese of Richmond condemned the memo and urged members of Congress who represent Virginia

---

8   O'Neil, Tyler. "BREAKING: FBI Rescinds Memo Citing Southern Poverty Law Center After Daily Signal Report." *The Daily Signal.* February 9, 2023. https://www.dailysignal.com/2023/02/09/breaking-fbi-rescinds-radical-traditionalist-catholic-ideology-document-citing-southern-poverty-law-center/ Accessed April 29, 2024.

to "exercise their role of oversight, to publicly condemn this threat to religious liberty, and to ensure that such offenses against the constitutionally protected free exercise of religion do not occur again."[9]

What Inspired the Memo?

In April 2024, the Justice Department Inspector General wrote a letter to Congress explaining the memo. It said that the Richmond FBI drafted it following an investigation into a domestic terrorism suspect who was indicted on federal charges in June 2023. This suspect pleaded guilty to vandalism (slashing the tires of a parked car) and agreed to avoid contact with firearms as part of his plea. Yet he used "increasingly violent rhetoric," threatening "pro-choice, Jewish, and LGBTQ individuals" in monitored communications, and said he planned to "make total war against the Satanic occultist government and the Zionist devil worshiping bankers who control it."

The suspect, upon his release from jail, began to attend a Catholic church and tried to recruit others at the church to his cause, according to the DOJ IG. He described himself as a "Fascist and Catholic" and spoke about carrying out an attack. The FBI's Richmond office placed a source in the church the suspect attended and found that he was planning to commit terrorist acts. The suspect pleaded guilty in March 2024 to possessing destructive devices while a convicted felon.

FBI analysts decided to start drafting the memo based on this one suspect. The analysts admitted that "there was no evidence that [the suspect] was being radicalized at [the church he attended]." [10]

9   O'Neil, Tyler. "Gov. Youngkin Demands 'Full Transparency and Accountability' From FBI in Wake of 'Radical-Traditional Catholic' Memo." The Daily Signal. February 16, 2023. https://www.dailysignal.com/2023/02/16/gov-youngkin-demands-full-transparency-accountability-fbi-wake-radical-traditional-catholic-memo/ Accessed April 29, 2024.

10   Horowitz, Michael E. to Senate and House committees. Department of Justice Office of the Inspector General. April 18, 2024. https://oig.justice.gov/sites/default/files/2024-04/4-18-2024-letter.pdf Accessed April 29, 2024.

So, Who Are These 'Radical-Traditional Catholics'?

The list of "radical-traditional Catholic hate groups" the FBI cited includes *The Remnant*, a newspaper and TV outlet in Forest Lake, Minnesota. Michael J. Matt, its editor, told *The Daily Signal* that many of the other groups on the list—including Catholic Apologetics International and Christ or Chaos—are either defunct or irrelevant, another entity on the list, Culture Wars, "regularly attacks *The Remnant*," and none of these groups represented a threat to begin with. According to Matt, "The SPLC are huge defenders of the Second Vatican Council, saying the Catholic Church was antisemitic, full of hate. So, anybody who likes the old Latin Mass, that's just code for hate, especially antisemitism. That's the broad brush that they paint traditional Catholics with."

He said the list dates back to 2007 and doesn't show much evidence of having been updated. "There has been an explosion of traditional Catholic groups since Pope Benedict XVI brought back the Latin Mass," Matt said. "None of the new groups who are in positions of real influence are targeted in the memo."

He also noted that Slaves of the Immaculate Heart of Mary in Town of Richmond, New Hampshire, is a convent full of nuns. (Note to the FBI: "Warrior Nun" is a *fiction* show on Netflix, not reality.)

THE SOUTHERN POVERTY LAW CENTER

Regardless of the FBI staff's intentions in drafting the memo, its reliance on the SPLC rightly set off alarms. The SPLC publishes an annual report about "hate groups" in the U.S., putting mainstream conservative and Christian nonprofits on a "hate map" with chapters of the Ku Klux Klan.

While the SPLC began by offering pro-bono legal representation to poor people in the South, it gained its strongest reputation by suing KKK groups into bankruptcy in the 1980s. SPLC lawyers quit over this new direction, comparing suing the Klan to "shooting fish in a barrel," but SPLC co-founder Morris Dees seemed to prefer it, in part because it proved a boon for fundraising.[11] As the SPLC succeeded in taking down the remnants of true evil, it ran out of "grand dragons" to conquer. The program it developed for monitoring the Klan, Klanwatch, morphed into The Intelligence Project, and started including broader categories of "hate."

In 2019, amid a racial discrimination and sexual harassment scandal that led the SPLC to fire its co-founder, a former employee came forward, calling the "hate" accusations a "highly profitable scam," explaining that by exaggerating hate, the SPLC scared donors into ponying up cash.[12]

In the early 2000s, the "hate map" started including conservative groups alongside the Klan. It added the Traditional Values Coalition, a now-defunct national social conservative lobbying group, as an "Anti-LGBT hate group" to the 2005 version of the map, and it added the Federation for American Immigration Reform, a mainstream conservative group advocating for enforcing immigration law, to the 2007 version.

The 2010 version of the "hate map" included a broad swath of conservative Christian groups, including the Family Research Council in Washington, D.C., which advocates against same-sex marriage and for traditional Christian sexuality, along with religious freedom and free speech.[13] The SPLC—which continues to put FRC on the "hate map"—accused FRC of linking "being gay with pedophilia" and portraying "LGBTQ people as sick, evil, perverted, incestuous and a danger to the nation."

---

11   O'Neil, Tyler. *Making Hate Pay: The Corruption of the Southern Poverty Law Center.* New York: Bombardier Books, 2020. pp. 63–64.

12   Moser, Bob. "The Reckoning of Morris Dees and the Southern Poverty Law Center." *The New Yorker.* March 21, 2019. https://www.newyorker.com/news/news-desk/the-reckoning-of-morris-dees-and-the-southern-poverty-law-center Accessed April 26, 2024.

13   "Anti-LBGTQ Hate Map." Southern Poverty Law Center website. https://www.splcenter.org/hate-map?year=2010&state=DC&ideology=anti-lgbt Accessed April 12, 2024.

FRC has countered these claims. "FRC has never said, and does not believe, that most homosexuals are child molesters," former FRC Senior Vice President Rob Schwarzwalder explained. "However, it is undisputed that the percentage of child abuse cases that are male-on-male is far higher than the percentage of adult males who are homosexual. This suggests that male homosexuality is a *risk factor* for child sexual abuse."

FRC's senior fellow for policy studies, Peter Sprigg, said his organization's position is that "Every person, no matter who they are sexually attracted to, is created in the image and likeness of God" and therefore is "equal in value and dignity and must be treated with respect." He said FRC opposes homosexual *conduct*, not LGBTQ people, and cited health risks associated with same-sex sexual activity.[14]

Americans and the SPLC have every right to oppose FRC's positions on these issues, but its stance does not justify placing FRC on a "hate map" with Klan chapters.

A Domestic Terror Attack

The SPLC's decision to brand FRC a "hate group" resulted in real-world harm.

Around the same time the SPLC added FRC to the "hate map," news outlets started reporting that Chick-fil-A was funding pro-family groups through its WinShape Foundation, including FRC. Activists protested Chick-fil-A, accusing it of supporting "hate."

Floyd Lee Corkins II, 28, an LGBT activist, entered the Family Research Council's office on August 15, 2012, with a nine-millimeter handgun and a bag of Chick-fil-A chicken sandwiches. Leo Johnson, FRC's building manager, confronted Corkins, who shot

---

14 O'Neil, Tyler. "5 Reasons the SPLC Is Profoundly Wrong About Two Notorious Christian 'Hate Groups.'" *PJ Media*. August 20, 2019. https://pjmedia.com/tyler-o-neil/2019/08/20/5-reasons-the-splc-is-profoundly-wrong-about-two-notorious-christian-hate-groups-n68219 Accessed April 29, 2024.

Johnson in the arm during the ensuing struggle. Johnson pinned Corkins until the police arrived, preventing a major tragedy.

Corkins later told the FBI that he had used the SPLC "hate map" to find FRC's location. "How did you find it earlier? Did you look it up online?" FBI interviewers asked.

"It was a, uh, Southern Poverty Law, lists, anti-gay groups," Corkins responded.

"I found them online. I did a little bit of research, went to the website ... stuff like that," he said. "I wanted to kill the people in the building and then smear a Chick-fil-A sandwich in their face ... to kill as many people as I could."[15]

FRC President Tony Perkins blamed the SPLC for inspiring the shooting. "The SPLC's reckless labeling has led to devastating consequences," he said at the time. "Because of its 'hate group' labeling, a deadly terrorist had a guide map to FRC and other organizations. ... The Southern Poverty Law Center, which has now been linked to domestic terrorism in federal court, should put an immediate stop to its practice of labeling organizations that oppose their promotion of homosexuality."

The SPLC condemned the attack. "The SPLC has listed the FRC as a hate group since 2010 because it has knowingly spread false and denigrating propaganda about LGBT people—not, as some claim, because it opposes same-sex marriage," Mark Potok, then an SPLC spokesman, said at the time of the shooting. "The FRC and its allies on the religious right are saying, in effect, that offering legitimate and fact-based criticism in a democratic society is tantamount to suggesting that the objects of criticism should be the targets of criminal violence."[16]

Yet the same SPLC would go on to claim that its hate accusations are a matter of opinion, not fact, when challenged on them in court.

---

15   O'Neil, *Making Hate Pay.* pp. 121–122.
16   Ibid. 123–124.

An Extreme Bias

The Family Research Council is far from alone among the SPLC's targets. Its "hate map" includes many conservative groups and very few liberal groups. It overlooks the left-wing activists who have engaged in vandalism and violence in recent years, such as the black bloc forces of Antifa, the pro-abortion vandals who call themselves "Jane's Revenge," and anti-Israel students who harass Jews on college campuses.

Meanwhile, the SPLC brands conservative groups such as the Federation for American Immigration Reform, the Center for Immigration Studies, and others that advocate for border enforcement, "anti-immigrant hate groups."

It brands conservatives who analyze the threat of radical Islamist terrorism, such as The Center for Security Policy and ACT for America, "anti-Muslim hate groups." In 2018, the SPLC released *Journalist's Manual: Field Guide to Anti-Muslim Extremists*, which attacked multiple current and former Muslims who warned against an Islamist ideology's potential to inspire terrorism. Ayaan Hirsi Ali, a Somali victim of female genital mutilation, and Maajid Nawaz, a Muslim reformer, both found themselves attacked in this document. Nawaz later sued for defamation, and the SPLC formally apologized for attacking him. It also rescinded the document.[17]

The SPLC also issued a formal apology to neurosurgeon and former presidential candidate Ben Carson in 2015, after placing him on its "extremist" list. The SPLC claimed that its "extremist file" on Carson "did not meet our standards." However, the SPLC went on to highlight statements from Carson it described as "extreme," including a statement insisting that "marriage is between a man and a woman."[18]

The "hate map" includes socially conservative law firms like Alliance Defending Freedom, Liberty Counsel, Pacific Justice

---

17 Dalmia, Shikha. "Southern Poverty Law Center Scraps Its Anti-Muslim Hate List." *Reason*. April 20, 2018. https://reason.com/2018/04/20/southern-poverty-law-center-scraps-its-h/ Accessed April 29, 2024.

18 "SPLC Statement on Dr. Ben Carson." Southern Poverty Law Center. February 11, 2015. https://www.splcenter.org/sites/default/files/d6_legacy_files/downloads/publication/splc-statement-carson.pdf Accessed April 26, 2024.

Institute, and the American Freedom Law Center. ADF has won multiple cases at the Supreme Court, and even its ideological opponents have condemned the SPLC's accusation against ADF. For example, former ACLU President Nadine Strossen noted that while she admires and supports the work of the SPLC, she must "respectfully dissent" from the claim that ADF is a "hate group."

"I consider ADF to be a valuable ally on important issues of common concern, and a worthy adversary (not an 'enemy') on important issues of disagreement; what I do not consider it to be, considering the full scope of its work, is a 'hate group,'" she wrote.

In 2023, the SPLC even added parental rights groups like Moms for Liberty and Parents Defending Education to the "hate map," suggesting that moms and dads who want a say in their kids' education are the modern equivalent of men in white hoods burning crosses.[19]

The SPLC also opened an "extremist file" on Chaya Raichik, the Jewish woman behind LibsofTikTok, a social media account exposing teachers and others who advocate CRT and gender ideology.[20]

In June 2024, the SPLC even added an openly gay group, Gays Against Groomers, to the list of "anti-LGBTQ hate groups." The group started with Jaimee Michell's X account, Gays Against Groomers. Michell started the effort to warn against the sexualization of children and to highlight the fact that not all people who identify as LGBTQ support sexualized lessons and events geared toward kids. The SPLC condemns the group for making "amplifying anti-trans and anti-drag messaging key to its online and in-person activity."[21]

19 O'Neil, Tyler. "Far-Left Group Puts Moms for Liberty on Map With KKK Chapters." *The Daily Signal.* June 6, 2023. https://www.dailysignal.com/2023/06/06/breaking-southern-poverty-law-center-adds-parental-rights-groups-hate-map/ Accessed April 26, 2024.

20 "Chaya Raichik." Southern Poverty Law Center Extremist File. https://www.splcenter.org/fighting-hate/extremist-files/individual/chaya-raichik Accessed April 26, 2024.

21 O'Neil, Tyler. "SPLC Adds Openly Gay Group to List of 'Anti-LGBTQ+ Hate Groups.'" *The Daily Signal.* June 5, 2024. https://www.dailysignal.com/2024/06/05/splc-gays-groomers-doctors-who-oppose-gender-affirming-care-hate-map-klan-chapters/ Accessed July 10, 2024.

What About Catholics?

The fact that the FBI would cite the SPLC on Catholicism is especially alarming.

The SPLC has suggested that the entire Roman Catholic Church should be considered a "hate group." When the center branded the Ruth Institute an "anti-LGBTQ hate group," it quoted the institute's president, Jennifer Roback Morse, in what SPLC characterized as an ostensibly damning statement—that the Catholic Church "is very clear that same-sex sexual acts are intrinsically disordered and can never be morally acceptable." Morse didn't come up with that idea, however. That language comes directly from the Catechism of the Catholic Church, the binding document stating the essential and fundamental content of the Catholic faith.

As I wrote in my book *Making Hate Pay*, "If this claim is enough to make an organization a 'hate group,' then the SPLC should call the entire Catholic Church a 'hate group.' Otherwise, it is being intellectually dishonest."[22]

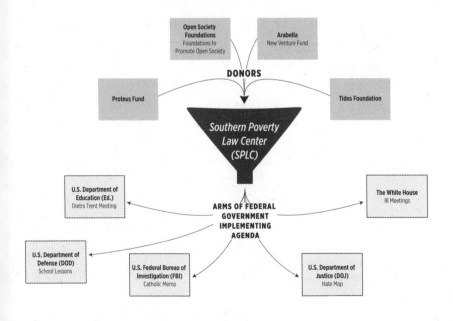

---

22 O'Neil, *Making Hate Pay*, p. 108.

Not Just the FBI

The SPLC's impact in the Biden administration has spread far beyond one now-retracted FBI memo.

President Biden twice nominated Nancy Abudu, then deputy legal director at the SPLC, to the U.S. Court of Appeals for the 11th Circuit, and the Senate confirmed her in May 2023.[23] The White House also touted the partnership of the SPLC in its "National Strategy to Counter Antisemitism."[24]

The White House has hosted SPLC leaders and staff at least eighteen times since Biden's inauguration. SPLC President Margaret Huang attended a meeting with Biden and eighteen others on May 20, 2021, when Biden signed the COVID-19 Hate Crimes Act into law.[25] Susan Corke, director of the Intelligence Project, who is responsible for the "hate map," has attended at least three White House meetings with John Picarelli, director of counterterrorism at the White House National Security Council. These meetings—one on January 6, 2023, and two on December 7, 2023—also included members of American University's Polarization & Extremism Research & Innovation Lab (PERIL). Cynthia Miller-Idriss, PERIL's founding director, also serves as a member of the SPLC's Tracking Hate and Extremism Advisory Committee.[26]

23 O'Neil, Tyler. "5 Things to Know About Nancy Abudu, Leftist SPLC Lawyer Biden Tapped for 11th Circuit." *The Daily Signal.* February 1, 2023. Updated May 18, 2023. https://www.dailysignal.com/2023/02/01/5-things-know-nancy-abudu-leftist-splc-lawyer-biden-tapped-11th-circuit   Accessed March 29, 2024.

24 "FACT Sheet: Biden-Harris Administration Releases First-Ever U.S. National Strategy to Counter Antisemitism." White House Briefing Room. May 25, 2023. https://www.whitehouse.gov/briefing-room/statements-re-leases/2023/05/25/fact-sheet-biden-harris-administration-releases-first-ev-er-u-s-national-strategy-to-counter-antisemitism/ Accessed March 29, 2024.

25 "Remarks by President Biden at Signing of the COVID-19 Hate Crimes Act." White House Briefing Room. May 20, 2021. https://www.whitehouse.gov/briefing-room/speeches-remarks/2021/05/20/remarks-by-president-biden-at-signing-of-the-covid-19-hate-crimes-act/ Accessed April 29, 2024.

26 White House Visitor Logs, analyzed by Tyler O'Neil, downloaded from https://www.whitehouse.gov/disclosures/visitor-logs/ on March 21, 2024.

Seeking Advice on 'Domestic Terrorism'

The SPLC has even advised the administration on domestic terrorism, according to SPLC President Margaret Huang. She bragged to donors in the fall of 2021 that, in the early days of the Biden administration, federal agencies reached out to "solicit our expertise" to "help shape the policies" to counter "the domestic terrorism threat."[27]

That's not just braggadocio—the Justice Department consulted with the SPLC right after it put Moms for Liberty on the "hate map." Hours before publishing the 2022 version of the "hate map" on June 6, 2023, the SPLC's senior policy counsel for "hate and extremism," Michael Lieberman, reached out to Robert Moossy Jr., deputy assistant attorney general at the Justice Department's Civil Rights Division, and Shiela Foran, acting head of the division's policy and strategy section.

Lieberman gave them a "quick embargoed peek" of the full report. "We'd love to work with you both and the policy team to set up a briefing for interested DOJ interdepartmental hate crime task force members this month," he wrote. "If you're interested, happy to talk about scheduling time with our report authors and SPLC Intelligence Project subject-matter experts."

The "sneak peek" summarized the report's key points, such as claims that "hate and anti-government extremist groups are descending on Main Street America"; that "far-right lawmakers are pushing legislation straight from the scripts of hate groups, including bills that seek to control the bodies of women and those who can give birth, whitewash black history in schools, and criminalize LGBTQ+ people"; and that "one group at the forefront of this 'anti-student inclusion' movement is Moms for Liberty," which the

---

27   O'Neil, Tyler. "ORWELLIAN NIGHTMARE: Biden Admin Consulted Anti-Christian Group for 'Domestic Terrorism' Strategy." *The Daily Signal.* January 11, 2024. https://www.dailysignal.com/2024/01/11/exclusive-biden-admin-approached-anti-christian-splc-help-shape-policies-counter-domestic-terror-threat/ Accessed April 26, 2024.

SPLC accused of attempting to "normalize assaults on inclusive education."

Foran responded by promising to share the report with the Hate Crimes Enforcement and Prevention Initiative and promising to "circle back" on "setting up a briefing." The Justice Department confirmed that a briefing did indeed take place.[28]

"It is sadly predictable that the Biden administration is echoing the anti-conservative activists at the Southern Poverty Law Center," Senator Ted Cruz (R-TX) told *The Daily Signal* after news of the briefing became public. "Even pretending to take them seriously demonstrates a serious lack of judgment."

"Biden's leadership at the DOJ are partisans using another partisan organization to legitimize prosecuting Biden's political opponents," Cruz added.[29]

Advising the Department of Education

SPLC staff also advised Dietra Trent, executive director at the White House initiative on Historically Black Colleges and Universities, who reports to Education Secretary Miguel Cardona. A July 5, 2022, meeting included Trent, Warren, Lieberman, and Kevin Miles, the deputy director of programs and strategy at the SPLC's education arm, Learning for Justice. Learning for Justice promotes Critical Race Theory, gender ideology, and other left-wing causes in schools, and has long opposed Moms for Liberty and other parental rights groups which criticize schools for promoting these ideas.

The Department of Education also shared slide decks from the far-left group Equality Federation that describe Moms for Liberty

---

28 O'Neil, Tyler. "SMOKING GUN: Biden DOJ Took Advice From Group Demonizing Concerned Parents, Docs Show." *The Daily Signal.* March 7, 2024. https://www.dailysignal.com/2024/03/07/exclusive-splc-tried-sic-do-js-hate-crimes-division-moms-liberty/ Accessed April 26, 2024.

29 O'Neil, Tyler. "Ted Cruz Slams Biden Justice Department's Collusion With Southern Poverty Law Center." *The Daily Signal.* March 9, 2024. https://www.dailysignal.com/2024/03/09/ted-cruz-slams-biden-dojs-collusion-southern-poverty-law-center/ Accessed May 21, 2024.

as "our opposition." The slide deck also lists the "Christian Right," Alliance Defending Freedom, and The Heritage Foundation.[30]

"It is shocking to see in writing the evidence that innocent parents were harassed and targeted by their own federal government for exercising their right to free speech and for speaking out during the COVID school shutdowns," Moms for Liberty co-founder Tiffany Justice told *The Daily Signal* about the documents, which Heritage's Oversight Project unearthed. "We have known for some time the Biden administration has made it their mission to attack parents who publicly advocate for their children's education. Attending public school board meetings and voicing concerns about our children's education should not put a target on our backs to be silenced by the federal government."

Influence in Pentagon Schools

Department of Defense Education Activity (DODEA) schools promoted lessons published by the SPLC's Learning for Justice. Multiple DODEA staffers revealed that they use SPLC materials in teacher trainings and classrooms, while speaking at a 2021 Equity and Access Summit, according to documents unearthed by the education nonprofit Open the Books in July 2024.

A DODEA middle school teacher, speaking at a presentation titled "Integrating Global Citizenship Education and Social Justice Standards," said Learning for Justice resources aligned with the DODEA's approach to teaching students about history and social studies. The SPLC lessons in question encourage students to pressure business and political leaders to take "action in response to a social justice issue."

The SPLC's Social Justice Standards, which a DODEA physical education staffer praised, embrace Critical Race Theory, teaching

---

30   O'Neil, Tyler. "BREAKING: Biden Education Department Met With SPLC Before Center Put Parental Rights Groups on Its 'Hate Map.'" *The Daily Signal.* January 29, 2024. https://www.dailysignal.com/2024/01/29/breaking-department-education-met-splc-center-put-parental-rights-groups-hate-map/ Accessed April 29, 2024.

that America is systemically racist and urging students to "plan and carry out collective action against bias and injustice in the world."[31]

COMPARING PARENTS TO DOMESTIC TERRORISTS

The SPLC's attacks on parental rights groups echoed another disturbing incident where the White House met with a group demonizing parents as domestic terrorists.

During the COVID-19 pandemic, most students attended class virtually, over Zoom. At the same time, outrage over the death of George Floyd, who had died while police held him on the ground, led educators to embrace Critical Race Theory and teach some of its ideas to their students. Parents were able to see on their children's computer screens the politically-charged lessons they were receiving in school, and they started speaking out at school board meetings.

Parents mostly complained about COVID-19 school closures, mask mandates, lessons pushing racial division, and policies allowing boys to access girls' bathrooms and locker rooms. Although some schools reported isolated threats (without any confirmed ties to the budding parental rights movement), most parents protested peacefully at school board meetings. A few faced charges for disrupting school board meetings in a few incidents which became notorious for school board misconduct.

On June 22, 2021, police arrested Loudoun County father Scott Smith on charges of disorderly conduct and resisting arrest because he lashed out in a school board meeting.

Yet Smith's angry outburst did not come out of a vacuum. A fifteen-year-old boy who identified as "gender-fluid" had sexually assaulted his daughter in a girls' restroom on May 28, at Stone Bridge High School in the northern Virginia city of Ashburn. The

---

31   Schmad, Robert. "EXCLUSIVE: Pentagon Schools Encouraged Students To Be Left-Wing Activists, Pushed DEI On Kids And Teachers, Docs Show." *The Daily Caller News Foundation.* July 11, 2024. https://dailycaller.com/2024/07/11/pentagon-schools-dei-kids-teachers/ Accessed July 11, 2024.

father had been responding to then-Superintendent Scott Ziegler, who said, "the predator transgender student or person simply does not exist." This statement understandably infuriated Smith.

The Loudoun County Juvenile Court found the perpetrator "not innocent" of charges of forcible sodomy and forcible fellatio. The perpetrator also pleaded "no contest" to charges of abduction and sexual battery for another sexual assault in a girls' restroom at Broad Run High School, also in Ashburn.[32] A special grand jury report on the fifteen-year-old's sexual assaults concluded that the school board "failed at every juncture" with "a stunning lack of openness, transparency, and accountability both to the public and the special grand jury." However, the report concluded that there had been no "coordinated cover-up between [Loudoun County] administrators and members of the [school board]."[33]

The case became a central flashpoint in the debate over parental rights in the 2021 Virginia gubernatorial election, where Republican businessman Glenn Youngkin prevailed over Democratic former Governor Terry McAuliffe. McAuliffe had notoriously declared, "I don't think parents should be telling schools what they should teach."

While a jury convicted Smith of disorderly conduct and resisting arrest, Youngkin pardoned him on September 10, 2023. "Scott Smith is a dedicated parent who's faced unwarranted charges in his pursuit to protect his daughter," Youngkin said at the time. "Scott's commitment to his child despite the immense obstacles is emblematic of the parent empowerment movement that started in Virginia. In Virginia, parents matter and my resolve to empower parents is unwavering."[34]

---

32 O'Neil, Tyler. "Loudoun County sexual assault victim's mother plans Title IX lawsuit against school board." Fox News. November 16, 2021. https://www.foxnews.com/politics/loudoun-county-victim-mother-title-ix Accessed March 29, 2024.

33 *Report of the Special Grand Jury on the Investigation of Loudoun County Public Schools.* December 2022. https://www.loudoun.gov/specialgrandjury Accessed March 29, 2024.

34 "Governor Glenn Youngkin Grants Pardon to Loudoun County Dad Whose Daughter was Sexually Assaulted in Public School." Governor Glenn Youngkin news release. September 10, 2023. https://www.governor.virginia.gov/newsroom/news-releases/2023/september/name-1013859-en.html Accessed March 29, 2024.

This well-publicized incident did not suggest a campaign of violent threats against school boards. Rather, it illustrated how a school board appeared to suppress parental concerns in an emotionally charged environment.

Yet on September 29, 2021, the National School Boards Association sent the Biden White House a letter comparing concerned parents to "domestic terrorists." The letter urges the White House to assemble "a joint collaboration among federal law enforcement agencies, state and local law enforcement, and with public school officials" to counter "acts of malice, violence, and threats against public school officials" that could be classified as "the equivalent to a form of domestic terrorism and hate crimes."

The letter requests "a joint expedited review by the U.S. Departments of Justice, Education, and Homeland Security," along with training from the FBI, its National Security Branch and Counterterrorism Division, and "any other federal agency with relevant jurisdictional authority and oversight." It also asks that the review "examine appropriate enforceable actions against these crimes and acts of violence under the Gun-Free School Zones Act, the PATRIOT Act in regards to domestic terrorism, the Matthew Shepard and James Byrd Jr. Hate Crimes Prevention Act, ... and any related measure."[35]

NSBA President Viola Garcia and interim Executive Director and CEO Chip Slaven co-signed the letter. Slaven's original September 17 draft of the letter asks Biden to deploy the "Army National Guard and its Military Police" to address "acts and threats of violence."[36]

---

35   "Re: Federal Assistance to Stop Threats and Acts of Violence Against Public Schoolchildren, Public School Board Members, and Other Public School District Officials and Educators." National School Boards Association letter to President Joe Biden. September 29, 2021. Retracted October 22, 2021. Accessed via appendix of exhibits in NSBA report on letter, Exhibit 82. https://nsba-cloud-drupal-files-nsba-dev.s3.amazonaws.com/s3fs-public/NSBA+Report-5-19-22+exhibits+only.pdf Accessed March 29, 2024.

36   NSBA report on letter, Exhibit 36. https://nsba-cloud-drupal-files-nsba-dev.s3.amazonaws.com/s3fs-public/NSBA+Report-5-19-22+exhibits+only.pdf Accessed April 25, 2024.

The Justice Department Responds

On October 4, 2021, Attorney General Merrick Garland issued a memo to the FBI, the U.S. Attorneys, and the Justice Department's Criminal Division, based on the NSBA letter.

Garland's memo notes a "disturbing spike in harassment, intimidation, and threats of violence against school administrators, board members, teachers, and staff who participate in the vital work of running our nation's public schools."

"I am directing the Federal Burau of Investigation, working with each United States Attorney, to convene meetings with federal, state, local, Tribal, and territorial leaders in each federal judicial district within 30 days of the issuance of this memorandum," he wrote. The meetings would focus on "strategies for addressing threats against school administrators, board members, teachers, and staff."[37]

According to an October 5, 2021, email between NSBA board members Pam Doyle and Beverly Slough, Slaven "knew about the U.S. AG directives before they were published."[38]

Loud Backlash

The school board associations of at least twenty-one states distanced themselves from the NSBA letter between September 29 and October 22. Those in Pennsylvania, Louisiana, Ohio, and Missouri formally withdrew from the NSBA altogether.[39]

---

37 Garland, Merrick. "Memorandum for Director, Federal Bureau of Investigation; Director, Executive Office for U.S. Attorneys; Assistant Attorney General, Criminal Division; United States Attorneys." October 4, 2021. https://www.justice.gov/ag/file/1170061-0/dl?inline= Accessed March 29, 2024.

38 Dillon, A.P. "Former NSBA director was aware of Garland memo targeting parents prior to its release." February 24, 2022. https://nsjonline.com/article/2022/02/former-nsba-director-was-aware-of-garland-memo-targeting-parents-prior-to-its-release/ Accessed March 29, 2024.

39 Dunn, Lauren. "National School Boards Association retracts letter after backlash." *WORLD*. October 27, 2021. https://wng.org/roundups/national-school-boards-association-retracts-letter-after-backlash-1635358517 Accessed April 26, 2024.

"The most recent national controversy surrounding a letter to President Biden suggesting that some parents should be considered domestic terrorists was the final straw," the Pennsylvania School Boards Association said in a letter to members. "This misguided approach has made our work and that of many school boards more difficult. It has fomented more disputes and cast partisanship on our work on behalf of school directors, when we seek to find common ground and support all school directors in their work, no matter their politics. Now is not the time for more politics and posturing, it is the time for solutions to the many challenges facing education."[40]

The American Freedom Law Center filed a lawsuit against Garland on behalf of parents in Virginia and Michigan. The lawsuit condemned Garland's policy as "government-sanctioned discrimination and censorship of free speech in violation of the First Amendment." The lawsuit sought an injunction against the policy "to use federal enforcement resources to silence parents and other private citizens who publicly object to and oppose the divisive, harmful, immoral, and racist policies of the 'progressive' Left that are being implemented by school boards and school officials in public school districts."[41]

In court, the government acknowledged that the concerned parents' protests "fall outside the scope of the memorandum and are fully protected by the Constitution." Therefore, they dismissed the parents' lawsuit for lack of standing, since the parents could not prove they suffered an injury.[42]

---

40   Downey, Caroline. "Ohio, Missouri, Pennsylvania School Board Groups Leave National Association over Letter Likening Parents to Domestic Terrorists." *National Review.* October 26, 2021. https://www.nationalreview.com/news/ohio-pennsylvania-school-board-groups-leave-national-association-over-letter-likening-parents-to-domestic-terrorists/ Accessed April 26, 2024.

41   Saline Parents v. Garland. Complaint. Filed October 19, 2021. https://www.americanfreedomlawcenter.org/wp-content/uploads/2021/10/Complaint-Saline-Parents-v-Garland-Filed.pdf Accessed April 26, 2024.

42   Saline Parents v. Garland. U.S. Court of Appeals for the District of Columbia Circuit. Decided December 15, 2023. https://www.cadc.uscourts.gov/internet/opinions.nsf/E1563773B5A6CDDA85258A86005344A3/$file/22-5258-2031663.pdf Accessed April 26, 2024.

As the backlash mounted, the NSBA apologized for the September 29 letter less than a month afterward, on October 22. "There was no justification for some of the language used in the letter," the organization admitted.[43] The NSBA ousted Slaven, the interim director and CEO, in November 2021, placing most of the blame for the letter on him. Slaven stood by the letter, denounced the apology, and said he felt "betrayed" by the NSBA.[44]

A Horrifying Backstory

Parents Defending Education, a parental rights group that reached out to the school boards associations across the country for comment in the wake of the NSBA letter, also filed a Freedom of Information Act request and turned up a document suggesting that NSBA did not act alone.

On October 5, 2021, NSBA Secretary-Treasurer Kristi Swett wrote in an email that Slaven "told the officers he was writing a letter to provide information to the White House, from a request by Secretary Cardona." That email, which Parents Defending Education released in January 2022, suggests that Education Secretary Miguel Cardona first suggested the idea of the NSBA letter to Slaven, who drafted it.[45]

The Internal Investigation

In May 2022, the NSBA released an independent review into the letter, which revealed that Slaven had been in contact with the White House regarding it. According to the review's timeline,

---

43   "NSBA Apologizes for Letter to President Biden." National School Boards Administration news release. October 22, 2021. https://www.nsba.org/News/2021/letter-to-members Accessed March 29, 2024.

44   "NSBA Announces Completion of Independent Review; Takes Action Based on Findings." The National School Boards Association. May 20, 2022. https://www.nsba.org/News/2022/independent-review Accessed April 26, 2024.

45   Swett, Kristi. "Statement to President Biden." Email October 5, 2021. https://defendinged.org/wp-content/uploads/2022/01/Maldonado-emails-Oct-5-2021_Redacted.pdf Accessed March 29, 2024.

Slaven participated in a virtual townhall with Cardona and Surgeon General Vivek Murthy on August 26. When Gina Patterson, executive director of the Virginia School Boards Association, emailed Slaven about the forthcoming September 29 letter, Slaven told her, "The statement needed to be released after [President Biden] finished the address and that he did not want to sour his relationship with the White House by releasing it prematurely."

On September 9, Slaven told NSBA leaders that he was on "a last-minute call ... with the White House" where he discussed the issue of threats to school board meetings. He noted that Ronn Nozoe, chief executive officer at the National Association of Secondary School Principals (NASSP), "jumped in" on the subject.[46] (NASSP would release its own statement "calling on federal officials to provide support for school leaders threatened by those who disagree with school guidelines on COVID-19 best practices" on September 16, 2021.[47] NASSP has not apologized or rescinded this release.)

Slaven also coordinated with the School Superintendents Association on a September 22 statement stating that "school leaders across the country are facing threats because they are simply trying to follow the health and scientific safety guidance issued by federal, state, and local health policy experts."[48] Noelle Ellerson Ng, asso-

---

46 Kiko, Philip G. "Table 6—Comprehensive Timeline of Events." *Final Report on the Events Surrounding the National School Boards Association's September 29, 2021, Letter to the President.* National School Boards Association website. p. 37. May 2022. https://nsba.org/-/media/Files/NSBA-Report.pdf?la=en&hash=A001354D23C9AE88B54D398270C9790D91B01FF9 Accessed March 29, 2024.

47 "NASSP Calls on Federal Officials to Protect School Leaders from Threats and Violence." National Association of Secondary School Principals news release. September 16, 2021. https://www.nassp.org/news/nassp-calls-on-federal-officials-to-protect-school-leaders-from-threats-and-violence/ Accessed March 29, 2024.

48 "NSBA, AASA Issue Joint Statement Calling for End to Threats and Violence Around Safe School Opening Decisions." NSBA news release. September 22, 2021. https://www.nsba.org/News/2021/end-threats-violence-joint-statement Accessed March 29, 2024.

ciate executive director at the School Superintendents Association, told *Education Week* that asking for federal involvement was "a recipe for disaster and not at all a role for the [federal government] in school board meetings."

Jane Mellow, NSBA's interim chief advocacy officer, forwarded that conversation to Slaven, noting that Ellerson Ng "will be surprised and likely pissed when we do our letter." She told Ellerson Ng that Slaven had been in regular communication with the White House about the issue.[49]

NSBA board member Pam Doyle suggested Slaven drafted the letter for political reasons, to ingratiate himself with the Biden administration. "I had one exec say they thought it was a coup between Chip [Slaven] and the White House in positioning Chip for a place in the Biden square," she wrote.[50] Slaven had served as director of federal policy and intergovernmental affairs for West Virginia Democratic Governor Robert E. Wise, as well as Wise's congressional district director while Wise served in the House of Representatives.

Slaven's Side of the Story

Slaven, speaking to Fox News Digital after his ouster, claimed the NSBA "betrayed" him and insisted that the Biden administration did not initiate or coerce the letter.

"That narrative that the White House has somehow orchestrated…is really disingenuous," he said. "I would say that not only did they not ask for the letter, [but] they [also] did not encourage a letter."

He did not dispute sending a summary of the letter's contents to Mary Wall at the White House, but he said he waited over a

---

49 Kiko, comprehensive timeline.

50 Lucas, Fred. "6 Takeaways From Emails Revealing White House Role in Targeting Parents Who Disagree With School Boards." *The Daily Signal.* November 16, 2021. https://www.dailysignal.com/2021/11/16/6-takeaways-from-emails-revealing-white-house-role-in-targeting-parents-who-disagree-with-school-boards/ Accessed March 29, 2024.

week, with no response from the Biden administration, before he released it.

When Fox News presented Slaven with Swett's email claiming that Cardona had requested the letter, he replied, "I can't understand why she [said] that." He pointed out that the word "parents" does not appear in the letter, and insisted that he meant to condemn groups like the Proud Boys. "Hindsight's 2020. So…I can't go back in time…but I am proud of what we did, and I stand by it. And I don't think we have anything to apologize for, for calling out the issue around violence and threats."[51]

'No Compelling' Justification

According to a March 2023 report from the Select Subcommittee on the Weaponization of the Federal Government and the House Judiciary Committee, the Biden administration had "no compelling nationwide law-enforcement justification" for the October 4 memo. In his October 2021 testimony to the Judiciary Committee, Garland conceded that the NSBA letter was the only basis for his memo.[52]

This incident reveals the lengths to which the Biden administration would go to justify cracking down on parents who disagreed with the administration's stances on education, from COVID-19 mandates to Critical Race Theory and transgender orthodoxy.

51   Grossman, Hannah. "Man behind infamous NSBA letter says organization's leaders 'completely backstabbed' him." Fox News. June 3, 2022. https://www.foxnews.com/media/man-behind-infamous-nsba-letter-says-organization-backstabbed-him Accessed April 26, 2024.

52   Committee on the Judiciary and the Select Subcommittee on the Weaponization of the Federal Government. A "Manufactured" Issue and "Misapplied" Priorities: Subpoenaed Documents Show No Legitimate Basis for the Attorney General's Anti-Parent Memo. Interim Staff Report. March 21, 2023. https://judiciary.house.gov/sites/evo-subsites/republicans-judiciary.house.gov/files/evo-media-document/2023-03-21-school-board-documents-interim-report.pdf Accessed March 29, 2024.

PROSECUTING PRO-LIFE PROTESTERS

The Department of Justice has charged pro-life protesters, some of whom are now serving prison sentences. Meanwhile, most pro-abortion vandals appear to have got off scot-free.

In the wake of the Supreme Court's decision to overturn the abortion ruling *Roe v. Wade* (1973) in *Dobbs v. Jackson Women's Health Organization* (2022), Biden warned that the Court's decision "will have devastating consequences in the lives of women around the country."[53] He also announced various actions to promote abortion.

The Justice Department's Civil Rights Division enforces the Freedom of Access to Public Entrances Act, or FACE Act. According to the Civil Rights Division, the FACE Act "protects all patients, providers, and facilities that provide reproductive health services, including pro-life pregnancy counseling services and any other pregnancy support facility providing reproductive health care."[54] In December 2022, then-Associate Attorney General Vanita Gupta, who supervised the Department of Justice's Civil Rights Division, said the overturning of *Roe* increased "the urgency of our work, including enforcement of the FACE Act, to ensure continued lawful access to reproductive services."[55]

---

53 "FACT SHEET: President Biden Announced Actions In Light of Today's Supreme Court Decision on Dobbs v. Jackson Women's Health Organization." White House Briefing Room. June 24, 2022. https://www.whitehouse.gov/briefing-room/statements-releases/2022/06/24/fact-sheet-president-biden-announces-actions-in-light-of-todays-supreme-court-decision-on-dobbs-v-jackson-womens-health-organization/ Accessed March 26, 2024.

54 "Protecting Patients and Health Care Providers." U.S. Justice Department Civil Rights Division. https://www.justice.gov/crt/protecting-patients-and-health-care-providers Accessed March 26, 2024.

55 "Associate Attorney General Vanita Gupta Delivers Remarks at the Civil Rights Division's 65th Anniversary." U. S. Department of Justice Office of Public Affairs. December 6, 2022. https://www.justice.gov/opa/speech/associate-attorney-general-vanita-gupta-delivers-remarks-civil-rights-divisions-65th Accessed March 26, 2024.

The Supreme Court's draft opinion for *Dobbs* leaked, in a historic first for the Court. Following that leak, pro-abortion vandals targeted pro-life pregnancy centers, pro-life groups, and Roman Catholic Churches. According to CatholicVote, pro-abortion vandals have targeted at least eighty-eight pro-life pregnancy centers and pro-life groups since the leak,[56] and vandals have attacked 240 Catholic churches since the leak, many of them using pro-abortion messages.[57]

Under Biden, the Justice Department's Civil Rights Division has charged about 130 pro-life protesters for violating the FACE Act outside abortion clinics, while it has leveled only five charges against pro-abortion activists who targeted pregnancy centers. Pro-life groups including Advancing American Freedom, Students for Life of America, CatholicVote, the Family Research Council, and more have demanded that Congress repeal the FACE Act.[58]

"The Biden administration has weaponized the FACE Act against peaceful pro-life sidewalk counselors and activists who want to save lives and change hearts and minds," Paul Teller, executive director at Advancing American Freedom, told The Daily Signal. "Justice should be blind. But pro-abortion activists who have scaled bridges shutting down main roads, posted the home addresses of Supreme Court justices, and vandalized and firebombed pro-life pregnancy centers have not faced the FBI showing up on their doorstep."

FACE Act Prosecutions

The letter came after a Nashville jury found six pro-life activists guilty of violating the FACE Act. They had peacefully protested in

---

56   "Tracking Attacks on Pregnancy Centers & Pro-Life Groups." CatholicVote. Updated January 28, 2024. https://catholicvote.org/pregnancy-center-attack-tracker/ Accessed March 26, 2024.

57   "Tracker: Over 400 Attacks on U.S. Catholic Churches Since May 2020." CatholicVote. Updated March 12, 2024. https://catholicvote.org/tracker-church-attacks/ Accessed March 26, 2024.

58   Olohan, Mary Margaret. "EXCLUSIVE: Conservative Leaders Call on Jordan, Johnson to Repeal 'Weaponized' FACE Act." *The Daily Signal.* February 7, 2024. https://www.dailysignal.com/2024/02/07/exclusive-conservative-leaders-call-jordan-johnson-repeal-face-act/ Accessed March 26, 2024.

the hallway outside an abortion clinic in Mount Juliet, Tennessee, in March 2021.[59] These protesters face up to eleven years in prison and $350,000 in fines.

Eva Edl, an eighty-eight-year-old woman who survived a death camp in Yugoslavia at age ten, now expects to die in prison. "When I was indicted, I began to prepare to die there," Edl told *The Daily Signal's* Mary Margaret Olohan.

Yugoslavia's Communist leader, Josip Broz, commonly known as Tito, rounded up Edl's family in a purge of Danube Swabians, a German-speaking ethnic minority in his country. She recalled getting shipped off in cattle cars to a concentration camp. "We were packed body to body, and being a small child, I could hardly breathe," she recalled. "We had no food, no water." She said many of those who went with her to the concentration camp died there and were buried in mass graves.

Yet Edl escaped and came to the United States, where she learned about the horror of abortion, and began protesting the killing of the unborn. She attempted to stop pregnant women from entering abortion clinics, a crime under the FACE Act. The Justice Department has charged Edl with violating FACE three times, twice in Michigan and once in Tennessee.

She compares her efforts to save the unborn to efforts her countrymen could have taken to save her in Yugoslavia:

> When we were rounded up to be killed, we were placed in cattle cars, and our train was headed toward the extermination camp. What if citizens of my country would have overcome their fear, and a number of them stood on those railroad tracks between the gate of the entrance to the death camp and the train? The train would have to stop, and while the guards on those

---

59 Olohan, Mary Margaret. "Pro-Lifers Targeted by Biden DOJ Found Guilty." *The Daily Signal.* January 30, 2024. https://www.dailysignal.com/2024/01/30/pro-life-activists-charged-biden-doj-face-11-years-prison-peaceful-protest/ March 26, 2024.

trains would be busy rounding up the ones that were in front of the train, another group could have come in, pried open our cattle car and possibly set us free, but nobody did.

So, when we place our bodies between the woman and the clinic, we buy time to get our sidewalk counselors the opportunity to speak with women, and hopefully open their hearts with love for their babies and let their babies live. After all, we offer them everything there is, including adoptions. I've offered to adopt babies on the spot … we're standing between the killer and the victim.[60]

Mark Houck, a Catholic father of seven, faced FACE Act charges for a 2021 incident in which Houck reportedly pushed an abortion clinic volunteer who was repeatedly harassing his son. Local authorities dismissed the matter, but the Biden DOJ filed charges and raided Houck's house, pointing guns at Houck, his wife, and his children. A jury found Houck not guilty of federal charges in January 2023.

Houck then announced a run for Congress in August 2023, and in November 2023, he filed a lawsuit against the Biden DOJ. Houck claims the DOJ violated his Fourth Amendment right to protection from unreasonable searches and seizures, "by using excessive force to arrest him on non-violent charges when he had not threatened law enforcement, did not own a gun, and had offered to turn himself in to authorities if indicted."[61]

---

60   Olohan, Mary Margaret. "EXCLUSIVE: She Survived a Death Camp. Facing Biden DOJ Charges, She Is Prepared to Die in Prison." *The Daily Signal.* April 21, 2024. https://www.dailysignal.com/2024/04/21/exclusive-she-survived-death-camp-facing-biden-doj-charges-shes-prepared-die-prison/ Accessed April 26, 2024.

61   Olohan, Mary Margaret. "Mark Houck, Family Sue Biden DOJ for 'Malicious and Retaliatory Prosecution.'" *The Daily Signal.* November 8, 2023. https://www.dailysignal.com/2023/11/08/mark-houck-family-sue-biden-doj-for-malicious-and-retaliatory-prosecution/ Accessed March 26, 2024.

The Pro-Abortion Narrative on Pro-Life Violence

The National Abortion Federation tracks threats, violence, and incidents of "stalking" at abortion facilities across the country. Its report for 2022 found 218 death threats or threats of harm against abortion facilities and their employees, ninety-two incidents of stalking, forty-three instances of burglary, twenty instances of "invasion," and four instances of arson. The federation also reported 112,086 instances of "picketing" (where pro-life protesters stand outside abortion facilities, urging mothers to keep their babies).

While most Americans rightly condemn acts of violence against abortion clinics, the federation's report shows a horrific double standard when it comes to pro-life pregnancy centers. "Anti-abortion centers, sometimes called 'crisis pregnancy centers' (CPCs), are fake clinics, often subsidized by taxpayer dollars, that use deceptive practices to dissuade people from seeking abortions," the report states. It does not mention the fact that these centers provide counseling, free maternal and baby resources, and childcare, among other things, but states, "CPCs are simply another tactic in the war on bodily autonomy and reproductive justice that work in tandem with others."

The federation faults the FBI for announcing a reward for anyone with information about a series of attacks in 2022, because "nine of the 10 organizations that the agency listed in its announcement are anti-abortion centers—not abortion clinics." The report minimizes attacks against pro-life pregnancy centers, stating that "the well-organized extremist violence against abortion providers should not be conflated with acts of vandalism against fake clinics."[62]

Brittany Fonteno, who became the NAF president in September 2023, attended one White House event featuring Vice President Harris in December 2023.

---

62 *2022 Violence & Disruption Statistics.* National Abortion Federation. https://prochoice.org/wp-content/uploads/2022-VD-Report-FINAL.pdf Accessed March 27, 2024.

Abortion and 'Racial Justice'

Gupta, the assistant attorney general who linked FACE Act enforcement to the Biden administration's response to *Dobbs*, had worked at the NAACP Legal Defense Fund and the American Civil Liberties Union, where she rose to become the ACLU's deputy legal director and director of its Center for Justice. After a stint in the Obama administration heading up the DOJ's Civil Rights Division, she became president and chief executive officer of the Leadership Conference on Civil and Human Rights.

Each of these organizations supports abortion and ties it to "racial justice." The NAACP Legal Defense Fund claims that "access to abortion care has been a fundamental part of reproductive health care for Black, Brown, and low-income people throughout the country."[63] Lauren Johnson, the director of the ACLU's Abortion Criminal Defense Initiative, claims that "the criminalization of abortion care" represents "another way in which our criminal legal system is being wielded to control the bodies and futures of people who are disproportionately Black, Brown and low-income."[64]

Maya Wiley, the president and CEO of The Leadership Conference on Civil and Human Rights, lamented *Dobbs*. "Our basic and accepted right to control our own bodies has fallen victim to an ideologically extremist majority of the Supreme Court that is now permitting states to police and criminalize millions of women, girls, and transgender and nonbinary people for making decisions about their bodies, health care, and private lives," she said.[65]

---

63 "Reproductive Rights and Racial Justice: Frequently Asked Questions." NAACP Legal Defense Fund. https://www.naacpldf.org/reproductive-rights-faq/ Accessed March 26, 2024.

64 Johnson, Lauren. "Criminalizing Abortion Care is Wrong, and We're Fighting Back." American Civil Liberties Union. February 28, 2023. https://www.aclu.org/news/reproductive-freedom/fighting-against-criminalization-abortion-rights-acdi Accessed March 26, 2024.

65 "In Unconscionable Decision, Supreme Court Overturns Right to Abortion." The Leadership Conference on Civil and Human Rights. June 24, 2022. https://civilrights.org/2022/06/24/in-unconscionable-decision-supreme-court-overturns-right-to-abortion/ Accessed March 26, 2024.

The Enforcer

Kristen Clarke, assistant attorney general for civil rights at the DOJ, also had a stint at the NAACP Legal Defense Fund, as co-director of the Political Participation Group, from 2006 to 2011. She then served as president and executive director at the Lawyers' Committee for Civil Rights Under Law from 2016 to 2021, before joining the DOJ in May 2021.[66]

Clarke's social media history suggests a bias against pro-lifers and Christians. She cited the Southern Poverty Law Center in condemning Alliance Defending Freedom, a pro-life and religious freedom law firm, as a "hate group." She said that those protesting Dr. Anthony Fauci, the controversial COVID-19 czar and former head of the National Institute for Allergy and Infectious Diseases, should be "publicly identified and named, barred from treatment at any public hospital if/when they fall ill and denied coverage under their insurance."[67]

She also submitted testimony to the U.S. Senate opposing Amy Coney Barrett's confirmation to the Supreme Court, in part because her record suggested Barrett would "restrict reproductive rights and ultimately dismantle *Roe v. Wade*." Clarke went on to claim that Barrett "will move our country backward to a time when not all Americans enjoyed the civil rights they now enjoy. Black people and people of color, as well as all other marginalized groups, should not once again suffer the indignity of second-class citizenship."[68]

---

66 "Kristen Clarke." LinkedIn Profile https://www.linkedin.com/in/kristen-clarke9/ Accessed March 26, 2024.

67 Olohan, Mary Margaret. "DOJ's Kristen Clarke: A Pro-Abortion Activist Enforcing the Law Against Pro-Lifers." *The Daily Signal.* October 26, 2022. https://www.dailysignal.com/2022/10/26/dojs-kristen-clarke-pro-abortion-activist-enforcing-law-pro-lifers/ Accessed March 26, 2024.

68 Clarke, Kristen. "Statement of Kristen Clarke, President and Executive Director, Lawyers' Committee for Civil Rights Under Law." Testimony before the U.S. Senate Committee on the Judiciary. https://www.judiciary.senate.gov/imo/media/doc/Clarke%20Testimony.pdf Accessed March 26, 2024.

While studying at Harvard University, Clarke wrote a letter to the editors of the *Harvard Crimson* claiming that black people have "superior physical and mental abilities," and that "melanin endows blacks with greater mental, physical, and spiritual abilities—something which cannot be measured based on Eurocentric standards."[69]

Clarke later explained to *The Forward* that she had been criticizing "The Bell Curve," a book written by psychologist Richard Herrnstein and political scientist Charles Murray. She said the book "was generating wide acclaim for its racist views" and that her article aimed to "hold up a mirror to reflect how reprehensible the premise of black inferiority was set." She said she meant "to express an equally absurd point of view—fighting one ridiculous absurd racist theory with another ridiculous absurd theory."[70]

While at Columbia Law School, Clarke promoted an essay from self-proclaimed Marxist Amiri Baraka defending cop-killer Mumia Abu-Jamal and comparing police officers to the Ku Klux Klan. "The Klan is now the police, with blue uniforms replacing the sheets and hoods," Baraka wrote in the essay, which Clarke forwarded to her then-professor, the late historian Manning Marable.[71]

When Biden nominated Clarke, pro-abortion groups wrote a letter supporting her confirmation, saying Clarke "is exactly the accomplished civil rights attorney who will bolster civil rights enforcement and ensure equal justice for all." Among other issues,

---

69 Safi, Marlo. "A Joe Biden Justice Department Pick Argued In 1994 That Blacks Have 'Greater Mental, Physical and Spiritual Abilities' Than Whites." *The Daily Caller.* January 12, 2021. https://dailycaller.com/2021/01/12/joe-biden-justice-department-kristen-clarke-civil-rights-division-harvard-letter-bell-curve/ Accessed March 27, 2024.

70 Kornbluh, Jacob. "Biden's Deputy AG touts record on antisemitism amid criticism of her college activity." *Forward.* January 14, 2021. https://forward.com/news/462089/bidens-deputy-ag-pick-touts-record-on-antisemitism-amid-criticism-of/ Accessed March 27, 2024.

71 Ross, Chuck. "Email Shows Biden Nominee Pushed Essay Comparing Cops to KKK, Defending Cop Killer Mumia Abu-Jamal." *The Daily Caller.* April 22, 2021. https://dailycaller.com/2021/04/22/kristen-clarke-amiri-baraka-mumia-abu-jamal/ Accessed March 27, 2024.

the pro-abortion groups noted that Clarke will oversee the criminal section of the Civil Rights Division, "which handles cases brought under the Freedom of Access to Clinic Entrances Act (FACE) and prosecutes hate crimes." Fifty-six organizations, including NARAL Pro-Choice America (now rebranded as Reproductive Freedom for All), the National Women's Law Center, Planned Parenthood Federation of America, and TIME'S UP Now, signed the letter.[72]

In April 2024, *The Daily Signal*'s Mary Margaret Olohan uncovered documents revealing that Clarke had been in a violent domestic dispute. Her ex-husband, Reginald Avery, claimed that in 2006, Clarke had attacked him with a knife, deeply slicing his finger to the bone. (Avery and Clark finalized their divorce in 2009, according to court records.) This resulted in her arrest, which was eventually expunged from her record.

However, during her Senate confirmation, Clarke denied ever having been arrested or having been accused of committing a violent crime.[73] In a statement to CNN, she admitted she did not disclose the arrest, saying she was not required to disclose something that had been expunged from her record. She also claimed that she was "subjected to years-long abuse and domestic violence at the hand of [her] ex-husband."[74] ("I deny it of course," Avery told *The*

---

72 "Gender Justice Coalition Letter in Support of Kristen Clarke to be Assistant Attorney General for the Civil Rights Division at the Department of Justice." National Women's Law Center to Sens. Dick Durbin and Chuck Grassley. April 8, 2021. National Women's Law Center. https://nwlc.org/wp-content/uploads/2021/04/Gender-Justice-letter-in-Support-of-Kristen-Clarke-1.pdf Accessed March 27, 2024.

73 Olohan, Mary Margaret. "EXCLUSIVE: DOJ's Kristen Clarke Testified She Was Never Arrested. Court Records and Text Messages Indicate She Was." *The Daily Signal.* April 30, 2024. https://www.dailysignal.com/2024/04/30/exclusive-dojs-kristen-clarke-testified-she-was-never-arrested-court-records-and-text-messages-indicate-she-was/ Accessed May 26, 2024.

74 Olohan, Mary Margaret. "DOJ's Kristen Clarke Confirms She Did Not Disclose Arrest, Alleges Domestic Abuse." *The Daily Signal.* May 1, 2024. https://www.dailysignal.com/2024/05/01/dojs-kristen-clarke-confirms-she-did-not-disclose-arrest-alleges-domestic-abuse/ Accessed May 26, 2024.

Daily Signal in response to the accusation. He called Clarke's claim "a sad and pathetic effort to make herself a victim.")

Senator Mike Lee (R-UT) demanded Clarke resign for having "lied under oath during her confirmation proceedings." He added, "She lied under oath to mask her arrest for committing a violent crime, yet she zealously prosecutes peaceful pro-life protesters."[75]

White House Ties

Leaders at the Lawyers' Committee for Civil Rights Under Law have visited the White House at least nine times. NAACP Legal Defense Fund leaders visited the White House at least seven times. ACLU leadership have visited the White House at least ten times.[76]

Center for American Progress

The Center for American Progress, a leftist group with various ties to the Biden administration (discussed in Chapter 4), released "A Proactive Abortion Agenda" in March 2021, which urges enforcement of the FACE Act. "The federal government must … actively enforce the FACE Act to prevent violence targeting abortion providers and patients," it states. "While important, the law has been unevenly enforced and has not provided sufficient protection from harassment and violence."

It warns that the anti-abortion movement has strengthened "ties to white supremacists, including far-right militias," and noted that "many of the same anti-abortion activists who harassed patients and providers participated in the January 6 coup attempt at the U.S. Capitol."[77]

75 Olohan, Mary Margaret. "'She Lied Under Oath': Sen. Mike Lee Calls for DOJ's Kristen Clarke to Resign." *The Daily Signal.* May 1, 2024. https://www.dailysignal.com/2024/05/01/she-lied-oath-sen-mike-lee-calls-dojs-kristen-clarke-resign/ Accessed May 26, 2024.

76 White House Visitor Logs.

77 Allsbrook, Jamille Fields, and Nora Ellman. "A Proactive Abortion Agenda." The Center for American Progress. March 17, 2021. https://www.americanprogress.org/article/proactive-abortion-agenda/ Accessed March 27, 2024.

Dark Money Funding

Each of the groups pushing federal law enforcement to demonize conservatives has ties to the Left's dark money network.

The SPLC has received:

- $20,000 from New Venture Fund in 2022 (Arabella)[78]
- $30,000 from The Proteus Fund between 2018 and 2021[79]
- $75,000 from The Foundation to Promote Open Society in 2016 (specifically earmarked for an "Anti-Hate Table")[80]
- $1 million from The Tides Foundation between 2018 and 2022[81]

The National School Boards Administration has received:

- $157,000 from the National Education Association between 2018 and 2022[82]

The Lawyers' Committee for Civil Rights Under Law has received:

- $225,000 from Hopewell Fund between 2018 and 2021 (Arabella)[83]
- $2 million from New Venture Fund between 2014 and 2022 (Arabella)[84]

---

78   "New Venture Fund." Form 990, Schedule I for 2022, accessed May 1, 2024.

79   "Proteus Fund." Form 990, Schedule I for 2018, 2020, 2021, accessed May 1, 2024.

80   "Awarded Grants" page search results for "Southern Poverty." Open Society Foundations. https://www.opensocietyfoundations.org/grants/past?filter_keyword=southern+poverty&grant_id=OR2016-30974 Accessed May 21, 2024.

81   The precise figure is $1,038,381. "Tides Foundation" Form 990 Schedule I for 2018-2022, accessed April 26, 2024.

82   "National Education Association." Form 990, Schedule I for 2018, 20202, and 2022, accessed May 26, 2024.

83   "Hopewell Fund." Form 990, Schedule I for 2018 and 2021, accessed April 26, 2024.

84   The figure is $2,062,000. "New Venture Fund." Form 990, Schedule I, for 2014–2022, accessed April 26, 2024.

- $25,000 from Sixteen Thirty Fund in 2016 (Arabella)[85]
- $1 million from The Tides Foundation between 2019 and 2022[86]
- $65,000 from the AFL-CIO between 2011 and 2017[87]
- $655,598 from Demos between 2012 and 2014[88]
- $40,000 from The National Education Association in 2010[89]

The NAACP Legal Defense Fund received:

- $240,000 from New Venture Fund between 2016 and 2022 (Arabella)[90]
- $1.2 million from The Tides Foundation between 2018 and 2022[91]
- $50,000 from Proteus Action League in 2012[92]
- $10,000 from the Human Rights Campaign in 2018[93]

The ACLU received:

- $176,000 from Proteus Action League between 2014 and 2016[94]

---

85 "Sixteen Thirty Fund." Form 990, Schedule I, for 2016, accessed April 26, 2024.

86 The exact number is $1,250,000. "Tides Foundation." Form 990, Schedule I for 2019–2022, accessed on April 26, 2024.

87 "American Federation of Labor-Congress of Industrial Orgs." Form 990, Schedule I for 2010, 2011, and 2016, accessed April 26, 2024.

88 "Demos A Network For Ideas And Action." Form 990, Schedule I for 2012-2014, accessed April 26, 2024.

89 "National Education Association of the United States." Form 990, Schedule I for 2010, accessed April 26, 2024.

90 "New Venture Fund." Form 990, Schedule I for 2016 and 2022, accessed April 26, 2024.

91 The exact figure is $1,205,949. "Tides Foundation." Form 990, Schedule I for 2018, 2020, and 2022, accessed April 26, 2024.

92 "Proteus Action League." Form 990, Schedule I for 2012, accessed April 26, 2024.

93 "Human Rights Campaign Inc." Form 990, Schedule I for 2018, accessed April 26, 2024.

94 "Proteus Action League." Form 990, Schedule I for 2016, 2018, accessed April 26, 2024.

- $30,000 from the American Federation of State, County & Municipal Employees in 2019[95]
- $15 million in grants from the Open Society Foundations in 2022[96]
- $500,000 from Tides Advocacy between 2018 and 2022[97]

The donors who propped up this effort urging federal law enforcement to demonize conservatives need to answer for their heinous attempt to silence opposition to their woke agenda. Americans should take note of the extreme bias of the SPLC, in particular, and regard its "hate" accusations with suspicion.

95 "American Federation Of State County & Municipal Employees." Form 990, Schedule I for 2019, accessed April 26, 2024.

96 "Awarded Grants" page search results for "American Civil Liberties Union" and "ACLU." Open Society Foundations. https://www.opensocietyfoundations.org/grants/past?filter_keyword=American%20Civil%20Liberties%20Union&page=2&grant_id=OR2022-84683 and https://www.opensocietyfoundations.org/grants/past?filter_keyword=ACLU Accessed March 22, 2024.

97 "Tides Advocacy." Form 990, Schedule I for 2018–2022, accessed April 26, 2024.

7

THE IMMIGRATION INDUSTRIAL COMPLEX

The Woketopus advised Biden officials to loosen border restrictions and enable the large influx of illegal aliens America has witnessed in the last few years, perhaps thinking that these aliens will support its causes. Under Biden and Harris, the administrative state has also worked with nonprofits to create an immigration industrial complex that sends illegal aliens throughout the country in the name of charity but with horrific effects on America. This record has drawn even more scrutiny after Biden left the presidential race in favor of Kamala Harris, whom he previously tasked with handling the immigration issue.

From his very first day in office, Biden rushed to reverse the policies former President Donald Trump set in place to curb illegal immigration and fortify the U.S.-Mexico border.

On Jan. 20, 2021, Biden signed executive orders reversing Trump's restrictions on immigrants from countries of terror concern (which Biden referred to as a "Muslim ban"), revoking Trump's executive order beefing up enforcement of immigration law, blocking the construction of the border wall, and cementing deferred action for illegal immigrants who arrive in the U.S. as children.[1]

---

1   "Fact Sheet: President-elect Biden's Day One Executive Actions Deliver Relief for Families Across America Amid Converging Crises." White House Briefing Room. Jan. 20, 2021. https://www.whitehouse.gov/briefing-room/statements-releases/2021/01/20/fact-sheet-president-elect-bidens-day-one-executive-actions-deliver-relief-for-families-across-america-amid-converging-crises/ Accessed April 1, 2024.

Biden has sought to reverse the Trump-era policy of requiring asylum seekers to remain in Mexico as the Department of Homeland Security began processing their asylum cases. This program remains in legal limbo due to a court challenge, but its operation ceased in October 2022.[2]

In January 2024, House Speaker Mike Johnson, R-La., released a list of 64 actions the Biden administration took to "intentionally" undermine border security.[3]

These policies sent a message that migrants, even if they entered the U.S. illegally, would receive welcome under Biden. When reporter Jorge Ventura asked a group of migrants crossing the U.S.-Mexico border what they would tell President Biden in March 2021, they said, "Thank you for supporting us."[4]

Also that month, a group of migrants went to a border crossing in Tijuana, Mexico, wearing T-shirts reading, "Biden, Please Let Us In."[5] The president responded to these trends by going on news outlets like ABC News, saying, "I can say quite clearly: Don't come."[6] The fact that Biden felt the need to say this clearly emphasized that his policies sent the opposite message.

2   "Rescission of the Migrant Protection Protocols: Litigation Developments." Congressional Research Service Legal Sidebar. Feb. 8, 2023. https://crsreports.congress.gov/product/pdf/LSB/LSB10915 Accessed April 1, 2024.

3   "64 Times the Biden Administration Intentionally Undermined Border Security." House Speaker Mike Johnson's Office. Jan. 9, 2024. https://www.speaker.gov/64-times-the-biden-administration-intentionally-undermined-border-security/ Accessed April 2, 2024.

4   X Post. @VenturaReport. March 21, 2021. 7:31 a.m. https://twitter.com/VenturaReport/status/1375047564345630722 Accessed April 1, 2024.

5   "Migrants wear Biden T-shirts at US-Mexico border, demand clearer policies." Fox10 Phoenix. March 5, 2021. https://www.fox10phoenix.com/news/migrants-wear-biden-t-shirts-at-us-mexico-border-demand-clearer-policies Accessed April 1, 2024.

6   Vasquez, Maegan and Kate Sullivan. "Biden tells migrants not to come to US: 'Don't leave your town.'" CNN March 16, 2021. https://www.cnn.com/2021/03/16/politics/joe-biden-migrant-children-border-immigration/index.html Accessed April 1, 2024.

A MASSIVE INFLUX OF ILLEGALS

Since Biden became president, the influx of immigrants has set new records, while the Woketopus pushed lax border policies. In the last fiscal year under Trump, Customs and Border Protection (CBP) encountered 646,822 illegal aliens. In the last full fiscal year under Biden (Oct. 1, 2022, to Sept. 30, 2023), CBP encountered a record 3.2 million illegal aliens.[7] Since Biden became president, CBP has encountered at least 8.7 million illegal aliens.[8]

This 8.7 million figure only includes the illegal aliens CBP encountered, not the millions who slip past authorities despite getting captured on camera. From fiscal year 2021 (starting in October 2020) to fiscal year 2023, 1,664,203 illegal aliens got away from

---

7   Allen, Virginia, and Ken McIntyre. "Biden Admin Reports Over 3 Million Illegal Aliens on America's Borders in Single Year." The Daily Signal. Oct. 21, 2023. https://www.dailysignal.com/2023/10/21/hold-biden-admin-reports-over-3-2-million-illegal-aliens-on-americas-borders-in-1-year/ Accessed April 1, 2024.

8   Analysis of CBP data, analyzing figures from February 2021 through February 2024. The exact figure, 8,711,529, comes from adding the Fiscal Year 2021 figure (minus the months of October, November, December, and January) of 1,591,840, the figures for Fiscal Years 2022 and 2023 (2,766,582 and 3,201,144), and the monthly figures through Feb. 2024, the most recent available figures: 240,988 encounters in October 2023 (CBP October 2023 monthly update released Nov. 14, 2023. https://www.cbp.gov/newsroom/national-media-release/cbp-releases-october-2023-monthly-update), 242,814 encounters in November 2023 (CBP November 2023 monthly update released Dec. 22, 2023. https://www.cbp.gov/newsroom/national-media-release/cbp-releases-november-2023-monthly-update), 302,034 encounters in December 2023 (CBP December 2023 monthly update released Jan. 26, 2024. https://www.cbp.gov/newsroom/national-media-release/cbp-releases-december-2023-monthly-update), 176,205 encounters in January (CBP January 2024 monthly update released Feb. 13, 2024. https://www.cbp.gov/newsroom/national-media-release/cbp-releases-january-2024-monthly-update), 189,922 encounters in February (CBP February 2024 monthly update released March 22, 2024. https://www.cbp.gov/newsroom/national-media-release/cbp-releases-february-2024-monthly-update) All accessed April 1, 2024.

authorities. As Fox News's Bill Melugin noted, in the decade from fiscal year 2010 through fiscal year 2020, Customs and Border Protection recorded about 1.4 million of these "gotaways," fewer than the number escaping authorities in the first three years of the Biden administration.[9]

Finally, the administration established a special parole program for Cubans, Haitians, Nicaraguans, and Venezuelans (CHNV in January 2023. According to documents obtained by the House Committee on Homeland Security, the Department of Homeland Security helped process more than 400,000 aliens into the country between January 2023 and February 2024.[10] While the federal government facilitated these aliens' entry into the country, that does not make them legal. The administration permitted them under the false pretense of "parole," helping them apply for asylum. While they may be "asylum seekers," they occupy a kind of legal limbo until asylum is granted, and the backlog causes long delays in these cases.

The Biden-Harris administration paused the CHNV program in mid-July amid reports of fraud. The Federation for American Immigration Reform (FAIR)—a pro-immigration enforcement group the SPLC brands an "anti-immigrant hate group"—obtained an internal report showing that forms from those applying for the problem included the same social security numbers, addresses, and phone numbers being used hundreds of times.

The DHS report FAIR obtained showed that 3,218 serial sponsors (those whose number appears on 20 or more forms) filled out 100,948 forms. The report also found that 24 of the 1,000 most used numbers belonged to a dead person, while 100 physical addresses were used between 124 and 739 times on over 19,000 forms. Those addresses included storage units.

---

9   X Post. @BillMelugin_ May 15, 2024. 12:35 p.m. Eastern time. https://x.com/BillMelugin_/status/1790783036713312574 Accessed May 17, 2024.

10   Shaw, Adam and Bill Melugin. "DHS docs reveal where paroled migrants under controversial Biden flight program are landing." Fox News. April 30, 2024. https://www.foxnews.com/politics/dhs-docs-reveal-where-migrants-under-controversial-biden-flight-program-are-landing Accessed May 22, 2024.

DHS told Fox News Digital that CHNV beneficiaries are "thoroughly screened and vetted prior to their arrival to the United States."[11]

The 8.7 million illegals encountered at the border, the 1.7 million gotaways, and the 400,000 aliens flown in under the CHNV program add up to 10.4 million illegal aliens. However, some of the 8.7 million have been deported, while many of the gotaways are involved in smuggling and have likely crossed the border back and forth. It remains unclear exactly how many illegals have entered the country and remain under Biden and Harris, but an estimate of 9 million seems reasonable.

Only 11 U.S. states have a population greater than 9 million, according to the U.S. Census Bureau's official population figures for 2020:[12]

- o California (40 million)
- o Florida (21.6 million)
- o Georgia (10.7 million)
- o Illinois (12.8 million)
- o Michigan (10 million)
- o New Jersey (9.3 million)
- o New York (20.2 million)
- o North Carolina (10.4 million)
- o Ohio (11.8 million)
- o Pennsylvania (13 million)
- o Texas (29.2 million)

11   Shaw, Adam. "Biden admin freezes controversial migrant flight program after fraud revelations." Fox News Digital. August 2, 2024. https://www.foxnews.com/politics/biden-admin-freezes-controversial-migrant-flight-program-after-fraud-revelations Accessed August 2, 2024.

12   U.S. Census Bureau. "Apportionment Population and Number of Representatives by State: 2020 Census." https://www2.census.gov/programs-surveys/decennial/2020/data/apportionment/apportionment-2020-table01.pdf Accessed May 17, 2024.

The population of the nine least-populous states (Alaska, Delaware, North Dakota, South Dakota, Vermont, Wyoming, Montana, Rhode Island, and Maine) adds up to a mere 8.2 million, still smaller than the number of illegal aliens who have crossed the border under Biden and Harris.

States receive seats in the U.S. House of Representatives based on their population numbers. The 9 million illegal aliens now residing in the U.S. can give more power to certain states by boosting their population. Virginia, for example, which had a population of 8.7 million in 2020, received 11 seats in the U.S. House of Representatives.

Illegal aliens also strain government safety nets and local law enforcement and education resources.

Facing this flood of illegals, the Republican governors of Texas and Florida sent illegals by bus to cities like New York and Chicago. These blue cities have adopted "sanctuary" policies that bar local law enforcement from working with federal law enforcement to enforce immigration law, advertising that illegal immigrants will not face deportation if they reside there. (Harris supported sanctuary policies when running for district attorney of San Francisco.)

As the flood of illegals continued, the Democratic governor of Colorado, Jared Polis, announced that he, too, would send illegals to The Big Apple and Chicago. The Democratic mayors of both cities have since petitioned the federal government for help.

"I don't know if we really understand the magnitude of dropping 30,000 people in the city that's already gone through a crisis," New York City Mayor Eric Adams said, referring to the recovery from the COVID-19 pandemic.[13]

His complaint seems rather ironic, given New York's sanctuary city policies. Yet it is also instructive that even pro-immigration Democrats are balking at the prospect of dealing with the horde of

---

13 Ward, Myah. "'We have been ignored': Democrat-led cities beg Biden for help with migrants." *Politico.* Jan. 4, 2023. https://www.politico.com/news/2023/01/04/biden-migrants-new-york-chicago-00076443 Accessed May 22, 2024.

illegals that has spread throughout the country. This massive migration has concrete impacts on America, often for the worse.

The Victims of the Border Crisis

Lax border enforcement has cost many lives, from contributing to the fentanyl crisis to enabling illegal alien criminals to kill Americans.

In 2022, fifteen-year-old Noah Dunn died after taking a Percocet pill that contained four times the lethal dose of fentanyl. Noah's father, Brandon, testified before the House Judiciary Committee in February 2023, asking, "How many pounds of fentanyl are coming across the thousands of miles of sparsely policed or monitored southern border?"[14]

According to the Centers for Disease Control and Prevention, opioid overdoses took the lives of more than 80,000 Americans in 2021, with synthetic opioids such as fentanyl accounting for 88 percent of the deaths.[15] Unintentional fentanyl overdose is likely the leading cause of death for Americans ages eighteen to forty-five.[16]

"What you don't hear from the Biden administration is that 95% of the fentanyl killing Americans comes from the wide-open southwest border," Mark Morgan, former head of U.S. Customs and Border Protection under Trump and now a visiting fellow at The Heritage Foundation's Border Security and Immigration Center,

---

14 Dunn, Brandon. Testimony before the House of Representatives Committee on the Judiciary. February 1, 2023, https://www.congress.gov/118/meeting/house/115264/witnesses/HHRG-118-JU00-Wstate-DunnB-20230201.pdf Accessed May 22, 2024.

15 Cosgray, Mary Elise. "Why the Sudden Rise in Fentanyl Deaths Among Young People?" *The Daily Signal.* April 12, 2024. https://www.dailysignal.com/2024/04/12/grieving-mother-lost-son-fentanyl-expert-shares-prevent-more-deaths/ Accessed May 22, 2024.

16 Mizan, Nusaiba. "Fact-check: Is fentanyl the leading cause of death among American adults?" *El Paso Times.* Feb. 2, 2023. https://www.elpasotimes.com/story/news/2023/02/02/fentanyl-overdose-cause-of-death-among-adults-greg-abbott/69867350007/ Accessed May 22, 2024.

told *The Daily Signal* in 2022. "How many more people have to die before we say enough is enough and secure our borders?"[17]

The border crisis has also more directly cost American lives. Laken Riley, a twenty-two-year-old nursing student at Augusta University, went for a run at the University of Georgia in Athens on Feb. 22, 2024, and she never came home.

Authorities arrested a suspect, José Antonio Ibarra, and charged him with felony murder, false imprisonment, and kidnapping. Ibarra entered the U.S. illegally in El Paso, Texas, in 2022. U.S. Immigration and Customs Enforcement detained Ibarra before releasing him "for further processing."

Ibarra had two run-ins with the law in 2023. New York City police charged him with endangering a child in August but released him before immigration officials could ask police to hold him in custody. Athens police arrested him in October for shoplifting and a judge issued a warrant in December when he failed to show up in court. Athens is a sanctuary city.[18]

Georgia passed a law to close some of the loopholes Ibarra went through, but Georgia state Representative Jesse Petrea, a Republican, told me the Georgia Department of Corrections reported holding more than 182 illegal aliens convicted of murder and held on ICE detainers.[19] (An ICE detainer is a document notifying state or local law enforcement that ICE intends to take an alien into custody once the law enforcement agency stops detaining that alien.)

17   Allen, Virginia. "How America's Unsecured Border Contributes to Fentanyl Crisis, Deaths." *The Daily Signal.* Aug. 18, 2022. https://www.dailysignal.com/2022/08/18/how-americas-unsecured-border-contributes-to-fentanyl-crisis-deaths/ Accessed May 22, 2024.

18   O'Neil, Tyler. "Georgia Bill Targets Lax Immigration Enforcement After Laken Riley Slaying, Allegedly at Hands of Venezuelan Immigrant." *The Daily Signal.* Feb. 28, 2024. https://www.dailysignal.com/2024/02/28/laken-riley-georgia-house-advances-immigration-enforcement-bill-illegal-alien-murders-coed-jog-sanctuary-city/ Accessed May 22, 2024.

19   Ibid.

Very few illegal aliens commit heinous crimes like murder, but preventing their illegal entry could have prevented the deaths of 182 people in Georgia, along with that of Laken Riley.

Creating the Border Crisis

Many of the Woketopus organizations I have mentioned in previous chapters helped the Biden-Harris administration create the policies enabling this horrific crisis. The American Civil Liberties Union, the Center for American Progress, and a nonprofit called America's Voice stand out.

When President-elect Joe Biden released his transition teams ahead of his Jan. 20, 2021, inauguration, his team for the Department of Homeland Security included two notable names: the team lead, Ur Mendoza Jaddou, and Andrea Flores.

Jaddou, now the head of U.S. Citizenship and Immigration Services (USCIS), served as director of DHS Watch, a project of the pro-immigration group America's Voice. America's Voice launched DHS Watch in 2018 "to uphold an immigration system that is competently administered, accountable, and adheres to long-held American values on immigration," according to its website.[20] The project heavily criticized the Trump administration but appears to have gone silent after Biden's election victory. The last archived post dates to Aug. 26, 2020.[21]

Jaddou previously served at USCIS in the Obama administration from July 2014 to January 2021.[22]

America's Voice hailed "undocumented immigrants" as "essential to our economy and essential to our democracy," citing a Center for American Progress report claiming that "an estimated 5 million

---

20 "About Us: DHS Watch." America's Voice. https://americasvoice.org/uncategorized/about-us-dhs-watch/ Accesssed July 29, 2024.
21 "DHS Watch Archives." America's Voice. https://americasvoice.org/tag/dhs-watch/ Accessed July 29, 2024.
22 "Ur Jaddou." America's Voice staff page. Archived April. 23, 2021. https://web.archive.org/web/20210423230150/https://americasvoice.org/staff/ur-jaddou/ Accessed July 29, 2024.

undocumented immigrants—nearly 3 in 4 undocumented immigrants in the workforce—are keeping the country moving forward as essential workers in the face of the pandemic."[23]

"They have earned a place at the American table," America's Voice Director of Communication Douglas Rivlin said in December 2020. "As a democratic nation, we can no longer tolerate a permanent underclass of people outside our democratic system."

"Addressing the status of millions who work with no clear route to fully participate in our society, through a long overdue path to citizenship, is essential both to our economy and to the broader health of our democracy," Rivlin added.

Biden nominated Jaddou to lead USCIS in April 2021, and the Senate confirmed her that July.[24]

Jaddou's elevation at USCIS received notice in the legacy media. The Associated Press reported that Biden had tapped her as one of two prominent "Trump critics."[25]

Yet Jaddou was not the only America's Voice leader Biden tapped for his administration. Pili Tobar, who served as managing director at America's Voice from March 2018 to July 2020, joined Biden's campaign in July 2020, served as the communications director on his inaugural committee, and then became White House deputy communications director in January 2021, a post she held until May 2022.[26]

---

23 "Undocumented Immigrants: Essential to Our Economy and Essential to Our Democracy." America's Voice. Press release. December 2, 2020. https://americasvoice.org/uncategorized/undocumented-immigrants-essential-to-our-economy-and-essential-to-our-democracy/ Accessed July 29, 2024.

24 "President Biden Announces His Intent to Nominate Key Members for the U.S. Department of Homeland Security." White House Briefing Room. April 12, 2021. https://www.whitehouse.gov/briefing-room/statements-releases/2021/04/12/president-biden-announces-his-intent-to-nominate-key-members-for-the-u-s-department-of-homeland-security/ Accessed July 29, 2024.

25 The Associated Press. "Biden picks 2 Trump critics for border, immigration roles." The Associated Press. April 12, 2021. https://apnews.com/article/joe-biden-arizona-immigration-immigration-policy-0cd569660a5de-61b5adb6505830f4aa6 Accessed July 29, 2024.

26 "Pili Tobar." LinkedIn profile. https://www.linkedin.com/in/pili-tobar-3a469a23/ Accessed July 29, 2024.

Politico reported that the influence of America's Voice in the budding Biden administration gave Democrats hope that Biden would weaken border protections more than Obama had.

"Democratic lawmakers and advocates said based on conversations with Biden's team—as well as Biden's comments—they are confident Biden will take a different approach to immigration than President Barack Obama," the outlet reported. "The immigration policy advisers Biden's added to his team from advocacy groups like America's Voice and The Immigration Hub are a positive sign, they said."[27]

Frank Sharry, founder and executive director of America's Voice, visited the White House in 2021. Vanessa Cárdenas, the group's executive director, has visited the White House fourteen times between April 2022 and March 2024.

America's Voice also has ties to the Left's dark money network. The group received:

- o $215,000 from New Venture Fund (Arabella) between 2019 and 2021[28]

- o $2.3 million from the Open Society Policy Center between 2018 and 2022 (the policy center sent another $200,000 to America's Voice Education Fund in 2017)[29]

- o $1.4 million from the Foundation to Promote Open Society between 2016 and 2020 (sent to America's Voice Education Fund)[30]

---

27 Barrón-López, Laura, and Sabrina Rodriguez. "Democrats ready immigration push for Biden's early days." *Politico.* January 15, 2021. https://www.politico.com/news/2021/01/15/biden-immigration-plans-459766 Accessed July 29, 2024.

28 "New Venture Fund." Form 990, Schedule I for 2019, 2021, accessed July 29, 2024.

29 The precise figure is $2,325,000. "Open Society Foundations grant search for "America's Voice." https://www.opensocietyfoundations.org/grants/past?filter_keyword=America%27s%20Voice&page=2&grant_id=OR2018-45646 Accessed July 29, 2024.

30 The precise figure is $1,365,000. "Open Society Foundations grant search for "America's Voice." https://www.opensocietyfoundations.org/grants/past?filter_keyword=America%27s%20Voice&page=2&grant_id=OR2018-45646 Accessed July 29, 2024.

THE ACLU

America's Voice was not the only left-wing group advising the Biden transition team on DHS. Andrea Flores, then deputy director of immigration policy at the ACLU, appeared on the list, as well.

After advising Biden's transition team on DHS, Flores became the director for border management at the White House National Security Council from January 2021 to October 2021.[31]

The ACLU published a series of blog posts "outlining a reimagined, just, and humane immigration system for the United States" in 2020. That series included a post on Biden's campaign pledge to put a moratorium on deportations at the beginning of his presidency.

"During a moratorium, the executive branch must immediately halt immigration enforcement and deportations while it works to undo policies like the Muslim ban, the public charge rule, the politicization of our immigration courts, and the evisceration of asylum," the ACLU's Madhuri Grewal wrote.[32]

Biden revoked the "Muslim ban" on his first day in office, and USCIS substantially altered the public charge rule, revoking Trump-era regulations early in 2021.[33] The public charge rule sets out parameters by which DHS bars certain noncitizens from entering the U.S. because they may become a "public charge," i.e. a person who needs government benefits to survive. Trump's DHS expanded the rule to apply to more noncitizens, and the Biden DHS shrunk it.

The ACLU set forth a vision for DHS that focused less on enforcing immigration law and preventing illegal aliens from entering the country and more on helping immigrants settle:

---

31   Andrea Flores. LinkedIn profile. https://www.linkedin.com/in/andrea-r-flores-17973911/ Accessed July 29, 2024.

32   Grewal, Madhuri. "A Deportation Moratorium, What Comes Next for Biden?" ACLU. December 22, 2020. https://www.aclu.org/news/immigrants-rights/a-deportation-moratorium-what-comes-next-for-biden Accessed July 29, 2024.

33   "Public Charge." U.S. Citizenship and Immigration Services. https://www.uscis.gov/archive/public-charge-0 Accessed July 29, 2024.

> A moratorium also provides an opportunity for the Biden-Harris administration to reject our existing immigration system's reliance on the punitive, enforcement-based approach driven by mass detention and mass deportation. This system costs taxpayers tens of billions of dollars a year.
>
> The executive branch should instead invest in a humane and effective system focused on helping people navigate a byzantine immigration system and on a pathway to citizenship.[34]

This change in mindset—from a law-enforcement focus on enforcing the border to a mandate to welcome noncitizens into the country—arguably characterizes much of the Biden administration's approach to the border crisis.

President Biden officially declared the COVID-19 pandemic crisis over on May 11, 2023, which entailed the automatic end of the Trump-era pandemic policy Title 42. Title 42 allowed law enforcement to expel illegal immigrants who recently came from countries where a communicable disease had been present. When Biden ended Title 42, he sent 1,500 active-duty U.S. troops to the border, ostensibly to maintain order.

Yet Frank Lopez, a retired Border Patrol agent, explained the troops' real purpose, as he saw it.

"It's a welcome wagon," Lopez told *The Daily Signal.* He noted that DHS said the troops would be helping with "non-law enforcement duties." Lopez said that means troops would be tasked with helping illegal aliens, rather than deporting them.

Lopez served in the Border Patrol for 30 years before retiring in 2018. While the situation at the border changes with each administration, he said, "the change under Biden was so drastic, so detrimental, and so anti-enforcement."[35]

---

34 Grewal.

35 Allen, Virginia. "Biden's 1,500 Troops Sent to Southern Border Are a 'Welcome Wagon,' Retired Border Patrol Agent Says." *The Daily Signal.* May 5, 2023. https://www.dailysignal.com/2023/05/05/bidens-1500-troops-southern-border-welcome-wagon-retired-border-patrol-agent-says/ Accessed July 29, 2024.

As mentioned in Chapter 6, the ACLU has received millions through the Left's dark money network, and its leaders and staff have visited the White House at least thirty-one times.

THE CENTER FOR AMERICAN PROGRESS

The Center for American Progress also played a role in Biden's border policy, and it also advocated the change in focus away from enforcement.

The center called for a "reorientation of cultural norms at DHS" in a massive report published on June 16, 2021.

> A change in policies alone will not achieve the goal of building a fair, humane, and workable immigration system. A shift toward a more service-driven department that treats immigration as an asset to be managed rather than a crime to be enforced against would go a long way in building a rational border management apparatus that facilitates the secure, efficient movement of people and goods while also ensuring a humane approach toward refugees requesting protection under U.S. asylum laws.[36]

One of the report's authors, Katrina Mulligan, joined the Department of Defense in November 2021 and became chief of staff to the secretary of the Army in July 2022, where she served until February 2024.[37] Another author, Philip Wolgin, served on the board of the Hebrew Immigrant Aid Society (more on this

36   Rudman, Mara; Rudy deLeon; Joel Martinez; Elisa Massimino; Silva Mathema; Katrina Mulligan; Alexandra Schmitt; and Philip E. Wolgin. "Redefining Homeland Security: A New Framework for DHS To Meet Today's Challenges." Center for American Progress. June 21, 2021. https://www.americanprogress.org/article/redefining-homeland-security-new-framework-dhs-meet-todays-challenges/ Accessed July 29, 2024.

37   "Katrina Mulligan." LinkedIn profile. https://www.linkedin.com/in/katrinaemmons/ Accessed July 29, 2024.

below) for nine years while also working as managing director of CAP's immigration department.[38]

Meanwhile, CAP's vice president for immigration policy, Tom Jawetz, left the center in March 2021 to become deputy general counsel at the Department of Homeland Security, where he served until June 2022.

In February 2021, just before joining DHS, Jawetz told Al Jazeera what Biden should do to reverse Trump's policies on immigration.

"There are so many things that they did comprehensively to prevent people from accessing the protections that are afforded to them under U.S. and international law—that you cannot single out one policy," Jawetz said. "Their overlapping nature means that any single one of them can have a significant effect on its own. All of them need to be addressed."

As mentioned in Chapter 4, the Center for American Progress has received millions through the Left's dark money network, and CAP leaders have visited the White House at least thirty-five times.

Abetting the Border Crisis

The administrative state under Biden has not just loosened border enforcement, however. It has actively helped resettle illegal aliens throughout the country, funneling billions into migrant resettlement programs. The nongovernmental organizations that help resettle illegals also oppose reforms that would close the border and enforce the law.

Homeland Security Secretary Alejandro Mayorkas has not attempted to hide the fact that his agency, among others, is directing taxpayer dollars to transport illegal aliens throughout the country.

In an April 2022 memorandum, Mayorkas laid out his agency's "Plan for Southwest Border Security and Preparedness." In that plan, "Border Security Pillar 4" involves "bolstering the capacity of non-governmental organizations (NGOs) to receive noncitizens

---

38 "Philip Wolgin." LinkedIn profile. https://www.linkedin.com/in/philip-wolgin/ Accessed July 29, 2024.

after they have been processed by CBP and are awaiting the results of their immigration removal proceedings."

DHS helps NGOs receive funding from the Federal Emergency Management Agency's Emergency Food and Shelter Program (EFSP). "The EFSP, administered by DHS through FEMA, supplements and expands ongoing work of local NGOs to meet the urgent needs of local agencies assisting the unique and vulnerable migrant population encountered by DHS," the document explains. It notes that Congress authorized $150 million for the program.[39]

WHERE DOES THE MONEY GO?

The Department of Health and Human Services directs billions in grants through programs to house and transport illegal aliens throughout the country.

The HHS Administration for Children and Families directed $1.99 billion through the Refugee and Entrant Assistance State/Replacement Designee Administered Programs grant in 2022 and another $3.78 billion through that program in 2023. As of April 1, 2024, ACF has already funneled $1.35 billion through the program this fiscal year. These numbers represent an over 500 percent increase over the program's $372 million in grants in the last full fiscal year under Trump.[40]

Where does the money go? Between Fiscal Year 2021 and Fiscal Year 2024:[41]

o $1.13 billion went to chapters of Catholic Charities

o $8.3 million went to The North Dakota and South Dakota chapters of Lutheran Social Services

39   Mayorkas, Alejandro. "DHS Plan for Southwest Border Security and Preparedness." Department of Homeland Security memo. April 26, 2022. https://www.dhs.gov/sites/default/files/2022-04/22_0426_dhs-plan-southwest-border-security-preparedness.pdf Accessed March 29, 2024. pp. 2, 3, 16.
40   HHS's Tracking Accountability in Government Grants System. "Refugee and Entrant Assistance State/Replacement Designee Administered Programs." https://taggs.hhs.gov/Detail/CFDADetail?arg_CFDA_NUM=93566 Accessed April 1, 2024.
41   Author's analysis of TAGGS data in previous footnote.

o   Nearly $410 million went to The U.S. Committee for Refugees and Immigrants

The ACF also awards grants for the "Unaccompanied Alien Children Program," which significantly increased under Biden. ACF awarded $2.9 billion in Fiscal Year 2022 and $3 billion in Fiscal Year 2023, and the agency awarded $1.45 billion so far in Fiscal Year 2024. It awarded $1.75 billion in 2020, the last full fiscal year under Trump.[42]

Between Fiscal Year 2021 and Fiscal Year 2024, this program gave: [43]

o $239 million to Lutheran Social Services

o $209 million to the U.S. Committee for Refugees and Immigrants

o $61 million to various chapters of Catholic Charities

o $386 million to Lutheran Immigration and Refugee Service, which rebranded as "Global Refuge" in January 2024

o $76 million to Church World Service

o $209 million to the U.S. Committee for Refugees and Immigrants

According to HHS, the U.S. Conference of Catholic Bishops received $145.6 million in grants from the Administration of Children and Families and the HHS generally in 2023 alone, mostly for refugee assistance and long-term foster care for unaccompanied alien children.[44]

---

42   HHS's Tracking Accountability in Government Grants System. "Unaccompanied Alien Children Program. https://taggs.hhs.gov/Detail/CFDADetail?arg_CFDA_NUM=93676 Accessed April 1, 2024.

43   Author's analysis of TAGGS data in previous footnote.

44   HHS's Tracking Accountability in Government Grants System. "United States Conference of Catholic Bishops." https://taggs.hhs.gov/Detail/RecipDetail?arg_EntityId=XTXz0kBrlFCzzFcd8P4WdQ%3d%3d Accessed April 19, 2024.

A Sizeable Chunk of Revenue

These nonprofits receive large portions of their revenue from federal grants.

According to *Forbes*, Catholic Charities USA received $1.4 billion of its $4.7 billion in revenue from government support, more than the $1 billion it received in private donations, in 2022.[45]

Global Refuge, formerly Lutheran Immigration and Refugee Service, received $180 million in government grants, more than seven times what it received in "all other contributions," namely $25 million, in 2022.[46]

Church World Service received $20.5 million in government grants in the fiscal year ending in June 2022, a sizeable chunk of its $51 million in total assets. It spent $3.8 million on advocacy during that same fiscal year.[47]

HIAS, formerly known as the Hebrew Immigrant Aid Society, notes in its report for 2021 that "the most significant source of HIAS's revenue are grants from the U.S. Government." HIAS received $37 million from the State Department and $3.9 million from HHS that year, making up 30 percent and 3 percent of its total revenues of $119 million.[48]

The U.S. Committee for Refugees and Immigrants reported receiving the vast majority of its revenue ($117.4 million of its $121.7 million) through government grants in 2020.[49]

45 *Forbes* Profile, Catholic Charities USA. https://www.forbes.com/companies/catholic-charities-usa/?sh=2d22e98d32b6 Accessed April 1, 2024.

46 Lutheran Immigration & Refugee Service, Inc. Form 990. https://www.globalrefuge.org/wp-content/uploads/2023/09/LIRS-2022-Form-990.pdf Accessed April 2, 2024.

47 Church World Service, Inc. Financial Statements June 30, 2022 and 2021. https://cwsglobal.org/wp-content/uploads/2023/01/BOD-6-CWS-Audited-Financial-Statements-as-of-June-30-2022.pdf Accessed April 2, 2024.

48 "Consolidated Financial Statements and Report of Independent Certified Public Accountants." HIAS, Inc. Dec. 31, 2021 and 2020. https://hias.org/wp-content/uploads/2021_hias_inc._fs-1.pdf Accessed April 2, 2024.

49 U.S. Committee for Refugees and Immigrants Form 990 for 2020. https://refugees.org/wp-content/uploads/2022/06/USCRI-2021-09-Tax-Form-990-Public-Disclosure-Copy.pdf Accessed April 2, 2024.

WHERE DO THE ILLEGAL ALIENS GO?

The Immigration Industrial Complex sends illegal aliens across the country, but the true scope of the problem only became clear after a year and a half of the Biden administration.

In 2022, two departments at The Heritage Foundation, the Oversight Project and the Border Security and Immigration Center, tracked how illegal aliens spread throughout the country after crossing the U.S.-Mexico border. The investigation proceeded in four phases.

First, the investigation examined 407 cell phone devices at the Val Verde Border Humanitarian Connection and Customs and Border Protection's Del Rio Station in Del Rio, Texas. The investigation tracked those devices to forty different U.S. states.

The second phase focused on twenty private organizations in Arizona, California, and Texas. The 22,000 unique cell phones detected at those locations made their way to 431 out of the 435 congressional districts nationwide.

The investigation's third phase involved following 5,000 cell phones detected at 13 organizations along the U.S.-Mexico border. Those devices traveled to 434 congressional districts—all but one in the entire country.

Finally, the investigation focused on Catholic Charities of the Rio Grande Valley. During January 2021, the investigation detected nearly 3,400 devices, which it traced to 433 congressional districts.[50]

The border crisis truly is a national crisis, and these organizations are helping to turn every state into a border state.

OPEN BORDERS ADVOCACY

The nonprofits that form the Immigration Industrial Complex wear noble missions on their sleeves, waxing eloquent about helping refugees, immigrants, and the most vulnerable. But their advo-

---

50   Bluey, Robert. "Who's Really Facilitating America's Border Crisis? Biden Isn't Acting Alone." *The Daily Signal.* Dec. 7, 2023. https://www.dailysignal.com/2022/12/07/whos-really-facilitating-americas-border-crisis-biden-isnt-acting-alone Accessed April 2, 2024.

cacy reveals a dark side—an opposition to the policies that would curb the crisis of illegal immigration. Some of them also have ties to the Left's dark money network.

These nonprofits opposed the vital bill to address the border crisis, H.R. 2, the Secure the Border Act of 2023.

According to Rep. Mark Green, R-Tenn., an original cosponsor of the bill, H.R. 2 "addresses the immediate impact of the crisis by focusing on mitigating and stopping the surge of illegal aliens and drugs flowing across the U.S. borders, mainly between ports of entry."[51]

The bill would require DHS to resume the construction of the U.S.-Mexico border wall, prohibit DHS from processing the entry of non-U.S. nationals arriving between ports of entry, limit asylum eligibility, authorize the removal of illegal aliens to a country other than that person's nationality, expand the types of crimes that may make aliens ineligible for asylum, impose penalties for overstaying a visa, and require DHS to create an electronic employment eligibility confirmation system modeled after E-Verify.[52]

Heritage Action for America praised H.R. 2 as "the strongest and most consequential border security and immigration enforcement legislation to date." The advocacy group noted that the bill would "end the inhumane catch and release practices of the Biden administration, prevent the exploitation of unaccompanied alien children, and curb the fraudulent abuse of asylum claims." The bill also "cuts off funds for non-governmental organizations that are being misused to process and transport illegal aliens into U.S. communities."[53]

51 Allen, Virginia and Samantha Aschieris. "House Passes Border Bill as Illegal Alien Encounters Surge on Southern Border." *The Daily Signal.* May 11, 2023. https://www.dailysignal.com/2023/05/11/house-passes-border-bill-illegal-aliens-encounters-surge-southern-border/ Accessed April 17, 2024.

52 H.R.2 – Secure the Border Act of 2023. Bill summary. https://www.congress.gov/bill/118th-congress/house-bill/2/summary/00 Accessed April 17, 2024.

53 "Key Vote: 'YES' on the Secure the Border Act (H.R. 2)." Heritage Action for America. May 9, 2023. https://heritageaction.com/key-vote/key-vote-yes-on-the-secure-the-border-act-h-r-2 Accessed April 17, 2023.

H.R. 2 passed the House of Representatives in a party-line vote of 219-213 on May 11, 2023, but it has yet to receive a hearing in the U.S. Senate.

Most of the organizations receiving government funding to house illegal aliens and transport them into the country oppose H.R. 2.

HIAS

HIAS, formerly known as Hebrew Immigrant Aid Society, launched in 1903 to continue the work of previous organizations aiming to assist Jews fleeing pogroms in Russia and Eastern Europe. HIAS now provides services to "refugees, asylum seekers, and other forcibly displaced and stateless persons around the world and advocates for their fundamental rights," according to its website.[54]

HIAS condemned H.R. 2, the Secure the Border Act of 2023.

"HIAS staunchly opposes H.R. 2, and we urge representatives to vote NO on it," Naomi Steinberg, HIAS vice president of U.S. policy and advocacy, said in a May 2023 statement. "If this bill were to become law, it would essentially end the U.S. asylum system. Among other things, it would eliminate the right to seek asylum for people who enter the U.S. between ports of entry, even though that is a violation of accepted international asylum law."[55]

One does not reference toothless international law when seriously attempting to solve a crisis of epic proportions.

HIAS has close ties to the Biden administration. Alejandro Mayorkas, the secretary of Homeland Security, served as a HIAS board member until Biden nominated him in November 2020.[56]

HIAS President Mark Hetfield has visited the White House seven times under Biden.[57]

54 "Who We Are." HIAS website. https://hias.org/who/ Accessed April 17, 2024.

55 "HIAS Opposes Secure the Border Act of 2023." HIAS news release. May 8, 2023. https://hias.org/statements/hias-opposes-secure-border-act-2023/ Accessed April 17, 2023.

56 "HIAS Congratulates Board Member Alejandro Mayorkas on DHS Nomination." HIAS news release. Nov. 23, 2020. https://hias.org/statements/hias-congratulates-board-member-alejandro-mayorkas-dhs-nomination/ Accessed April 17, 2024.

57 White House Visitor Logs.

Catholic Charities

According to its website, Catholic Charities aims "to provide service to people, families and communities in need, to advocate for justice in social structures and to call the entire church and other people of good will to do the same." The group claims to have served "more than 15 million of our at-risk neighbors" in 2023, and it includes 168 diocesan Catholic Charities agencies. Each agency falls under the authority of its local bishop or archbishop in the Roman Catholic Church.[58] The organization dates to 1910 with the National Conference of Catholic Charities.

In 2017, the Arabella Network group New Venture Fund contributed $150,000 to Catholic Charities USA.[59]

On May 8, 2023, Catholic Charities President and CEO Sister Donna Markham sent a letter to then-House Speaker Kevin McCarthy, R-Calif., and Minority Leader Hakeem Jeffries, D-N.Y., urging them to oppose H.R.2, the "Secure the Border Act of 2023."

Why did Catholic Charities oppose the bill? The nonprofit's then-president, Donna Markham, wrote that the bill "would severely restrict vulnerable people's access to asylum, detain more families including children, undermine U.S. efforts to effectively manage immigration, and dismantle the public-private infrastructure currently in place to manage the humanitarian crisis at the southern border and its impact throughout the country."

"The gospel calls us to provide shelter for those who are homeless, feed the hungry, and 'welcome the stranger,'" Markham added. "The work of Catholic Charities is humanitarian not political. While we do not oppose all the provisions in H.R. 2, several of them, if enacted, would severely hinder the government and nongovernmental organizations (NGOs) from aiding migrants who need services, care, and assistance."[60]

58 "About Us." Catholic Charities website. https://www.catholiccharitiesusa.org/about-us/mission/ Accessed April 17, 2024.

59 "New Venture Fund." Form 990 Schedule I for 2017, accessed April 17, 2024.

60 Markham, Donna. Letter to House Speaker Kevin McCarthy and Minority Leader Hakeem Jeffries. May 8, 2023. https://www.catholiccharitiesusa.org/wp-content/uploads/2023/05/Opposition-to-HR-2-Catholic-Charities-USA.pdf Accessed April 17, 2024.

The claim that H.R. 2 would "undermine U.S. efforts to effectively manage immigration" seems absurd, and some supporters of H.R. 2 might say that undermining the "public-private infrastructure" that helps illegal aliens settle throughout the country might be part of the point.

Markham has traveled to the White House at least eight times during Biden's tenure.[61]

Anthony J. Granado—who served as vice president of government relations for Catholic Charities until August 2023, when he re-joined the U.S. Conference of Catholic Bishops—visited the White House at least nine times.[62]

The U.S. Conference of Catholic Bishops

The United States Conference of Catholic Bishops runs a Migration and Refugee Services ministry separate from Catholic Charities.

The USCCB previously listed ten types of grants it receives from the federal government, but the web page with this list appears to have been deleted. The list included a Department of Homeland Security grant "for the processing, reception and placement of Cuban and Haitian entrants paroled by DHS into the U.S.," an HHS grant to provide "enhanced services to newly arrived refugees at sites selected for their proven success in resettlement," and a grant to serve "unaccompanied children who have been apprehended by immigration officials."[63]

Bishop Mark J. Seitz of El Paso, Texas, chairman of the USCCB's Committee on Migration, released a statement opposing H.R. 2. He wrote to lawmakers in Congress, expressing the

---

61   White House Visitor Logs.

62   White House Visitor Logs.

63   "Federal Government Grants To Support USCCB MRS Programs and Services." USCCB web page preserved via the Internet Archive. Captured on Aug. 18, 2020. https://web.archive.org/web/20200818224850/https://www.usccb.org/committees/migration/federal-government-grants-support-usccb-mrs-programs-and-services Accessed April 19, 2024.

USCCB's "strong opposition to H.R. 2, the 'Secure the Border Act of 2023.'"

"If enacted, this measure would fundamentally weaken our nation's decades-long commitment to humanitarian protection," he wrote. He warned that the bill "would endanger unaccompanied children and inflict harm on other vulnerable persons, decimate access to asylum, mandating damaging detention and removal practices, restrict access to legal employment, limit—and potentially eliminate—federal partnerships with faith-based and other nongovernmental organizations, undermine the rule of law, and more."[64]

All policy involves tradeoffs, and fixing the border crisis needs to be a priority. H.R. 2 would not stop America's generosity to immigrants, it would merely decrease some of the extreme leniency in recent years in order to bring order to a crisis.

The U.S. Conference of Catholic Bishops' Committee on Migration urged members of the U.S. House of Representatives to oppose a bill codifying Title 42 into law, claiming it would "unjustly deprive vulnerable persons of the legal right to seek humanitarian protection in the United States."[65]

Three USCCB leaders, Archbishop Timothy P. Broglio (the president), Archbishop William E. Lori (the vice president) and Rev. Michael J.K. Fuller (the general secretary), met with John McCarthy, special assistant to President Biden, at the White House on July 20, 2023.

The conference's associate general secretary, Rev. Paul B.R. Hartmann, had a White House meeting on Sept. 17, 2023.[66]

---

64 Rev. Mark Seitz. Letter to representatives. May 5, 2023. https://www.usccb. org/resources/USCCB%20Letter%20on%20H.R.%202.pdf   Accessed April 19, 2024.

65 U.S. Conference of Catholic Bishops letter to representatives, Jan. 17, 2023. https://www.usccb.org/resources/USCCB%20Letter%20Opposing%20 H.R.%2029.pdf Accessed April 2, 2024.

66 White House Visitor Logs.

A Note on Catholic Social Teaching

While I am a Protestant myself (an Anglican), I have a healthy respect for the Roman Catholic tradition, and I find it shocking that Catholic nonprofits like Catholic Charities and the U.S. Conference of Catholic Bishops would abet this border crisis. Some Catholics claim that Catholic Social Teaching encourages open borders, but that is simply not the case.

Former Congressman Tim Huelskamp, now advisor to the conservative Roman Catholic nonprofit Catholic Vote, explained in an interview for this book that Catholic social teaching does not require Catholics to support illegal immigration. In fact, he argued that abetting the border crisis conflicts with Catholic social teaching.

"Facilitating lawlessness at America's southern border and throughout the country is completely inconsistent with Catholic social teaching," Huelskamp said. "Catholic groups promoting an open border are defying centuries of teaching, and they must be held accountable for enabling the resulting historic and humanitarian border crises of massive human trafficking, the deadly drug trade, and an influx of criminal aliens."

Huelskamp wrote a chapter in the book "For God, Country, & Sanity: How Catholics Can Save America," dedicated to exploring Catholic social teaching on the immigration issue.

He noted that the Catechism of the Catholic Church places obligations on immigrants, as well as on the governments that deal with them.

"Immigrants are obliged to respect with gratitude the material and spiritual heritage of the country that receives them, to obey its laws and to assist in carrying civic burdens," the Catechism states.[67]

"By extension, these fundamental obligations logically fall upon those assisting immigrants, including charitable and religious organizations such as Catholic Charities USA," Huelskamp writes. "It is well documented that tens and thousands of these charitable entities and employers, not to mention the immigrants themselves,

---

67 "Catechism of the Catholic Church." Washington, D.C.: United States Conference of Catholic Bishops. First Printing Nov. 2019. Paragraph 2241 p. 541

have promoted and developed lawless, often cash-only economies specifically designed to avoid detection, hide income from taxation, and illegally qualify for government benefits."

"As a result, legal immigrant workers and just employers who seek to obey the law and 'assist in carrying civic burdens' are pressured by competition, lax social mores, lack of clear Church teaching, economic hardship, or even bureaucratic complexity to ignore this obligation," the former congressman adds.

"Under no Catholic doctrine is one country, no matter how wealthy, meant to be the band-aid for the wounds of another country, for the Church in another nation, or for the people and families of another homeland," he concludes.[68]

Global Refuge

Global Refuge, formerly Lutheran Immigration and Refugee Service, began in 1939 as American Lutherans responded to the needs of Europeans displaced in World War II.[69]

When Biden won the 2020 election, Global Refuge President Krish O'Mara Vignarajah called the results "a new dawn in America for immigrants, refugees, asylum seekers, DREAMers, and all those who stand for welcome." (DREAMer refers to a child brought to the U.S. as an illegal immigrant.)

Vignarajah called the Trump years "a dark chapter for our immigrant brothers and sisters." She called his pause on immigration from countries of terror concern a "xenophobic Muslim ban," and accused him of an "assault on DACA and DREAMers," among other things.[70]

68 Huelskamp, Tim. "Immigration Apocalypse: A Catholic Social Teaching Response." RealClearReligion. April 29, 2024. https://www.realclearreligion.org/articles/2024/04/29/immigration_apocalypse_a_catholic_social_teaching_response_1028229.html Accessed May 8, 2024.

69 "Our History." Global Refuge website. https://www.globalrefuge.org/who-we-are/history/ Accessed April 17, 2024.

70 "LIRS Statement: 2020 Presidential Election Results." Global Refuge news release. Nov. 9, 2020. https://web.archive.org/web/20201128142936/https://www.lirs.org/statement-presidential-election-2020/ Accessed via Internet Archive on April 17, 2024.

The nonprofit has also condemned policies enacted by the Biden-Harris administration, even though they are considerably more lax than Trump's were.

Global Refuge condemned what it called Biden's "punitive enforcement and deterrence measures." The nonprofit launched a campaign urging Americans to "tell the Biden administration to end the asylum ban and restore access to asylum at the border! Let elected leaders know we want welcome, not harsh policies!"

The campaign also urges readers to "join us in urging [elected leaders] to … develop solutions that welcome and honor the dignity of the protection-seeking migrant and support organizations assisting migrants at the border and across the country."[71]

Vignarajah, the nonprofit's president, previously served as policy director to first lady Michelle Obama. She has visited Biden's White House six times, taking a one-on-one meeting with President Biden on Dec. 9, 2022.[72]

One Global Refuge leader's resume reveals the ties between the administration and the nonprofits that send illegal aliens to settle across the country.

Ashley Feasley spent two years as a migration policy advisor at the U.S. Conference of Catholic Bishops, then joined Catholic Legal Immigration Network as director of advocacy for about a year, and then returned to USCCB to become director of migration policy and public affairs. After leading USCCB's migration policy from September 2016 to March 2021, she joined U.S. Customs and Border Protection for eight months, and then moving to the White House where she became "Director of Transborder Security" at the National Security Council.

In January 2023, she joined the Administration for Children and Families at HHS (which oversees many of the grants groups like USCCB receive). She worked there through March 2023 before

---

71 "Urge the Biden Administration and Congress To Choose Welcome Over Harsh Policies!" Global Refuge on Quorum. https://globalrefuge.quorum.us/campaign/47850/ Accessed April 2, 2024.

72 White House Visitor Logs, analyzed by Tyler O'Neil, downloaded from https://www.whitehouse.gov/disclosures/visitor-logs/ on March 21, 2024.

hopping over to become vice president of policy and advocacy at Global Refuge in April 2024.[73]

The U.S. Committee for Refugees and Immigrants

The U.S. Committee for Refugees and Immigrants, also known as USCRI, provides legal services, social services, and health services to "refugees, unaccompanied migrating children, trafficking survivors, and other immigrants in all 50 states, El Salvador, Honduras, Kenya, and Mexico," according to its website. The committee also advocates for refugees and immigrants in law and policy.[74]

The U.S. Committee for Refugees and Immigrants has received $75,000 in grants from the Foundation to Promote Open Society between 2017 and 2021. A 2021 grant supported the committee in developing "a community sponsorship program that will expand resettlement support for refugees and other forcibly displaced populations."[75]

The committee condemned some of the provisions in H.R. 2, calling them "anti-asylum" and "anti-immigrant proposals."[76]

Church World Service

Seventeen Christian denominations came together to form Church World Service in 1946, delivering more than 11 million pounds

73 "Ashley Feasley." LinkedIn Profile. https://www.linkedin.com/in/ashley-feasley-85a6347b/details/experience/ Accessed May 8, 2024.

74 "Who We Are." U.S. Committee for Refugees and Immigrants. https://refugees.org/who-we-are/ Accessed April 17, 2024.

75 Open Society Foundations, "Awarded Grants" page search results for "Committee for Refugees." https://www.opensocietyfoundations.org/grants/past?filter_keyword=Committee+for+refugees&grant_id=OR2017-38528 Accessed April 2, 2024.

76 "Trafficking Survivors Lost in the Funding Debate's Asylum Stipulations." U.S. Committee for Refugees and Immigrants. Jan. 30, 2024. https://refugees.org/trafficking-survivors-lost-in-the-funding-debates-asylum-stipulations/ Accessed April 18, 2024.

of food, clothing, and medical supplies for Europe and Asia in the aftermath of World War II. The group also resettled more than 100,000 refugees in its first ten years, according to CWS's website.[77]

The Sixteen Thirty Fund, part of the network established by Arabella Advisors, donated $25,000 to Church World Service between 2014 and 2015.[78]

On May 9, 2023, Church World Service urged its members to contact their representatives in Congress to vote against H.R. 2. CWS presented a script for a phone call, urging Americans to tell their representatives to "reject legislation that would further entrench anti-asylum, anti-immigrant, anti-family policies."[79]

CWS also denounced Texas Republican Gov. Greg Abbott for signing SB 4, a bill making it a felony for a person to illegally cross the U.S.-Mexico border into Texas. Church World Service dismissed the fact that federal law already prohibits illegal entry, claiming that the law "will charge migrants seeking safety in the United States a state crime."[80]

Church World Service has urged Americans to contact their representatives in Congress, urging them "to robustly fund key refugee and immigrant accounts, include key authorizing language to improve and expand services, and reallocate funding away from border militarization and ICE detention facilities."

The organization launched its campaign after Congress passed an appropriations bill that included fewer funds for migrant grant programs—programs from which Church World Services directly benefits. Church World Services urged Americans to write their

---

77 "CWS: A Brief History." Church World Service website. https://cwsglobal.org/about/history/ Accessed April 17, 2024.

78 "Sixteen Thirty Fund." Form 990, Schedule I for 2014 and 2015, accessed April 17, 2024.

79 "TAKE ACTION: Tell Our National Leaders to Support Welcoming, Humane Border Solutions." Church World Service action alert. May 9, 2023. https://cwsglobal.org/action-alerts/take-action-tell-our-national-leaders-to-support-welcoming-humane-border-solutions/ Accessed April 17, 2024.

80 "Abbott Actively Undermines Texas' Ability to Grow and Welcome." Church World Service news release. Dec. 19, 2023.

legislators, saying "I urge you to support … $4.447 billion for the Migration and Refugee Assistance (MRA) account."[81] Between Nov. 15, 2022, and Sept. 30, 2023, Church World Service received $28 million from the Migration and Refugee Assistance Program.[82]

Mary Elizabeth Margolis, senior director of communications at Church World Service, told me in remarks for this book that CWS only receives federal funds to resettle migrants who came to the U.S. legally:

> Church World Service has provided humanitarian assistance to refugees for over 75 years. Federal funding from the Migration and Refugee Assistance account is allocated for implementing reception and placement services for refugees being resettled via the U.S. Refugee Admissions Program (USRAP), as well as eligible Afghan evacuees. All individuals arriving in the U.S. via these programs are in the United States lawfully, having been granted admission from the U.S. Government following rigorous vetting.

Lora Ries, director of The Heritage Foundation's Border Security and Immigration Center, cried foul.

> Having done refugee resettlement for decades, CWS well-knows that the Left has greatly watered down the standards to grant refugee status to economic migrants who make weak claims of fear from ineligible conditions like general crime, civil strife, and climate change. Our refugee system has strayed significantly from what the

---

81 "TAKE ACTION: Urge Congress to Support Refugees in FY 2025 and Supplemental Funding Efforts." Church World Services. April 1, 2024. https://cwsglobal.org/action-alerts/take-action-urge-congress-to-support-refugees-in-fy-2025-and-supplemental-funding-efforts/ Accessed April 2, 2024.

82 USASpending.gov. Cooperative Agreement, Federal Award Identification Number SPRMCO23CA0013. Department of State to Church World Service. https://www.usaspending.gov/award/ASST_NON_SPRMCO23CA0013_1900/ Accessed April 2, 2024.

U.S. committed to following WWII. Refugee protection is the second most important immigration benefit the U.S. provides (after citizenship). We need to return to a system with integrity, not use resettlement as just another pathway to bring more aliens into the U.S.

With respect to vetting, the Department of Homeland Security Inspector General has repeatedly found that the Biden administration's vetting was inadequate with Afghan evacuees and other aliens released into the U.S. Furthermore, the sheer volume of aliens the U.S. has released into the U.S. belies the administration's and CWS' claim that they have undergone "vigorous vetting." Also, the number of killed and harmed Americans at the hands of criminal aliens and the historic number of encountered aliens on the terror watchlist prove otherwise.

CWS's claims echo the Biden-Harris administration's strategy of creating "lawful pathways" to make it seem like illegal aliens are legal immigrants, but only Congress has the ability to establish legal avenues of immigration, and Biden's policies do not change the fundamental status of aliens outside those avenues.

None of the other groups that make up the immigration industrial complex responded to my questions about whether they ensure that the aliens they resettle across the country are legally in the U.S.

INFLUENCING ELECTIONS?

The influx of at least 9 million illegal immigrants may impact America's elections. Even if only a few illegal immigrants register to vote and successfully cast ballots, they may have the potential to swing an election.

A peer-reviewed study from Just Facts estimates that 10-17 percent of non-citizens are registered to vote, and based on previous elections and federal data, at least 1-2.7 million non-citizens will vote in the 2024 presidential election.[83]

---

83   Agresti, James. "Study: 10% to 27% of Non-Citizens Are Illegally Registered to Vote." May 13, 2024. https://www.justfacts.com/news_non-citizen_voter_ registration Accessed May 22, 2024.

In April 2024, a journalist discovered flyers at a resource center for migrants heading to the United States. The flyers urged migrants to vote for Biden after they crossed the U.S.-Mexico border, in order to keep the border open.

"Reminder to vote for President Biden when you are in the United States," the flyers read. "We need another four years of his term to stay open."

The flyers, first reported by The Heritage Foundation's Oversight Project, appeared in porta-potties at the center, which is just south of the U.S. border. The city of Matamoros, located in the Mexican state of Tamaulipas, borders Brownsville, Texas, where President Biden spoke in February.[84]

Resource Center Matamoros describes itself as "the home for HIAS, which is providing legal assistance and assistance with obtaining formal documents for job search and integration into the city of Matamoros as they wait to access the asylum process in the U.S." HIAS told The Associated Press that is has not rented space from the center or had any ties to it since 2022.

Gaby Zavala, founder and executive director of Resource Center Matamoros, told The Associated Press that her organization did not know who made the flyers. She insisted that her group "does not encourage immigrants to register to vote or cast ballots in the U.S."[85]

Yet Zavala has publicly admitted that she founded her organization in part to fight U.S. policy.

"I founded the Asylum Seeker Network of Support as an effort to fight policy, U.S. policy," Zavala said in a video posted

---

84   Lucas, Fred. "Illegals Instructed to Vote Biden for Border NGO to 'Stay Open.'" The Daily Signal. April 15, 2024. https://www.dailysignal.com/2024/04/15/group-in-mexico-displays-flyers-urging-illegal-aliens-to-vote-for-biden Accessed April 19, 2024.

85   Gonzalez, Valerie and Ali Swenson. "Dubious claims about voting flyers at a migrant camp show how the border is inflaming US politics." The Associated Press. April 17, 2024. https://apnews.com/article/migrants-shelter-flyer-mexico-voting-conspiracy-theories-e02f14ef0763684f2919dc84e9ef2458 Accessed April 19, 2024.

online. In other videos, she attributed the immigration crisis to climate change.[86]

Republicans condemned the flyers and claimed that Democrats are trying to "import a new electorate."

"Democrats want permanent power and they are willing to import a new electorate to get it," Rep. Jim Banks, R-Ind., told *The Daily Signal* after news of the flyers broke. "The endgame of the Biden border crisis is to disenfranchise American citizens by diluting their votes."[87]

Democrats disavow this political strategy, and left-wing groups claim that it is a conspiracy theory. Yet the very plausibility of this narrative shows just how dangerous it is to allow millions of illegal aliens to cross America's borders and settle in the country.

MOBILIZING 'WORKER POWER'

The Woketopus has a system for protecting illegal aliens once they enter the country and for encouraging immigrants to become voters.

The ACLU launched an "Immigrants' Rights Project" aimed at "expanding and enforcing the civil liberties and civil rights of immigrants" and "combating public and private discrimination against them."[88] The ACLU has sued to block even the Biden administration's belated responses to the immigration crisis. In June 2023, the Immigrants' Rights Project sued to block a Department of Homeland Security rule that would have enabled a rapid deportation process for some illegal aliens.

---

86   X Post. @JosephTrimmer_ April 17, 2024. 10:56 p.m. https://twitter.com/JosephTrimmer_/status/1780792443023011881 Accessed April 19, 2024.

87   Lucas, Fred. "'Import a New Electorate': Congress Alarmed by Flyers in Mexico Urging Illegal Aliens to Vote Biden." The Daily Signal. April 17, 2024. https://www.dailysignal.com/2024/04/17/import-a-new-electorate-congress-alarmed-by-flyers-in-mexico-urging-illegal-aliens-to-vote-biden/ Accessed April 19, 2024.

88   Immigrant Rights Project website. American Civil Liberties Union. https://www.aclu.org/issues/immigrants-rights Accessed May 31, 2024.

"Asylum seekers cannot be pushed out of the country without a fair chance to make their claims for protection before a judge," The ACLU project's managing attorney, Katrina Eiland, said at the time.[89]

The Biden administration encourages illegal aliens to apply for asylum; thus they become "asylum seekers." It also established a "lawful pathways" system that grants illegal aliens parole if they cross at a port of entry using a government app, enabling them to claim certain rights and forestall deportation.[90]

The ACLU and its allies appear to operate on the assumption that violating immigration law and entering the country illegally are not serious crimes that warrant deportation. Their advocacy makes it harder for the U.S. to enforce its laws and handle the immigration crisis.

Meanwhile, some parts of the Woketopus help migrants on the path to citizenship, explicitly with an eye toward voting and enhancing "worker power."

In March 2024, the labor union SEIU sent out an email to supporters stating that there are "9 million lawful permanent Residents…eligible to apply for U.S. citizenship" and "5.2 million newly naturalized U.S. citizens with the potential to vote for worker power."[91] In order to encourage these green card holders to "take the brave step and become citizens," the SEIU announced it

89 "Immigrants' Rights Advocates Sue Government Over Asylum Ban and Rapid Deportation Process That Places Asylum Seekers in Grave Danger." American Civil Liberties Union. June 23, 2023. https://www.acludc.org/en/press-releases/immigrants-rights-advocates-sue-government-over-asylum-ban-and-rapid-deportation Accessed May 31, 2024.

90 Allen, Virginia. "18 States Sue Biden Administration Over Redefining 'Illegal Border Crossings' as 'Lawful Pathways.'" *The Daily Signal*. June 1, 2023. https://www.dailysignal.com/2023/06/01/18-states-sue-biden-administration-aiming-redefining-illegal-border-crossings-lawful-pathways/ Accessed May 31, 2024.

91 SEIU email obtained by the Freedom Foundation. https://www.freedomfoundation.com/wp-content/uploads/2024/04/SEIU-immigration-and-voting-email.pdf Accessed May 31, 2024.

would work to naturalize immigrants "ahead of the 2024 presidential election" through the union's annual Virtual U.S. Citizenship Workshop.

The SEIU urged supporters to counter "extremist politicians" who "try to divide and hold us back by pushing racist laws or attacking worker's rights." The union concluded the email saying, "we can push worker power from ALL angles that impact our lives."

While Americans should celebrate when legal immigrants become naturalized U.S. citizens, the SEIU's rhetoric about translating immigrants into votes for "worker power" is alarming.

A WORD ON THE 'BORDER CZAR'

Kamala Harris, who became the presumptive nominee of the Democratic Party in the 2024 presidential election in July, appears to be running away from Biden's record on immigration.

The legacy media appeared to go into overdrive to protect her, without numerous outlets claiming that it was false to call her Biden's "border czar."

Axios, a more straight-shooting news outlet than many others on the Left, went so far as to fact-check itself. Axios noted that Biden tapped Harris "to lead the administration's coordination with Guatemala, Honduras and El Salvador, which were key sources of migration to the border," and added that "the announcement led to near-immediate confusion… with Republicans and some news outlets, including Axios, giving Harris the unofficial monicker of 'border czar.'"[92]

While former DHS Secretary Jeh Johnson told Fox News, "She is not the border czar," news reports from March 2021 suggest otherwise.

When NBC News reported the meeting where Biden announced he appointed Harris to handle border issues, it did not

---

92   Kight, Stef. "Harris border confusion haunts her new campaign." July 24, 2024. https://www.axios.com/2024/07/24/kamala-harris-border-czar-immigratin Accessed August 1, 2024.

seem limited to the Central American countries often referred to as the Northern Triangle.[93]

> A senior administration official said Harris' role would focus on "two tracks": both curbing the current flow of migrants and implementing a long-term strategy that addresses the root causes of migration. Cabinet members, including the secretary of state, are expected to work closely with Harris on these issues.

Whatever Harris claims, she served four years in Biden's White House, and most of that tenure came after Biden tapped her to address the border crisis, a crisis that reached historic levels on her watch.

The Woketopus' influence in favor of open borders, the growth of the Immigration Industrial Complex, and the influx of illegal aliens continued after Biden tapped her to address the issue, and she cannot distance herself from this record, even if she wants to.

93 Egan, Lauren; Gabe Guttierrez; and Dareh Gregorian. "Biden tasks Harris with 'stemming the migration' on southern border." NBC News. March 24, 2021. https://www.nbcnews.com/politics/white-house/biden-taps-harris-lead-coor-dination-efforts-southern-border-n1261952 Accessed August 1, 2024.

8

THE ANTI-ISRAEL PRESSURE CAMPAIGN

While the Woketopus' agenda often aligns with that of President Biden, the Left's dark money network has funded a pressure campaign within the administrative state to try to force Biden away from supporting Israel in its current war. This pressure campaign acts like a "deep state," combating Biden's official policy from within, while other parts of it exert influence from outside the government.

On October 7, 2023, Hamas terrorists invaded Israel under cover of rocket fire. They spread into southern Israel, slaughtering Israeli security forces and civilians alike. They raped women. They murdered infants. They massacred attendees at a music festival. They used GoPros and smartphones to broadcast their assault to the world. In one particularly chilling phone call, a Hamas terrorist calls his parents to brag about slaughtering Jews. "Look how many I killed with my own hands!" the young man says (according to an English translation). "Your son killed Jews!" He later adds, "Mom, your son is a hero."[1]

Hamas terrorists chose a historic date for their attack: The joyous festival of Simchat Torah, as well as the Sabbath day of rest and the fiftieth anniversary of the Yom Kippur War.

---

1   "IDF publishes audio of Hamas terrorist calling family to brag about killing Jews." *The Times of Israel.* October 25, 2023. https://www.timesofisrael.com/idf-publishes-audio-of-hamas-terrorist-calling-family-to-brag-of-killing-jews/ Accessed May 3, 2024.

A November 2023 analysis from Agence France-Press put the final death toll at 695 Israeli civilians (including 36 children), 373 security forces, and 71 foreigners, giving a grisly total of 1,139. This does not include five more people, four of them Israelis, who appear on the Israeli prime minister's list of the missing.[2]

President Biden immediately declared his support for Israel amid the attack. "In this moment of tragedy, I want to say to [the people of Israel] and to the world and to terrorists everywhere that the United States stands with Israel," he declared. "We will not ever fail to have their back."

"Israel has the right to defend itself and its people. Full stop," the president added. "There is never justification for terrorist acts." He described his administration's support for Israel as "rock solid and unwavering."[3]

Yet ever since that day, a loud chorus of anti-Israel activists, nonprofits, and rioters has attempted to create as much daylight between Biden and the Jewish state as possible, and some groups funded by the Left's dark money network have apparently convinced Biden to take concrete policy steps against Israel.

A TAINTED BEGINNING

Anyone familiar with the politics of the Middle East already distrusted Biden's remarks on October 7. Although the administration has stood by Israel in important ways, it has also abetted Israel's primary opponent in the region, the Islamic Republic of Iran.

Unlike in so many policy arenas, Biden did not rush to reverse Trump's policies on Israel. Trump had outraged the foreign policy

2 "Israel social security data reveals true picture of Oct 7 deaths." Agence France-Press. December 15, 2023. https://www.france24.com/en/live-news/20231215-israel-social-security-data-reveals-true-picture-of-oct-7-deaths Accessed May 1, 2024.

3 "Remarks by President Biden on the Terrorist Attacks in Israel." White House Briefing Room. October 7, 2023. https://www.whitehouse.gov/briefing-room/speeches-remarks/2023/10/07/remarks-by-president-biden-on-the-terrorist-attacks-in-israel/ Accessed May 1, 2024.

establishment by moving the U.S. Embassy in Israel from Tel Aviv to Jerusalem.[4] Biden did not reverse this, nor did he reverse Trump's decision to recognize Israeli settlements in Judea and Samaria, even after House Democrats demanded that he do so in 2021.[5]

Biden also attempted to build on the Abraham Accords, a process of peace and diplomatic reconciliation between Israel and its Arab neighbors. Under Trump, Bahrain, the United Arab Emirates, Sudan, and Morocco normalized relations with Israel.[6] Biden has since leaned in on the Abraham Accords in attempting to convince Saudi Arabia to also recognize the Jewish state.[7]

Yet Biden's rapprochement with Iran has arguably undermined those efforts. He significantly weakened America's opposition to Iran, moving toward restoring the Obama administration's Joint Comprehensive Plan of Action (better known as the Iran Nuclear Deal).[8] That deal involved loosening U.S. sanctions in exchange for Iran's promises to roll back its nuclear program.

Critics like James Phillips, a former visiting fellow at The Heritage Foundation, argued that the agreement amounted to "lit-

---

4   Dalton, Ben. "Trump ignores warnings with 'reckless Jerusalem move.'" Al Jazeera. December 7, 2017. https://www.aljazeera.com/news/2017/12/7/trump-ignores-warnings-with-reckless-jerusalem-move Accessed May 3, 2024.

5   "Congressional Democrats urge Biden to reverse Trump moves on Israel." Rep. Sarah Jacobs, D-Calif., news release. June 25, 2021. https://sarajacobs.house.gov/news/in-the-news/congressional-democrats-urge-biden-to-reverse-trump-moves-on-israel Accessed May 3, 2024.

6   O'Neil, Tyler. "Yet Another Muslim Country Joins Abraham Accords With Israel." *The Daily Signal.*" December 10, 2020. https://pjmedia.com/tyler-o-neil/2020/12/10/breaking-yet-another-muslim-country-joins-abraham-accords-with-israel-n1202421 Accessed May 3, 2024.

7   Khalid, Asma. "Biden is building on the Abraham Accords, part of Trump's legacy in the Middle East." NPR. July 9, 2022. https://www.npr.org/2022/07/09/1110109088/biden-is-building-on-the-abraham-accords-part-of-trumps-legacy-in-the-middle-eas Accessed May 3, 2024.

8   Lee, Matthew. "Biden attempt to resurrect Iran nuke deal off to bumpy start." *The Associated Press.* February 23, 2021. https://apnews.com/article/donald-trump-iran-iran-nuclear-diplomacy-middle-east-fe94f33feaa974d-244c0e3cdd6c33dfc Accessed May 3, 2024.

tle more than a diplomatic speed bump that will delay, but not permanently halt, Iran's drive for a nuclear weapons capability." He argued that Obama negotiated from a position of weakness, as his administration wanted the deal more than Iran did, and this enabled Iran to keep its nuclear infrastructure largely intact.[9]

The Biden negotiations have arguably emboldened Iran even further. The Islamic Republic has demanded the U.S. drop sanctions on the Islamic Revolutionary Guard Corps, the military division that controls Iran's ballistic missiles, orchestrates Iran's proxy terrorist network, and dominates important sectors of the country's economy. Iran has also demanded that the U.S. pledge not to withdraw from the new agreement, after Trump withdrew from the previous deal in 2018.

Phillips presciently predicted that "the resurrection of the flawed 2015 agreement would not defuse tensions in the Middle East, but would fuel them."[10]

Biden has also loosened the enforcement of sanctions on Iran. According to my analysis, Iran netted approximately $71.02 billion more under Biden than it would have under Trump in the lead-up to the October 7 attacks. This does not include the notorious $6 billion prisoner exchange deal in September 2023,[11] which the U.S. and Qatar agreed to block shortly after the Hamas terrorist attacks.[12]

---

9   Phillips, James. "The Most Glaring Flaws in Obama's Iran Deal." The Heritage Foundation. July 14, 2015. https://www.heritage.org/global-politics/commentary/the-most-glaring-flaws-obamas-iran-deal Accessed May 3, 2024.

10   Phillips, James. "Dangerous Ramifications of Reshuffled Iran Nuclear Deal." *The Daily Signal.* March 25, 2022. https://www.dailysignal.com/2022/03/25/dangerous-ramifications-of-reshuffled-iran-nuclear-deal/ Accessed May 3, 2024.

11   "Background Press Call by Senior Administration Officials on the Return of American Detainees from Iran." White House Briefing Room. September 17, 2023. https://www.whitehouse.gov/briefing-room/press-briefings/2023/09/17/background-press-call-by-senior-administration-officials-on-the-return-of-american-detainees-from-iran/ Accessed May 3, 2024.

12   Alba, Monica, Elyse Perlmutter-Gumbiner, and Katherine Doyle. "U.S. and Qatar agree not to release Iran's $6B." NBC News. October 12, 2023. https://www.nbcnews.com/politics/white-house/us-qatar-agree-not-release-iran-6-billion-prisoner-swap-rcna120135 Accessed May 3, 2024.

In contrast to Trump's "maximum pressure" sanctions on Iran, Biden campaigned on restoring the Iran deal and loosening the sanctions, which sent a strong signal to global markets, according to Benham Ben Taleblu, a senior fellow at the Foundation for the Defense of Democracies. "Markets are real, markets work, and when you send the wrong incentives, you get a whole bunch of risk-tolerant buyers becoming more active," he told *The Daily Signal*.

According to my analysis, this loosening of sanctions has enabled Iran to rake in $52.2 billion more in oil revenues than it would have under Trump. The Biden administration also signed a national security waiver allowing Iraq, which depends on Iranian electricity, to deposit $10 billion in payments to Iran. Iran has netted $3.8 billion more than its 2020 rate in petrochemical sales, and $1.6 billion more in steel exports. Finally, the International Monetary Fund sent Iran $3.42 billion in special drawing rights, which Biden could have blocked.

This amounts to a $71.02 billion windfall for Iran ahead of the October 7 terrorist attacks.[13]

Biden has claimed that there is no "specific evidence" showing that Tehran had any involvement in the Hamas attack, but Iran has funded Hamas for years. Hamas spokesman Ghazi Hamad told the BBC that Iran gave the green light for the attack.[14]

Robert Greenway, director of The Heritage Foundation's Center for National Defense, led a team to plan and execute the most significant U.S. economic sanctions against Iran under Trump. He served as a principal architect of the Abraham Accords, working as dep-

13 O'Neil, Tyler. "$6B Prisoner Swap Was 'Just a Drop in the Bucket' for Iran. Here's How Much Tehran Has Raked in Under Biden." *The Daily Signal.* October 18, 2023. https://www.dailysignal.com/2023/10/18/not-just-6b-heres-how-much-money-biden-admin-freed-iran-hamas-terror-attack-israel/ Accessed May 3, 2024.

14 Said, Summer. "Israel at War With Hamas: Live Updates." *The Wall Street Journal.* October 10, 2023. https://www.wsj.com/livecoverage/israel-hamas-gaza-rockets-attack-palestinians/card/hamas-says-attacks-on-israel-were-backed-by-iran-kb2ySPwSyBrYpQVUPyM9 Accessed May 3, 2024.

uty assistant to Trump and senior director of the National Security Council's Middle East and North African Affairs Directorate.

He said that by loosening the sanctions on Iran, Biden encourages other countries to pay Tehran. "We're encouraging everyone else to do this," he told *The Daily Signal*. "Everybody in the region is paying Iran not to attack them…. This is extortion."

Then Greenway spoke as though he were Biden, speaking to the Israelis. "I literally paid the people who attacked you," he said. "No one should be defending this. No one in Israel can think that Biden is their friend."[15]

Between a Rock and a Hamas Place

Richard Goldberg, senior advisor at the Foundation for the Defense of Democracies and former director for countering Iranian weapons of mass destruction for the White House National Security Council, warned that Biden is attempting to triangulate to the middle of where he sees the Democratic Party on the issue of Israel.

"The president in his own mind, he's always looking to triangulate to where he thinks the center of the Democratic Party is," Goldberg said in an interview for this book.[16]

Fearing backlash early in his term, Biden's administration "made a political decision at the time that they would put the more radical policies that would be considered hostile to Israel—favorable to the Palestinians—to some extent on hold." They would "avoid outright political warfare against the state of Israel the way you saw from President Obama."

After October 7, Biden rhetorically tied the Hamas attacks to Russian President Vladimir Putin's invasion of Ukraine. In an Oval Office address on October 19, 2023, he said:

> Hamas and Putin represent different threats, but they share this in common. They both want to completely annihilate a neighboring democracy—completely

15   O'Neil, "$6B Prisoner Swap."
16   Richard Goldberg interview. May 1, 2024.

annihilate it. Hamas's stated purpose for existing is the destruction of the state of Israel and the murder of Jewish people. Hamas does not represent the Palestinian people. Hamas uses Palestinian civilians as human shields, and innocent Palestinian families are suffering greatly because of them.

"American leadership is what holds the world together," Biden added. "American values are what make us a partner that other nations want to work with. To put all that at risk if we walk away from Ukraine, if we turn our backs on Israel, it's just not worth it."[17]

Yet many on the Left started heavily criticizing Biden for his stance on Israel. Protesters took to the streets of U.S. cities, to college campuses, and even to the White House itself, condemning Israel even before it launched a military campaign to wipe out Hamas and prevent another October 7. Less than two weeks after the Hamas attacks, Secret Service arrested thirty-three protesters at a demonstration outside the White House. The protesters blocked White House entrances and chanted pro-Palestine slogans, denouncing Israel's anticipated response as "genocide."[18]

Activists have demanded a "cease-fire" in Gaza, even though Hamas took 240 people, including Americans, hostage on October 7. (Israel has estimated that 116 of the hostages remain in Gaza, not all of them alive, after a November 2023 truce and a successful rescue mission in June.[19]) Israeli Prime Minister Benjamin Netanyahu

---

17 "Full Transcript: Biden's Speech on Israel-Hamas and Russia-Ukraine Wars." *The New York Times.* October 19, 2023. https://www.nytimes.com/2023/10/19/us/politics/transcript-biden-speech-israel-ukraine.html Accessed May 3, 2024.

18 Alexander, Harriet. "Jewish pro-Palestinian protesters BLOCK White House entrances: Secret Service arrest demonstrators demanding Biden push Israel to a ceasefire and 'stop genocide' in Gaza." *The Daily Mail.* October 16, 2023. https://www.dailymail.co.uk/news/article-12637641/white-house-blockade-jewish-pro-palestine-arrests.html Accessed May 3, 2024.

19 "Hamas hostages: Stories of the people taken from Israel." The BBC. July 1, 2024. https://www.bbc.com/news/world-middle-east-67053011 Accessed July 11, 2024.

initially opposed a cease-fire on the grounds that it would only benefit Hamas, but in November 2023, the fighting paused for a week as Hamas returned 81 hostages in exchange for about 180 Palestinian prisoners held in Israel.[20] Then Hamas reignited the conflict by firing rockets into Israel.

This lopsided exchange illustrates Israel's willingness to make a deal and Hamas's intransigence. Apparently, Israel values a cease-fire more than twice as much as Hamas does, and yet protesters still condemn the Jewish state's actions as a "genocide."

DEEP STATE REVOLTS

Protests did not just take place outside the White House and other government agencies. An internal rebellion not dissimilar to the "deep state" efforts to undermine former President Trump rose up against Biden's policies, as members of the administrative state voiced their opposition to U.S. support for Israel.

First, dozens of State Department employees signed internal memos to Secretary of State Antony Blinken expressing serious disagreement with the administration's approach to Israel. Staff sent two of the memos during the first week of the war, sources told *The New York Times*, using a dissent channel established during the Vietnam War. They sent a third memo in mid-November. Each of the three memos urged Biden to call for a cease-fire in Gaza. One of the memos also asked Biden to offer a serious plan for a long-term peace agreement between Israel and the Palestinians that would create a Palestinian state.[21]

---

20 "Live updates: Israel releases 30 prisoners after Hamas frees 12 hostages in extended truce deal." *The Associated Press*. November 29, 2023. https://apnews.com/article/israel-hamas-war-live-updates-11-28-2023-d11ff-273b41ac9fcb37cf8d043e802dd Accessed May 26, 2024.

21 Crowley, Michael and Edward Wong. "State Department employees send Blinken 'dissent' cables over Gaza policy." *The New York Times*. November 13, 2023. https://www.nytimes.com/2023/11/13/us/politics/state-dept-israel-gaza-cease-fire.html Accessed May 3, 2024.

More than 1,000 officials in the U.S. Agency for International Development signed a letter urging the Biden administration to demand an immediate cease-fire. USAID staff published the letter November 2, according to Reuters.

> (W)e are alarmed and disheartened at the numerous violations of international law; laws which aim to protect civilians, medical and media personnel, as well as schools, hospitals, and places of worship.... We believe that further catastrophic loss of human life can only be avoided if the United States Government calls for an immediate ceasefire in Gaza.[22]

More than five hundred political appointees and staff members representing roughly forty government agencies sent a letter to Biden on November 14, calling on the president to seek an immediate cease-fire and to push Israel to allow humanitarian aid into the Gaza strip. The signatories, like those who signed the USAID letter, remained anonymous, saying they withheld their names out of "concern for our personal safety and risk of potentially losing our jobs."

"Although the Biden administration has recently started voicing concern over the high numbers of Palestinian civilians killed while urging Israel to show restraint, that budding criticism does not appear to be placating many in the U.S. government," *The New York Times* reported.

Two political appointees who helped organize the letter said most of the 502 signatories are political appointees who work throughout the government, from the National Security Council, to the FBI, to the Justice Department.[23]

---

22   Pamuk, Humeyra and Simon Lewis. "Over 1,000 USAID officials call for Gaza ceasefire in letter." *Reuters.* November 10, 2023. https://www.reuters.com/world/over-1000-usaid-officials-call-gaza-ceasefire-letter-2023-11-10/ Accessed May 3, 2024.

23   Abi-Habib, Maria, Michael Crowley, and Edward Wong. "More Than 500 U.S. Officials Sign Letter Protesting Biden's Israel Policy." *The New York Times.* November 14, 2023. https://www.nytimes.com/2023/11/14/us/politics/israel-biden-letter-gaza-cease-fire.html Accessed May 3, 2024.

One State Department official did not remain anonymous, however. Josh Paul, director of congressional and public affairs at the Bureau of Political-Military Affairs, published an open letter on October 18, explaining his resignation. He wrote that his "responsibilities lie solidly in the arms transfer space."

> I cannot work in support of a set of major policy decisions, including rushing more arms to one side of the conflict, that I believe to be shortsighted, destructive, unjust, and contradictory to the very values that we publicly espouse, and which I wholeheartedly endorse: a world built around a rules-based order, a world that advances both equality and equity, and a world whose arc of history bends toward the promise of liberty, and of justice, for all.[24]

Paul then joined Democracy for the Arab World Now as a senior advisor.[25]

Democracy for the Arab World Now

Saudi journalist Jamal Khashoggi started the process of founding Democracy for the Arab World Now before his 2018 assassination in Saudi Arabia. DAWN launched in September 2020. Soros's Open Society Foundations gave DAWN $525,000 between 2020 and 2022.[26]

---

24 Paul, Josh. Resignation letter. Published on LinkedIn. October 18, 2023. https://www.linkedin.com/posts/josh-paul-655a25263_explaining-my-resignation-activity-7120512510645952512-APhR/ Accessed May 3, 2024. Archived here: https://web.archive.org/web/20231019014209/https://www.linkedin.com/posts/josh-paul-655a25263_explaining-my-resignation-activity-7120512510645952512-APhR/

25 "Josh Paul." Democracy for the Arab World Now profile. https://dawnmena.org/experts/josh-paul/ Accessed May 3, 2024.

26 "Awarded Grants" page search results for "Arab World Now." Open Society Foundations. https://www.opensocietyfoundations.org/grants/past?filter_keyword=Arab+World+Now Accessed May 3, 2024.

Nihad Awad, co-founder and executive director of the Council for American-Islamic Relations, sits on DAWN's board. Mongi Dhaouadi, another DAWN board member, previously served as executive director of CAIR's Connecticut chapter. Both DAWN's executive director, Sarah Leah Whitson, and its communications director, Omid Memarian, came from the left-leaning Human Rights Watch. Whitson, director of HRW's Middle East and North Africa division, reportedly raised money "from wealthy Saudis by highlighting HRW's demonization of Israel."[27]

The Atlantic's Jeffrey Goldberg pressed HRW Executive Director Ken Roth about the accusation, and Roth danced around the issue. Ultimately, Goldberg asked, "did your staff person attempt to raise funds in Saudi Arabia by advertising your organization's opposition to the pro-Israel lobby?" Roth responded, "That's certainly part of the story."[28]

DAWN Presses Biden to Go Further

Biden began to change his policies in November. The president reportedly sent a memo in mid-November, directing senior aides "to develop policy options for expeditious action against those responsible for the conduct of violence in the West Bank."[29]

Richard Goldberg, the analyst at the Foundation for the Defense of Democracies, told me that when Biden received backlash, he and his team "perceived that they're no longer in the center

---

27 Bernstein, David. "Human Rights Watch Goes to Saudi Arabia." *The Wall Street Journal.* July 15, 2009. https://www.wsj.com/articles/SB124528343805525561 Accessed May 3, 2024.

28 Goldberg, Jeffrey. "Fundraising Corruption at Human Rights Watch." *The Atlantic.* July 15, 2009. https://www.theatlantic.com/international/archive/2009/07/fundraising-corruption-at-human-rights-watch/21345/ Accessed May 3, 2024.

29 Ward, Alexander. "Biden orders top aides to prepare reprimands for violent Israeli settlers in West Bank." *Politico.* November 18, 2023. https://www.politico.com/news/2023/11/18/biden-orders-top-aides-to-prepare-reprimands-for-violent-israeli-settlers-in-west-bank-00127940 Accessed May 3, 2024.

of the Democratic Party, they're in the right wing." Yet Biden still fears alienating the pro-Israel faction of his party, particularly Senate Majority Leader Chuck Schumer (D-NY). "It almost seems like the president wouldn't go all the way to cut off military support," Goldberg said. "So, he authorizes his administration to unleash political warfare on Israel as a make-good for not completely abandoning Israel."

During the 1967 Six-Day War, Israel had captured the West Bank and East Jerusalem from Jordan, the Gaza Strip and the Sinai Peninsula from Egypt, and the Golan Heights from Syria. Israelis established communities in those territories. Many foreign countries consider these settlements illegal and an obstacle to peace, because Palestinians hope to establish a state in the West Bank and Gaza.[30]

The United Nations and the Israeli human rights group B'Tselem have claimed that more than one thousand Palestinians have fled their homes in the West Bank since the October 7 Hamas terror attacks.[31]

On February 1, 2024, President Biden issued an executive order imposing sanctions on Israeli "settlers" in the West Bank whom he accused of "undermining peace, security, and stability." Biden said he found "that the situation in the West Bank—in particular high levels of extremist settler violence, forced displacement of people and villages, and property destruction—has reached intolerable levels and constitutes a serious threat to the peace, security, and stability of the West Bank and Gaza, Israel, and the broader Middle East Region."

---

30 Al Lawati, Abbas. "Who are Israeli settlers and why are they so controversial?" CNN. February 2, 2024. https://www.cnn.com/2024/02/02/middleeast/who-are-israeli-settlers-palestinian-land-intl/index.html   Accessed May 3, 2024.

31 Stancati, Margherita, and Fatima Abdul Karim. "Palestinians in West Bank Flee After Settler Violence: 'We Were Forced to Leave." *The Wall Street Journal.* December 3, 2023. https://www.wsj.com/world/middle-east/palestinians-in-west-bank-flee-after-settler-violence-we-were-forced-to-leave-7d3c1988?mod=article_inline Accessed May 3, 2024.

He declared a "national emergency" to deal with the "threat," and imposed new sanctions on "settlers."[32]

Rabbi Steven Pruzansky, who serves as the Israel regional vice president at the Coalition for Jewish Values, called Biden's sanctions a "farce." He noted that the four "settlers" sanctioned do not face charges in Israel. "So-called settler violence, never murderous, against Arabs is down in the past year, even as Arab violence against settlers is up," Pruzansky wrote.[33]

Yet *The Guardian* reported that "human rights groups" pressured Biden to expand the sanctions. The outlet quoted two DAWN staffers, Josh Paul and Michael Schaeffer Omer-Man, DAWN's research director for Israel-Palestine.

"I think the order could and should implicate members of the current Israeli government," Paul said, specifically naming Israel's national security minister, Itamar Ben-Gvir. "The problem isn't violent settlers. They're low-hanging fruit. The problem is the settlement enterprise and that is an enterprise that is funded, supported, enabled through U.S. private donations and through U.S. government tacit support." Omer-Man said the sanctions could prove effective "to completely defund the settlement movement and the organizations that support it."[34]

On April 19, the State Department sanctioned Ben-Zion Gopstein, who has family ties to Ben-Gvir. Ben-Gvir responded by

---

32   "Executive Order on Imposing Certain Sanctions on Persons Undermining Peace, Security, and Stability in the West Bank." White House Briefing Room. February 1, 2024. https://www.whitehouse.gov/briefing-room/presidential-actions/2024/02/01/executive-order-on-imposing-certain-sanctions-on-persons-undermining-peace-security-and-stability-in-the-west-bank/ Accessed May 3, 2024.

33   Pruzansky, Rabbi Steven. "The empty toolbox." *Israel National News.* February 6, 2024. https://www.israelnationalnews.com/news/384783 Accessed May 3, 2024.

34   McGreal, Chris. "Biden urged to include politicians in sanctions on violent Israeli settlers." *The Guardian.* February 10, 2024. https://www.theguardian.com/us-news/2024/feb/10/biden-expand-sanctions-banks-israeli-settlers Accessed May 3, 2024.

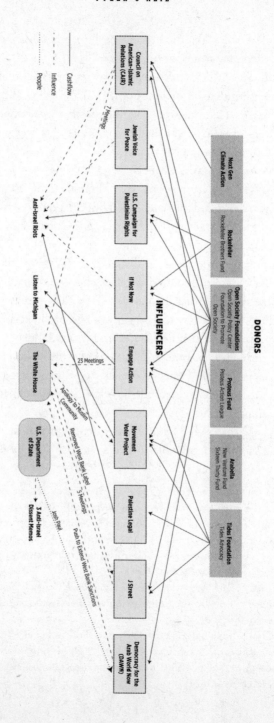

condemning what he called harassment against Gopstein's group, Lehava, and "our dear settlers who have never engaged in terrorism or hurt anyone." Ben-Gvir called the accusations of violence a "blood libel" and urged Western countries to "stop cooperating with these antisemites and end this campaign of persecution against the pioneering Zionist settlers."[35]

The administration has applied sanctions against at least nine people under the executive order.[36] These sanctions show Biden bending to pressure to act against Israel, while stopping short of fully opposing the Jewish state's war in Gaza.

THE COUNCIL ON AMERICAN-ISLAMIC RELATIONS

The Council on American-Islamic Relations (CAIR), which bills itself as "America's largest Muslim civil liberties organization,"[37] has longstanding ties with the Biden administration.

On May 25, the White House released its "National Strategy to Counter Antisemitism." At the same time, it released a factsheet touting "commitments" from various partners, including the Southern Poverty Law Center and the Council on American-Islamic Relations. The document stated:

> The Council on American-Islamic Relations will launch a tour to educate religious communities about

---

35 Lewis, Simon. "U.S. sanctions ally of Israeli minister, fundraisers over settlers." Reuters. April 19, 2024. https://www.reuters.com/world/us/us-slaps-sanctions-entities-that-raised-funds-west-bank-settlers-2024-04-19/ Accessed May 3, 2024.

36 Hussein, Fatima, Matthew Lee, and Julia Frankel. "US sanctions three Israeli West Bank settlers and their outposts for violence against Palestinians." *The Associated Press*. March 14, 2024. https://apnews.com/article/sanctions-west-bank-gaza-israel-war-hamas-57a673cd9836590856c8259e-f7a895e1 Accessed May 3, 2024.

37 "About Us" page on the Council on American-Islamic Relations website. https://www.cair.com/about_cair/about-us/ Accessed April 11, 2024.

steps they can take to protect their houses of worship from hate incidents, such as instituting appropriate security measures, developing strong relationships with other faith communities, and maintaining open lines of communication with local law enforcement.[38]

The Coalition for Jewish Values, which represents more than 2,500 Orthodox Jewish rabbis across the U.S., condemned Biden's antisemitism strategy for including the SPLC and CAIR.

"SPLC not only fails to identify radical Islam as a source of antisemitic hatred, but targets allies of the Jewish community as 'hate groups,'" Rabbi Yaakov Menken, the coalition's managing director, told *The Daily Signal.* "CAIR, for its part, issued a report at the end of 2021 identifying mainstream Jewish charities as investors in 'anti-Muslim hate.'"

"How are they expected to become partners fighting antisemitism after years of inciting it?" he asked.

The coalition has long slammed CAIR, citing the fact that its founders previously worked at the Islamic Association for Palestine, or IAP, which the FBI's counterterrorism chief described as a "front organization for Hamas that engages in propaganda for Islamic militants."

When a jury convicted the Holy Land Foundation of funneling millions to Hamas (a State Department-identified terrorist group), the FBI listed CAIR as an unindicted co-conspirator in the case. CAIR received two $5,000 payments from the Holy Land Foundation. CAIR has pushed back on these claims, noting that "there is no legal implication to being labeled an unindicted co-conspirator, since it does not require the Justice Department to

---

38   "FACT SHEET: Biden-Harris Administration Releases First-Ever U.S. National Strategy to Counter Antisemitism." White House Briefing Room. May 25, 2023. Archived version May 26, 2023. https://web.archive.org/web/20230526013348/https://www.whitehouse.gov/briefing-room/statements-releases/2023/05/25/fact-sheet-biden-harris-administration-releases-first-ever-u-s-national-strategy-to-counter-antisemitism/ Accessed via Internet Archive May 3, 2024.

prove anything in a court of law." CAIR also has cited a 2010 case in which the 5th U.S. Circuit Court of Appeals ruled that the Justice Department violated the Fifth Amendment rights of groups such as CAIR by including them on the list of unindicted co-conspirators.

Menken noted that CAIR organized a series of rallies calling for the release of Pakistani national Aafia Siddiqui from a U.S. prison, the cause that motivated Malik Faisal Akram to hold hostages in a Texas synagogue. Menken also said that Zahra Billoo, executive director of CAIR's San Francisco office, identified "Zionist synagogues" and "polite Zionists"—including the Anti-Defamation League—as "your enemies." CAIR has claimed Billoo was "misquoted.[39]

CAIR's board members have visited the White House at least three times. Robert S. McCaw, director of government affairs at CAIR, has visited the White House at least four times. He also took part in a "listening session on Islamophobia" on May 2, 2023 with second gentleman Doug Emhoff, White House Domestic Policy Advisor Susan Rice, and others.[40] That meeting also included two leaders at Emgage, an organization that would support a political pressure campaign against Biden.

McCaw last visited the White House on September 28, 2023, and there is no record of him visiting 1600 Pennsylvania Avenue since October 7. McCaw's absence at the White House correlates with CAIR's falling out with Biden.

39 O'Neil, Tyler. "DISTORTED PICTURE: Biden Antisemitism Push Celebrates CAIR, SPLC, Ignores Left-Wing Jew-Hatred." The Daily Signal. June 1, 2023. https://www.dailysignal.com/2023/06/01/biden-touts-cair-splc-antisemitism-push-muddies-waters-israel-hours-major-jewish-holiday/ Accessed May 3, 2024.

40 "Readout of White House Listening Session on Islamophobia." White House Briefing Room. May 3, 2023. https://www.whitehouse.gov/briefing-room/statements-releases/2023/05/03/readout-of-white-house-listening-session-on-islamophobia/ Accessed May 3, 2024.

A Break From the White House

On November 4, 2023, Nihad Awad spoke at the American Muslims for Palestine convention in Chicago. According to a translation from the Middle East Media Research Institute (MEMRI) —a translation Awad disputed—he said:

> The people of Gaza only decided to break the siege, the walls of the concentration camp, on October 7. And yes, I was happy to see people breaking the siege and throwing down the shackles of their own land, which they were not allowed to walk in…. And yes, the people of Gaza have the right to self-defense, have the right to defend themselves, and yes, Israel, as an occupying power, does not have that right of self-defense.[41]

MEMRI published that translation on December 7, and on December 8, the White House condemned Nihad Awad's remarks. "We condemn these shocking, antisemitic statements in the strongest terms," Andrew Bates, a White House spokesman, said. "The horrific, brutal terrorist attacks committed by Hamas on October 7 were, as President Biden said, 'abhorrent' and represent 'unadulterated evil.'"[42]

The White House removed CAIR from the Islamophobia strategy document sometime after December 7 at 1:51 p.m. EST

---

41 "CAIR Executive Director Nihad Awad At American Muslims For Palestine (AMP) Convention: I Was Happy To See The People Of Gaza Break The Siege On October 7; They Were Victorious; The People Of Gaza Have The Right To Self-Defense—Israel Does Not." MEMRI. December 7, 2023. https://www.memri.org/reports/cair-executive-director-nihad-awad-american-muslims-palestine-amp-convention-i-was-happy-see Accessed May 6, 2024.

42 Baker, Peter. "White House Disavows U.S. Islamic Group After Leader's October 7 Remarks." *The New York Times.* December 8, 2023. https://www.nytimes.com/2023/12/08/us/politics/white-house-cair-nihad-awad.html Accessed May 3, 2024.

and before December 8 at 1:23 p.m. EST.[43] Awad claimed he had condemned antisemitism in his speech, and that his reference to "breaking the siege" involved a few Palestinians stepping foot outside Gaza to symbolically put their foot on Israeli soil without attacking anyone.[44]

The Left's dark money network has funded CAIR, which has received:

- $7,000 from the Proteus Fund in 2018[45]
- $335,000 from NextGen Climate Action, a 501(c)4 founded by environmentalist billionaire Tom Steyer, between 2017 and 2019[46]
- $350,000 from the Foundation to Promote Open Society in 2017, directed to CAIR chapters in California, Florida, New York, and Texas[47]

While it remains unclear if CAIR is influencing the White House, its allies—including those who met with McCaw at the White House—continue to have sway in Biden's circles. It took heinous comments for Biden to finally distance himself from this

43 Analysis of Internet Archive results on search terms: "FACT SHEET: Biden-Harris Administration Releases First-Ever U.S. National Strategy to Counter Antisemitism" to examine different versions https://web.archive.org/web/20230601000000*/https://www.whitehouse.gov/briefing-room/statements-releases/2023/05/25/fact-sheet-biden-harris-administration-releases-first-ever-u-s-national-strategy-to-counter-antisemitism/

44 "Statement By Nihad Awad on Remarks at Palestine Human Rights Conference." Council on American-Islamic Relations news release. December 7, 2023. https://www.cair.com/press_releases/statement-by-nihad-awad-on-remarks-at-palestine-human-rights-conference/ Accessed May 6, 2024.

45 "Proteus Fund." Form 990, Schedule I for 2018, accessed May 1, 2024.

46 "Nextgen Climate Action." Form 990, Schedule I for 2017-2019, accessed May 1, 2024.

47 The exact figure is $366,010. "Awarded Grants" page search results for "American-Islamic Relations." Open Society Foundations. https://www.opensocietyfoundations.org/grants/past?filter_keyword=American-Islamic+Relations&grant_id=OR2016-32098 Accessed May 6, 2024.

group, but the president never should have included CAIR in the antisemitism effort in the first place. The fact that he did so speaks volumes.

THE MICHIGAN INFLUENCE CAMPAIGN

President Biden's reelection campaign has reached out to Muslim communities across the U.S., and some have refused to meet with him, demanding a ceasefire in Gaza. Some Islamic groups have launched a pressure campaign, using the impending election as leverage to demand concessions regarding the war.

In late January 2024, Arab and Muslim leaders in Michigan canceled a meeting with Biden's reelection campaign manager, Julie Chavez Rodriguez. "For us, you have to have that conversation with policymakers. Those who are actually influencing decision-making," Dearborn Mayor Abdullah Hammoud said. "It's actually dehumanizing to send campaign staff to ask us what it would take to earn your support in November when you have an active genocide that is being funded and supported and defended by the current administration."[48]

Biden sent top administration officials—who were not publicly identified—to meet with the Arab and Muslim leaders a little more than a week after they canceled the event.[49]

In the lead-up to the February 27 Michigan Democratic primary, the group Listen to Michigan rallied Democrats to vote

---

48   Samra, Ibrahim. "Arab leaders in Michigan decline meeting with Biden campaign team amid Israel-Hamas war backlash." CBS News Detroit. January 26, 2024. https://www.cbsnews.com/detroit/news/arab-leaders-in-michigan-decline-meeting-with-biden-campaign-team-amid-israel-hamas-war-backlash/ Accessed May 3, 2024.

49   Cappelletti, Joey and Corey Williams. "Biden aides meet in Michigan with Arab American and Muslim leaders, aiming to mend political ties." *The Associated Press*. February 8, 2024. https://apnews.com/article/biden-gaza-protest-hamas-michigan-election-5bf3f88529d625a129e786bab29c4fde Accessed May 3, 2024.

"uncommitted" to shame President Biden and support a cease-fire in Gaza.[50]

According to Open Secrets, two organizations funded Listen to Michigan: The Movement Voter Project and Arab Americans for Progress.[51] Arab Americans for Progress does not appear to receive any grants from other organizations, but the Movement Voter Project has received millions through the Left's dark money network. Many donations to the project appear in the project's corporate name, "All Hands on Deck Network."

The Movement Voter Project received:

- $25,000 from New Venture Fund in 2019 (Arabella)[52]
- $18,000 from Sixteen Thirty Fund in 2016 (Arabella)[53]
- $187,400 from the Open Society Policy Center in 2020[54]
- $446,000 from Tides Advocacy between 2018 and 2020[55]
- $9.5 million from The Tides Foundation between 2018 and 2022[56]

While Biden won the Michigan Democratic primary on February 27 with 81 percent of the vote—625,221 votes—the "uncommitted" option exceeded its goal, racking up 101,623 votes, 13.19 percent of the vote, according to the Michigan Secretary

---

50 "Listen to Michigan" home page. https://www.listentomichigan.com/ Accessed May 1, 2024.

51 "Top Organizations Disclosing Donations to Listen to Michigan, 2024." Open Secrets. https://www.opensecrets.org/outside-spending/detail/2024?cmte=C00870311&tab=donors Accessed May 1, 2024.

52 "New Venture Fund." Form 990, Schedule I for 2019, accessed May 1, 2024.

53 "Sixteen Thirty Fund." Form 990, Schedule I for 2016, accessed May 1, 2024.

54 "Open Society Policy Center." Form 990, Schedule I for 2020, accessed May 1, 2024.

55 "Tides Advocacy." Form 990, Schedule I for 2018, 2020, accessed May 1, 2024.

56 The exact figure is $9,546,480. "Tides Foundation." Form 990, Schedule I for 2018–2022, accessed May 1, 2024.

of State.[57] The campaign aimed to get more than 10,000 votes, approximately the margin by which Trump defeated Hillary Clinton in 2016.

"We have led a movement that is far exceeding expectations, using the ballot box to urge America to stop killing our families," Listen to Michigan spokesman Abbas Alawieh said at an election watch party.[58]

Alaweih's past demonstrates the anti-Israel bias of the Listen to Michigan campaign. He previously worked as a legislative director for Representative Rashida Tlaib (D-MI) and then as chief of staff to Representative Cori Bush (R-MO).[59] The House of Representatives censured Tlaib for condemning Israel's "blockade," "occupation," and "apartheid" less than twenty-four hours after October 7, and for declaring half of the slogan, "From the river to the sea, Palestine will be free" in a video condemning Israel.[60]

Bush, who also loudly condemned Israel, denounced the twenty-two Democrats who voted alongside Republicans to censure Tlaib, accusing them of "blatantly attempting to silence the only Palestinian American representative" in Congress. She then intro-

57 Michigan Secretary of State election results, Michigan Voter Information Center. February 27, 2024. Final results published March 19, 2024. https://mvic.sos.state.mi.us/votehistory/Index?type=C&electionDate=2-27-2024 Accessed May 1, 2024.

58 Moore, Elena. "The push to vote 'uncommitted' to Biden in Michigan exceeds goal." NPR. February 28, 2024. https://www.npr.org/2024/02/27/1234279958/biden-uncommitted-democrats-michigan-primary-election-2024- Accessed May 1, 2024.

59 "Abbas Alawieh." LinkedIn profile. https://www.linkedin.com/in/abbasalawieh/ Accessed May 1, 2024.

60 H.Res.845 "Censuring Representative Rashida Tlaib for promoting false narratives regarding the October 7, 2023, Hamas attack on Israel and for calling for the destruction of the state of Israel." 118th Congress. https://www.congress.gov/bill/118th-congress/house-resolution/845/text Accessed May 1, 2024.

duced a House resolution urging Biden to push for a cease-fire, which gathered more than a dozen co-sponsors, including Tlaib.[61]

Alawieh, who was working for Bush at the time, visited the White House fifteen times between March 2021 and July 2023.

The Muslim group Emgage Action publicly backed the "Listen to Michigan" campaign, even though its leaders have close ties to the White House. "Supporting 'Listen to Michigan' goes beyond a mere political stance—it mirrors our relentless pursuit of justice and peace," Emgage Action Michigan Executive Director Hira Khan said in a statement at the time. "Emgage Action is proud to back this call for pivotal policy reforms, ensuring that our collective voice leads to meaningful action."[62]

Wa'el Alzayat, CEO of Emgage Action, is a frequent White House guest, visiting it at least twenty-three times between November 15, 2021, and October 26, 2023.

Before the White House broke with CAIR, Biden rushed to apologize to the American Muslim community after expressing mistrust in the Hamas-run Gaza Health Ministry's figures for civilian deaths. "I'm sure innocents have been killed and it is the price of waging war," Biden said on October 25, 2023. "I have no confidence in the number that the Palestinians are using," he added, referring to the Health Ministry figures.

CAIR demanded an apology. "We are deeply disturbed and shocked by the dehumanizing comments," CAIR Executive Director Nihad Awad said in a news release on the day Biden made the comments. "President Biden should apologize for his comments, con-

---

61   Rosenbaum, Jason. "Rep. Cori Bush doubles down on Israel criticism as primary opponent calls for nuance." NPR. November 8, 2023. https://www.npr.org/2023/11/08/1211483318/rep-cori-bush-doubles-down-on-israel-criticism-as-primary-opponent-calls-for-nua Accessed May 1, 2024.

62   "Emgage Action supports Listen to Michigan campaign to advocate for policy change on Gaza ahead of primary." Emgage Action news release. February 26, 2024. https://emgageusa.org/press-release/emgage-action-supports-listen-to-michigan-campaign-to-advocate-for-policy-change-on-gaza-ahead-of-primary/ Accessed May 3, 2024.

demn the Israeli government for deliberately targeting civilians, and demand a ceasefire before more innocent people die."[63]

President Biden personally apologized to Alzayat and a few other Muslim community leaders the very next day, on October 26.[64]

Emgage Action is not only connected to the White House; it also enjoys funding from the Left's dark money network. Emgage Action has received:

- ♦ $460,000 from Tides Advocacy between 2020 and 2022[65]
- ♦ $80,000 from Proteus Action League between 2017 and 2022[66]
- ♦ $600,000 from Open Society Policy Center between 2021 and 2022[67]

REMOVING A LABEL

In November 2020, then-Secretary of State Mike Pompeo issued new guidelines directing producers to label goods made in Israeli-controlled areas of the West Bank as "Made in Israel," when export-

63 "BREAKING: CAIR Calls on President Biden to Apologize for 'Shocking and Dehumanizing' Remarks on Palestinian Civilian Casualties." Council on American-Islamic Relations news release. October 25, 2023. https://www.cair.com/press_releases/breaking-cair-calls-on-president-biden-to-apologize-for-shocking-and-dehumanizing-remarks-on-palestinian-civilian-casualties/ Accessed May 3, 2024.

64 Shah, Zoreen, and Ayesha Ali. "New details on Biden's private apology to Muslim Americans for rhetoric on Palestinian civilians." ABC News. November 29, 2023. https://abcnews.go.com/Politics/new-details-bidens-private-apology-muslim-americans-rhetoric/story?id=105214648 Accessed May 3, 2024.

65 "Tides Advocacy." Form 990, Schedule I for 2020, 2022, accessed May 3, 2024.

66 "Proteus Action League." Form 990, Schedule I for 2017, 2022, accessed May 3, 2024.

67 "Open Society Policy Center." Form 990, Schedule I for 2021–2022, accessed May 3, 2024.

ing those goods to the United States. The goods had previously been labeled "Made in the West Bank."[68]

In February 2021, six left-leaning Jewish groups—J Street, the New Israel Fund, Partners for Progressive Israel, Ameinu, Americans for Peace Now, and T'ruah: The Rabbinic Call for Human Rights—sent a letter to Homeland Security Secretary Alejandro Mayorkas, urging him to reverse the policy.

"By inaccurately and misleadingly treating settlement and other products from Area C of the West Bank as if they were made in Israel, the [Trump-era notification] attempts to reverse decades of U.S. policy that makes a firm distinction between Israel and the West Bank," the groups wrote. [69] (Area C, which comprises 60 percent of the West Bank, is run by Israel, while Palestinians govern the smaller Areas A and B.)

While Biden's administration did not act on this recommendation at the time, the administration started drawing up plans to reverse Pompeo's move in April 2024, unnamed officials told The Financial Times.[70]

J Street leaders have visited the White House at least five times. National Security Council Chief of Staff Curtis Ried met with three J Street leaders on January 19, 2024 (Founder and President Jeremy Ben-Ami, Director of policy Deborah Shusan, and Vice President and Chief of Staff Adina Vogel-Ayalon). The group may have pressed Ried and other bureaucrats on the issue then.

---

68   Magid, Jacob. "In major shift, Pompeo says US to label settlement products 'Made in Israel.'" *The Times of Israel.* November 19, 2020. https://www.time-sofisrael.com/in-major-shift-pompeo-says-us-to-label-settlement-products-made-in-israel/ Accessed May 3, 2024.

69   Ahmed, Akbar Shahid. "Key Jewish Groups Ask Joe Biden To Revoke Trump's Parting Gift for Israel's Netanyahu." *HuffPost.* February 24, 2021. https://www.huffpost.com/entry/biden-trump-settlements-label_n_60358163c5b-62bef36792568 Accessed May 3, 2024.

70   Schwartz, Felicia. "US plans to label goods from Jewish settlements in occupied West Bank." *The Financial Times.* April 5, 2024. https://www.ft.com/content/f0df1d24-2824-41a1-bc7a-56285ab3720d Accessed May 3, 2024.

The Left's dark money network has ties to J Street, as well. J Street has received:

- $125,000 from The Tides Foundation in 2022[71]
- $2 million from The Open Society Policy Center between 2020 and 2022[72]

DARK MONEY DEFENDING RIOTERS IN COURT

In late April 2024, protests erupted on college campuses across the country, as pro-Hamas rioters demanded schools divest from Israel. Police arrested more than 2,000 people in the opening weeks.[73]

Rioters shouted antisemitic slogans and physically blocked Jewish students while they were trying to walk on campus.[74] Pro-Palestine agitators set up an encampment on the New York City campus of Columbia University on April 17, demanding the university divest from companies with ties to Israel. An anonymous Jewish student sued the university for allegedly failing to provide "a safe educational environment"; his lawyer, Jay Edelson, said, "There are straight-out calls for the genocide of Jews."

The lawsuit states:

71 "Tides Foundation." Form 990, Schedule I for 2022, accessed May 6, 2024.

72 "Open Society Policy Center." Form 990, Schedule I for 2020–2022, accessed May 6, 2024.

73 Watson, Julie, Christopher L. Keller, Carolyn Thompson, and Stefanie Dazio. "More than 2,100 people have been arrested during pro-Palestinian protests on US college campuses." *The Associated Press.* May 2, 2024. https://apnews.com/article/israel-palestinian-campus-student-protests-war-ec3f-62c51c08599f8fcecd99f7cf9e33 Accessed May 6, 2024.

74 O'Neil, Tyler. "Omar Shrugs Off Harassment of Jewish Student, Faults UCLA for Not Protecting Anti-Israel Protesters." *The Daily Signal.* May 23, 2024. https://www.dailysignal.com/2024/05/23/ilhan-omar-shrugs-harassment-jewish-student-faults-ucla-not-protecting-anti-israel-protesters/ Accessed May 26, 2024.

The encampment has been the center of round-the-clock harassment of Jewish students, who have been punched, shoved, spat upon, blocked from attending classes and moving freely about campus, and targeted by pro-terrorist hate speech—both verbal and in written form on massive banners and signs—with statements such as: "Death to the Jews"; "Long live Hamas"; "Globalize the Intifada."[75]

Eric Schorr, a former Israeli Defense Force intelligence officer, "wholeheartedly" suggested that "Jewish students not only leave campus but potentially seek new institutions for their continued education."

"As a security professional, [I can say] the campus is no longer safe, it is time for the Jewish community, students, faculty and alumni donors, to vacate and abandon it entirely," he added on Sunday, April 21.

The NYPD warned that extremist groups may engage in violence during the Jewish holiday of Passover. [76]

Although the NYPD repeatedly cleared the "encampment" and arrested agitators, the agitators returned, and some of them would go on to take over a campus building, trapping a janitor inside.

What happens after the arrests? Many find their legal defense with Palestine Legal, which states that its mission is "to bolster the Palestine solidarity movement by challenging efforts to threaten, harass and legally bully activists into silence and inaction." Palestine Legal filed a civil rights complaint *on behalf of the instigators* on April 25, demanding an investigation into "Columbia University's

---

75 Lonas, Lexi. "Columbia student's lawyer 'There are straight-out calls for the genocide of Jews.'" *The Hill.* April 30, 2024. https://thehill.com/homenews/education/4632357-columbia-students-protest-genocide-jews/ Accessed May 6, 2024.

76 Impelli, Matthew. "Jewish Students Told to Leave Columbia After Passover Warning." *Newsweek.* April 22, 2024. https://www.newsweek.com/columbia-university-jewish-students-protests-passover-1892747 Accessed May 6, 2024.

discriminatory treatment of Palestinian students and their allies, including by inviting NYPD officers in riot gear—for the first time in decades—to arrest over a hundred students peacefully protesting Israel's genocide last week."

Many of these agitators act as though they are the victims of "repression." Palestine Legal quoted a Palestinian student, Maryam Alwan, who claims she suffered harassment, doxing, and discrimination due to her identity and her activism. "I'm horrified at the way Columbia has utterly failed to protect me from racism and abuse, but beyond that, the university has also played a role in this repression by having me arrested and suspended for peacefully protesting Israel's genocide in Gaza," Alwan said. "The violent repression we're facing as peaceful anti-war protesters is appalling."[77]

"Columbia's vicious crackdown on student protests calling for Palestinian freedom amidst an ongoing genocide should alarm us all," Palestine Legal Staff Attorney Sabiya Ahamed said. "We urge federal civil rights officials to do what Columbia has disgracefully failed to: ensure the rights of Palestinian and allied students are protected at a moment when their voices are most essential."

Who, exactly, is representing these pro-Hamas rioters? Palestine Legal's website doesn't hide its dies to the Left's dark money network: "Palestine Legal is a fiscally sponsored project of the Tides Center, which is a 501(c)(3) non-profit organization."

The Tides Center will help defend the rioters once they face charges, but the Open Society Foundations bankrolls the groups behind the riots on the front end. The U.S. Campaign for Palestinian Rights (USCPR), for example, provides up to $7,800 for its community-based "fellows," and between $2,880 and $3,660 for its campus-based "fellows," in return for spending eight hours a week organizing "campaigns led by Palestinian organizations." USCPR goes by the name "Education for a Just Peace in the Middle East"

77 "Columbia Students File Civil Rights Complaint After NYPD Arrests, National Guard Threat." Palestine Legal news release. April 25, 2024. https://palestinelegal.org/news/2024/4/25/columbia-students-file-civil-rights-complaint-after-nypd-arrests-national-guard-threat Accessed May 6, 2024.

for business purposes, so checks and other legal documents with that name involve USCPR.

The Foundation to Promote Open Society sent USCPR $700,000 between 2018 and 2022.[78] The Rockefeller Brothers Fund has awarded it three grants consisting of $515,000 between 2019 and 2023.[79]

Police have arrested USCPR leaders at campus protests across the country.

Politico analyzed the donors behind two groups supporting the protests, Jewish Voice for Peace and IfNotNow. Both enjoy funding from the Tides Foundation and different Open Society entities founded by George Soros.[80] Jewish Voice for Peace received $525,000 from the Foundation to Promote Open Society between 2017 and 2022, while its action fund received $350,000 from the Open Society Policy Center between 2019 and 2021.[81] The Rockefeller Brothers Fund gave Jewish Voice for Peace $490,000 between 2019 and 2023.[82] If Not Now received $400,000 from the Foundation to Promote Open Society between 2019 and 2021.[83]

---

78   Open Society Foundations grant search for "Just Peace in the Middle East." https://www.opensocietyfoundations.org/grants/past?filter_keyword=-Just+Peace+in+the+Middle+East&grant_id=OR2018-45969   Accessed May 6, 2024.

79   "Education for Just Peace in the Middle East." Rockefeller Brothers Fund grantee page. https://www.rbf.org/grantees/education-just-peace-middle-east Accessed May 6, 2024.

80   Kapos, Shia. "Pro-Palestinian protesters are backed by a surprising source: Biden's biggest donors." *Politico*. May 6, 2024. https://www.politico.com/news/2024/05/05/pro-palestinian-protests-columbia-university-funding-donors-00156135 Accessed May 26, 2024.

81   "Awarded Grants" page search results for "Jewish Voice for Peace." Open Society Foundations. https://www.opensocietyfoundations.org/grants/past?-filter_keyword=Jewish+Voice+for+Peace Accessed May 26, 2024.

82   Rockefeller Brothers Fund grantee page for "A Jewish Voice for Peace, Inc." https://www.rbf.org/grantees/jewish-voice-peace-inc Accessed May 26, 2024.

83   "Awarded Grants" page search results for "If Not Now." Open Society Foundations.   https://www.opensocietyfoundations.org/grants/past?filter_keyword=If+Not+Now Accessed May 26, 2024.

On April 30, pro-Palestine rioters invaded Columbia University's Hamilton Hall, covering the cameras, moving in with zip ties, duct tape, and masks, and barricaded themselves inside. "They came from both sides of the staircases," Mario Torres, a forty-five-year-old janitor who was on duty when the rioters seized the building, later told *The Free Press*. "They came through the elevators and they were just rushing. It was just like, they had a plan."

He described feeling trapped. "I was freaking out," the janitor explained. "At that point, I'm thinking about my family. How was I gonna get out? Through the window?" He said he avoided campus in the days after the incident because he did not feel safe there.[84] Torres, who has worked at Columbia for five years, pushed one of the masked rioters against a wall, revealing his face. That rioter turned out to be James Carlson, a forty-year-old trust fund kid who owns a Brooklyn townhouse worth $2.3 million. (Carlson later faced five felony charges, including burglary and reckless endangerment for the incident.) He has a rap sheet going back to 2005.[85]

Agitators at Columbia's "Gaza Solidarity Encampment" displayed an astonishing degree of entitlement. Not only did they seize the building by force after acting like they were the victims, but they had the gall to demand the university bring food to the occupiers—which they called "humanitarian aid."[86]—as if they had not essentially declared war on the university by using force to seize land and property. They enjoyed delivery pizza, coffee from Dunkin' Donuts, free sandwiches worth $12.50 from Pret a Manger, organic

84 Block, Francesca. "Exclusive: Columbia Custodian Trapped by 'Angry Mob' Speaks Out." *The Free Press.* May 6, 2024. https://www.thefp.com/p/exclusive-columbia-custodian-trapped Accessed May 26, 2024.

85 Moore, Tina, Chris Harris, and Matthew Sedacca. "'Violent' Columbia protester is heir to ad empire, has mansion, model babymama—and long rap sheet." *The New York Post.* May 4, 2024. https://nypost.com/2024/05/04/us-news/columbia-protester-is-heir-to-ad-empire-has-long-rap-sheet/ Accessed May 26, 2024.

86 The Post Millennial (@TpostMillennial). X Post. April 30, 2024. 3:10 p.m. Eastern. https://twitter.com/TPostMillennial/status/1785386376755900611 Accessed May 6, 2024.

tortilla chips, and $10 rotisserie chickens, according to *The New York Post.*[87]

The NYPD cleared about forty people from the hall on April 30. Police went on to post photos of the "tools of agitators" that the NYPD discovered among the tents. "Gas masks, ear plugs, helmets, goggles, tape, hammers, knives, ropes, and a book on TERRORISM," NYPD Deputy Commissioner Kaz Daughtry wrote. "These are not the tools of students protesting, these are the tools of agitators, of people who were working on something nefarious."[88]

The Left's dark money network helped prop up these riots, which appear part of the pressure campaign to push Biden away from Israel.

THE HAMAS WING OF THE ADMINISTRATIVE STATE

While the Woketopus helps the effort to influence Biden from inside and outside the administration, some administration staff have praised the October 7 terrorist attacks, and others have former ties to an organization close to Hamas.

One of the staffers tasked with determining official U.S. policy for migrants and asylum seekers has openly celebrated the Hamas terrorist attacks. Nejwa Ali, an adjudication officer at the U.S. Citizenship and Immigration Services (USCIS) agency, posted a picture on Instagram on October 8 showing a Hamas terrorist flying on a paraglider outside the Dome of the Rock in Jerusalem

---

87 Vincent, Isabel. "George Soros is paying student radicals who are fueling nationwide explosion of Israel-hating protests." *The New York Post.* April 26, 2024. https://nypost.com/2024/04/26/us-news/george-soros-maoist-fund-columbias-anti-israel-tent-city/ Accessed May 6, 2024.

88 "NYPD official: Items found at Columbia show protesters were far from benign." *The Times of Israel.* May 4, 2024. https://www.timesofisrael.com/nypd-official-items-found-at-columbia-show-protesters-were-far-from-peaceful/ Accessed May 6, 2024.

with the message, "Free PALESTINE." On October 9, she posted a video captioned "F*** Israel and any Jew that supports Israel" on Facebook.

Ali had formerly worked as a public affairs officer in 2016 and 2017 at the Palestine Delegation to the U.S., the Palestine Liberation Organization's "office in D.C." The U.S. has designated the PLO, the quasi-government of the West Bank, a foreign terrorist organization since 1987. (Hamas, which controls the government in Gaza, is separate from the PLO.)

USCIS told The Daily Wire that it holds employees "to high ethical standards both on and off duty, including their presence on social media," It remains unclear what actions, if any, USCIS has taken against Ali, but it appears not to have fired her. [89] The Heritage Foundation's Oversight Project filed a Freedom of Information Act request for information about Ali, and USCIS denied Oversight's request for expedited processing.[90]

In another alarming development, many bureaucrats in the administrative state once worked for a United Nations agency that appears to have long colluded with Hamas. The United Nations Relief and Works Agency (UNRWA) provides aid to those struggling in Gaza and the West Bank, but it has also faced longstanding accusations of collusion with Hamas, which is the official government of Gaza. In January 2024, the United States, Germany, Britain, and seven other countries paused their funding of the agency, after Israel alleged that some UNRWA staff took part in the October 7 terrorist attacks.[91]

---

89 Rosiak, Luke. "The U.S. Gov't Hired A Pro-Hamas PLO Spokeswoman To Handle Asylum Claims." *The Daily Wire*. October 18, 2023. https://www.dailywire.com/news/the-u-s-govt-hired-a-pro-hamas-plo-spokeswoman-to-handle-asylum-claims Accessed May 8, 2024.

90 Oversight Project (@OversightPR). X Post. October 31, 2023. 3:27 p.m. Eastern Time. https://twitter.com/OversightPR/status/1719436046365044777 Accessed May 8, 2024.

91 "UNRWA could shut down by end of February if funding does not resume." Reuters. February 1, 2024. https://www.reuters.com/world/middle-east/unrwa-could-shut-down-by-end-february-if-funding-does-not-resume-2024-02-01/ Accessed May 1, 2024.

Israel later revealed that Hamas operated a tunnel right underneath UNRWA's headquarters in Gaza City. UNRWA chief Philippe Lazzarini insisted that the agency "did not know what is under its headquarters." However, part of the parking lot at the headquarters began to sink in 2014, likely due to the Hamas tunnel. "No one talked about what was causing the collapse," a former UNRWA official said. "But everyone knew."

U.N. Watch's Hillel Neuer revealed what he claimed to be a chat group with 3,000 UNRWA teachers celebrating the October 7 attacks.

The State Department under Secretary Mike Pompeo halted funding for UNRWA in 2018, but the Biden administration announced plans to pour $235 million into the agency in 2021.[92]

Two women who had served as America's ambassador to the United Nations under Obama and would go on to take key roles in the Biden administration condemned Pompeo's decision to cut UNRWA aid. Susan Rice, who would later become director of the U.S. Domestic Policy Council from 2021 to 2023, and Samantha Power, who would later become administrator of the U.S. Agency for International Development under Biden, signed a letter backing UNRWA funding in 2018.

"This financial gap puts into question the ability of UNRWA to continue to deliver education and health care services to millions of people, and has national security ramifications for our closest allies, including Israel and Jordan," Rice and Power wrote, alongside other former diplomats.[93]

These "education" services have been documented to foment hatred against Israel. Long before October 7 and Pompeo's decision

---

92 O'Neil, Tyler. "Biden Empowered Iran Proxies Attacking US Forces and Threatening Wider War Against Israel." *The Daily Signal.* February 16, 2024. https://www.dailysignal.com/2024/02/16/biden-empowered-iran-proxies-now-attacking-us-forces-threatening-wider-war-israel/ Accessed May 1, 2024.

93 "American ex-UN envoys urge restoration of Palestinian refugee funds." *The Times of Israel.* July 2, 2018. https://www.timesofisrael.com/american-ex-un-envoys-urge-restoration-of-palestinian-refugee-funds/ Accessed May 1, 2024.

to cut UNRWA funding, journalists released videos of UNRWA summer camps, in which teachers tell children that "Jews are the wolf," and encourage them to conquer Israeli cities by force. "We teach the children about the villages they came from," camp director Amina Hinawi says in a video released in 2013. "This way, every child will be motivated to return to their original village." She encouraged the children to identify where their ancestors lived, in cities that are now part of sovereign Israel.[94]

In 2019, the U.S. Government Accountability Office released a report showing that UNRWA schools have an anti-Israel bias bordering on incitement to violence. "It is unacceptable that the textbooks that are used to delegitimize Israel and demonize the Jewish people, it is unacceptable that this program attempts to engrain this hatred in the hearts of children," Representative Lee Zeldin (R-NY) said when the report became public.[95] These videos may have helped radicalize the very terrorists who attacked Israel on October 7.

At least one former UNRWA staffer now works in the Biden administration. Elizabeth Campbell, deputy assistant secretary for population, refugees, and migration at the State Department, directed UNRWA's office in Washington, D.C.[96]

In remarks for this book, the State Department condemned any antisemitism in UNRWA education materials and clarified that it paused funding of UNRWA after Israel claimed twelve UNRWA employees helped Hamas in the October 7 attacks.

---

94 Berman, Lazar. "Palestinian kids taught to hate Israel in UN-funded camps, clip shows." *The Times of Israel.* August 14, 2013. https://www.timesofisrael.com/palestinian-kids-taught-to-hate-israel-in-un-funded-camps-clip-shows/ Accessed May 1, 2024.

95 Bresky, Ben. "Declassified US document: PA schools teaching hate." *The Jerusalem Post.* February 8, 2019. https://www.jpost.com/Arab-Israeli-Conflict/Declassified-US-document-shows-PA-schools-teaching-hate-580100 Accessed May 1, 2024.

96 "Elizabeth H. Campbell." State Department biography. https://www.state.gov/biographies/elizabeth-h-campbell/ Accessed May 1, 2024.

As for Campbell, the spokesperson insisted that her responsibilities do not involve UNRWA. "Rules and regulations governing ethics and conflict of interest pertain to all State Department employees, and accordingly Ms. Campbell has recused herself from working on anything related to UNRWA."

This statement does not allay concerns about Campbell's potential bias or involvement in the dissent cables.

It remains unclear whether Ali or Campbell had any role in the deep state efforts to pressure Biden to abandon his support for Israel, but their statements and histories raise serious red flags. Bureaucrats like these can shape U.S. policy in subtle ways, especially if they become entrenched.

The fact that even Biden, who generally favors the woke leanings of the administrative state, can face a deep state effort to undermine his policy reveals a great deal about the power of entrenched bureaucrats and their willingness to buck the elected president. The Woketopus generally favors Biden, but it still has a mind of its own.

9

THE DARK MONEY FEDERAL
TAKEOVER OF ELECTIONS

Manipulating the federal government becomes much more difficult if your figurehead leaves office, so the Woketopus has developed a cunning strategy to try to prevent that from happening.

The latest scheme involves turning the federal government into a get-out-the-vote machine aimed to bolster Democrats. President Biden issued an executive order based on one left-wing group's template, and then federal agencies started to collaborate with that same left-wing group to carry it out.

If you've ever worked on a political campaign, you'll know that contacting voters who are likely to support your candidate, and motivating them to vote, is half the battle. Most campaigns do this in two phases: first by registering voters, and then by contacting them closer to Election Day to remind them to cast a ballot. Campaign workers call this kind of work "get out the vote."

What if, instead of relying on campaign volunteers and staff, you could get the government to start the process? That's exactly what the Woketopus is doing, and it's providing the framework and the resources to make it happen. The first step is to make it easier for likely Democratic voters to vote, in part by loosening election integrity laws. The second—and more crucial—step is to use government agencies for targeted voter registration under the guise of general civic-mindedness.

Voter registration is an easy sell because it's something everyone supports. Most American citizens have the right to vote, and states use voter registration systems to make sure that everyone who casts a ballot is legally qualified to do so. Although these systems are hard to maintain, they are a necessary check on fraud.

Yet if government agencies can help register voters, they can also target people who receive federal aid—people who may be more likely to vote for more government programs. Federal government voter registration may serve as a powerful tool to keep the Woketopus' favored politicians in power.

SUBVERTING CONGRESS

The story starts with H.R. 1—the For the People Act. This bill would:

- o mandate that federal agencies remind citizens about voter registration in the course of regular duties,

- o eviscerate voter ID laws,

- o prevent states from updating their voter registration rolls,

- o force states to automatically register voters,

- o authorize the IRS to investigate and consider the policy positions of nonprofit organizations when they apply for tax-exempt status,

- o and set up a public funding problem for candidates running for Congress.[1]

---

1   von Spakovsky, Hans. "8 Ways That HR 1, 'For the People Act,' Imperils Free and Fair Elections." *The Daily Signal.* March 15, 2021. https://www.dailysignal.com/2021/03/15/8-ways-that-hr1-the-for-the-people-act-imperils-free-and-fair-elections/ Accessed April 19, 2021.

Following their election victories in 2020, House Democrats passed the bill on a party-line vote on March 3, 2021, but the Senate never considered the bill.

Perhaps knowing that the bill would fail in the 50-50 Senate, Biden issued an executive order on March 7, 2021, directing federal agencies to implement some of these agenda items in lieu of legislation.[2] It directed each agency to focus on providing access to voter registration and vote-by-mail ballot applications, developing a plan to "promote voter registration and voter participation…in the course of activities or services that directly engage with the public," and to submit it to Susan Rice, director of the White House Domestic Policy Council. Such efforts include "distributing voter registration and vote-by-mail ballot application forms," "assisting applicants in completing voter registration and vote-by-mail ballot application forms," and "soliciting and facilitating approved, nonpartisan third-party organizations and state officials to provide voter registration services on agency premises."

THAT SOUNDS FAMILIAR...

These proposals did not come out of a vacuum.

After Biden won the 2020 presidential election, the left-wing group Demos released a policy brief, urging the incoming Biden administration to "make voting more accessible by directing specified federal agencies, in their administration of federal programs, to act as voter registration agencies." Demos noted that agencies could start "providing voter registration applications, assisting clients to complete applications, and transmitting completed applications to state authorities." The group explicitly called for "an executive order

---

2 "Executive Order on Promoting Access to Voting." White House Briefing Room. March 7, 2021. https://www.whitehouse.gov/briefing-room/presidential-actions/2021/03/07/executive-order-on-promoting-access-to-voting/ Accessed March 22, 2024.

directing federal agencies serving under-registered populations to provide voter registration services."[3]

Demos has many ties to the Biden administration. None other than Barack Obama served as one of the group's founding board members when he was an Illinois state senator.

In August 2022, K. Sabeel Rahman left his role as president at Demos to become senior counselor at the Office of Information and Regulatory Affairs, part of the White House Office of Management and Budget.[4]

In March 2021, Chiraag Bains left Demos, where he worked as director of legal strategies, to become a special assistant to the president for criminal justice on Biden's Domestic Policy Council. He had also served as a senior fellow at the Open Society Foundations.[5]

It remains unclear whether Rahman or Bains had any role in drafting Biden's executive order.

The current president of Demos, Taifa Smith Butler, visited the White House once, as did Candace Bond-Theriault, associate director of movement building at Demos, and Phi U. Ngyuen, director of democracy at Demos. [6] Xavier de Souza Briggs, vice chair of Demos' Board of Trustees, has visited the White House at least ten times. As mentioned in Chapter 4, Briggs—a member of the Biden presidential transition agency review team—serves as senior advisor

---

3   "Executive Action to Advance Democracy: What the Biden-Harris Administration and the Agencies Can Do to Build a More Inclusive Democracy." Demos Policy Brief. December 3, 2020. https://www.demos.org/policy-briefs/executive-action-advance-democracy-what-biden-harris-administration-and-agencies-can Accessed March 22, 2024.

4   Rozen, Courtney. "Biden Names K. Sabeel Rahman to Key Regulatory Post in White House." Bloomberg. August 31, 2022. https://www.bloomberg.com/news/articles/2022-08-31/k-sabeel-rahman-named-to-key-regulatory-post-in-white-house Accessed March 22, 2024.

5   "White House Announces Additional Policy Staff." White House Briefing Room. March 5, 2021. https://www.whitehouse.gov/briefing-room/statements-releases/2021/03/05/white-house-announces-additional-policy-staff/ Accessed March 22, 2024.

6   White House Visitor Logs.

and co-founder of What Works Plus, a donor collaborative pushing climate projects.[7]

DARK MONEY FUNDING

The Left's dark money network has contributed generously to Demos. The group has received:

- $5.375 million from the Open Society Foundations between 2016 and 2020[8]
- $536,000 from the Proteus Fund between 2014 and 2020[9]
- $175,000 from Hopewell Fund in 2020 (Arabella)[10]
- $120,000 from New Venture Fund between 2014 and 2017 (Arabella)[11]
- $344,350 from The Tides Foundation between 2018 and 2022[12]
- $550,000 from the Wyss Foundation in 2022[13]
- $10,000 from the AFL-CIO in 2014[14]

7   White House Visitor Logs.

8   "Awarded Grants" page search results for "Demos." Open Society Foundations. https://www.opensocietyfoundations.org/grants/past?filter_keyword=Demos&page=2&grant_id=OR2018-44293 Accessed March 22, 2024.

9   "Proteus Fund Inc." Form 990 Schedule I for 2015–2020, accessed April 19, 2024.

10 "Hopewell Fund." Form 990 Schedule I for 2020, accessed April 19, 2024.

11 "New Venture Fund." Form 990 Schedule I for 2014 and 2017, accessed April 19, 2024.

12 "Tides Foundation." Form 990 Schedule I for 2018–2022 accessed April 19, 2024.

13 Wyss Foundation 2022 grants page. https://www.wyssfoundation.org/grants Accessed May 20, 2024.

14 "American Federation Of Labor & Congress Of Industrial Orgs" Form 990 Schedule I for 2014, accessed April 19, 2024.

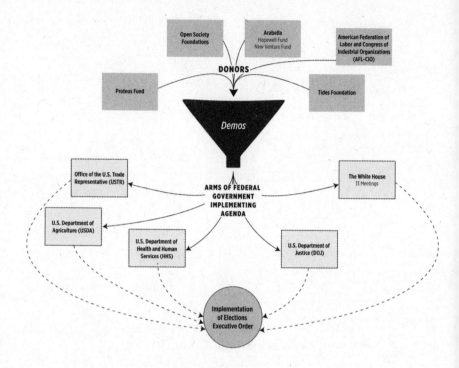

A WOKETOPUS PARTY

The Biden administration didn't just rely on Demos to craft the executive order. Administrative agencies partnered with Demos to implement it. The work apparently started on July 12, 2021, when the Department of Justice, White House staff, and other government agencies held a "listening session" inviting "nonpartisan nonprofit organizations engaged in voting rights advocacy to provide their recommendations and thoughts on best practices."

These groups may be nominally nonpartisan, but their leaders are aligned with one side of the political spectrum. The Heritage Foundation's Oversight Project checked the party affiliation or political donation history of each attendee for the meeting, and every attendee was Democratic, except for one Green Party member.[15]

Groups at the meeting included many of the main characters in this book:

- o AFL-CIO
- o AFSCME
- o The American Civil Liberties Union
- o The Brennan Center for Justice
- o Demos
- o Lawyers' Committee for Civil Rights
- o National Education Association
- o Open Society Policy Center
- o The Southern Poverty Law Center

During the meeting, the ACLU suggested using the Social Security process to register benefit recipients, saying, "They are lower income and have disabilities." Demos suggested the Department of Housing and Urban Development as a vehicle to register low-income people in public housing by "requiring public housing authorities to include this."

Notes from the meeting quote Laura Williamson, a Demos staffer, as saying, "don't stop at registration. It's just the first hurdle." She recommended making the offer to register to vote something "integrated into service, must offer help in completing it, and an office to transmit the registration form."[16]

---

15 Heritage Foundation Oversight Project memorandum. "New Document Highlights Partisan Application of Biden's FedGov Get-Out-The-Vote Operation." May 1, 2024. https://oversight.heritage.org/OP_Memo_on_EO_14019_Partisan_Implementation_5.1.2024.pdf?_gl=1*1pnhduf*_ga*MjEzMjc4NDM4My4xNzEzOTk0NTMx*_ga_W14BT6YQ87*MTcxNjQzMjgwMS4xOS4wLjE3MTY0MzI4MDEuNjAuMC4w Accessed May 23, 2024. p. 2.

16 Ibid. Appendix p. 5–6

AGENCY AFTER AGENCY...

Much of the federal bureaucracy brought in Demos to help implement the executive order.

According to documents unearthed by The Heritage Foundation's Oversight Project, the U.S. Department of Agriculture worked closely with Demos. In early July 2021, Dylan Tureff, a lobbyist with the Democratic-leaning firm The Raben Group, reached out to USDA staff offering a meeting with Demos "to discuss the implementation of the Executive Order to Promote Voting Access."[17] Demos met with Agriculture staff on August 3, 2021, via Microsoft Teams, "to discuss the executive order to promote voting access implementation and ways USDA can continue to play a role in the implementation." [18]

Adam Lioz, then a senior counsel at Demos, followed up with USDA staff on August 9, 2021, thanked them for a "productive conversation," and promised to give the agency a "best practices" slide, along with data on voter registration.[19] Lioz also said he and other Demos staff were "eager to schedule follow up conversations to dig into specific programs and help with integration in any way we can." (Lioz later left Demos in September 2021 to join the NAACP Legal Defense Fund as a senior policy counsel for political participation.)

Before Demos reached out, bureaucrats at the Department of Agriculture had come up with "top five suggestions" for implementing Biden's order. One of those recommendations involved

---

17   Lucas, Fred. "EXCLUSIVE: Harvesting Voters? These Left-Wing Groups Are Teaming With USDA." *The Daily Signal*. May 2, 2024. https://www. dailysignal.com/2024/05/02/exclusive-under-biden-order-usda-teams-with-left-wing-groups-to-grow-new-voters/ Accessed May 24, 2024.

18   Lucas, Fred. "USDA Colludes With Left-Wing Group to Turn Out Voters Under Biden Order, Documents Reveal." *The Daily Signal*. February 20, 2024. https://www.dailysignal.com/2024/02/20/usda-colludes-with-left-wing-group-to-turn-out-voters-under-biden-order-documents-reveal/ Accessed March 22, 2024.

19   "Adam Lioz." NAACP Legal Defense Fund staff profile. https://www. naacpldf.org/about-us/staff/adam-lioz/ Accessed March 22, 2024.

"Voter Registration & Information at Food and Nutrition Service Program Sites Through WIC and SNAP sites." WIC refers to an Agriculture Department food program for "women, infants, and children," while SNAP—better known as "food stamps"—refers to the Supplemental Nutrition Assistance Program.[20]

While those who lawfully receive such benefits likely also have the right to vote, offering voter registration services alongside federal subsidies may give beneficiaries the impression that they must vote to receive these benefits, or it may encourage them to vote for candidates who are likely to prioritize those benefits over other public concerns.

The Indian Health Service (IHS), part of the U.S. Department of Health and Human Services, is also working with Demos and the American Civil Liberties Union to implement Biden's executive order. "As part of efforts to promote awareness of national voter registration resources, the Indian Health Services has worked with groups such as the National Congress of American Indians, the Native American Rights Fund, Demos, and the ACLU," Joshuah Marshall, senior advisor to IHS Director Roselyn Tso, told *The Daily Signal*.[21]

The U.S. Office of Trade Representative (USTR), an agency within the Executive Office of the President, released its plan to implement Biden's order: "partner with nonpartisan, public service and civic engagement organizations (e.g., Asian Americans Advancing Justice, Mexican American Legal Defense and Education Fund, National Pan-Hellenic Council, Brennan Center for Justice) in developing and amplifying content" for social media posts on key dates important to voting.[22]

---

20   Lucas, "Harvesting Voters"

21   Lucas, Fred. "EXCLUSIVE: Demos, ACLU Among 'Voter Advocacy Groups' Helping Federal Agencies Turn Out Vote on Biden's Order." *The Daily Signal*. June 7, 2023. https://www.dailysignal.com/2023/06/07/exclusive-demos-aclu-among-voter-advocacy-groups-helping-federal-agencies-turn-out-vote-on-bidens-order/ Accessed March 22, 2024.

22   Lucas, Fred. "EXCLUSIVE: Here Are the Left-Wing Groups the White House Trade Office Is Scheming With to Get Out the Vote." *The Daily Signal*. March 10, 2024. https://www.dailysignal.com/2024/03/10/exclusive-biden-trade-agency-plans-partnership-with-liberal-legal-groups-to-turn-out-vote/ Accessed March 22, 2024.

"The Brennan Center for Justice at NYU Law has not partnered with, coordinated with, or otherwise worked with the Office of the U.S. Trade Representative," Brennan Senior Media Strategist Kendall Karson Verhovek told me in remarks for this book.

While these documents have shown the federal government colluding with Demos and the ACLU to help register voters and drive turnout, some agencies have refused to hand over documents. The Justice Department, for example, cited presidential privilege in refusing to hand over documents that The Foundation for Government Accountability has requested via the Freedom of Information Act.[23]

Many of the groups advising the White House and these agencies on implementing the executive order have made previous appearances in this book, but two organizations stand out for their rhetoric on voting and their ties to the Left's dark money network.

THE ACLU

Most Americans think of the ACLU as the civil liberties law firm that so prized the principle of free speech that it defended Nazis' right to protest back in the 1960s. The ACLU still takes some cases like this, but the organization has taken a decidedly woke turn in recent years, championing abortion, gender ideology, and commonsense bills responding to the border crisis.

When it comes to election integrity, the ACLU has also gone woke, claiming that "voter suppression laws…make it harder for Americans—particularly black people, the elderly, students, and people with disabilities—to exercise their fundamental right to cast a ballot." The organization opposes "cuts to early voting, voter ID laws, and purges of voter rolls."[24]

---

23   Lucas, Fred. "DOJ Keeps Plan Secret for Biden's Election Executive Order." *The Daily Signal.* March 11, 2024. https://www.dailysignal.com/2024/03/11/doj-keeps-plan-secret-for-bidens-election-executive-order/ Accessed March 22, 2024.

24   "Fighting Voter Suppression." ACLU issues page. https://www.aclu.org/issues/voting-rights/fighting-voter-suppression Accessed March 22, 2024.

These claims echo the "voter suppression" narrative, which my colleague Fred Lucas debunks in his book, *The Myth of Voter Suppression*.

During the Jim Crow era—from the end of the Civil War to the post-WWII civil rights legislation—election officials in the South used pretexts to prevent blacks from legally voting. Other election officials created "machines" like the infamous "Tammany Hall" to fabricate votes by stealing ballots, burning ballots, importing voters who lived outside the precinct, and recording votes cast by dead or fictional people.

Election integrity laws can and should prevent both kinds of election meddling.[25] The 1965 Voting Rights Act made voter intimidation illegal, and "voter denial"—any attempt to prevent a legally eligible voter from casting a ballot—is also illegal under federal law. The law also prevents vote dilution—an intentional effort to dilute the votes of one group of people.

Yet federal law is completely silent on "voter suppression." J. Christian Adams, a former Justice Department attorney, explains that the term "seeks to blur the line between the legal and illegal in order to taint and smear constitutionally protected activity, or perfectly legal state laws." According to Lucas, under the cover of fighting "voter suppression," Democrats are pushing legislation "to establish a legal structure for making fraud easier and installing long-term majorities."

As mentioned in Chapter 6, the ACLU has received millions through the Left's dark money network, and its leaders and staff have visited the White House at least thirty-one times.

ANOTHER 'VOTER SUPPRESSION' ALLIANCE

While the U.S. Office of Trade Representative ultimately did not work with the Brennan Center for Justice at New York University School of Law, there is a reason why the USTR suggested that it might do so, and the Brennan Center did appear at the listening session for implementing the executive order. The Brennan Center

---

25   Lucas, Fred V. *The Myth of Voter Suppression: The Left's Assault on Clean Elections*. New York: Bombardier Books, 2022. pp.3–5.

also parrots the "voter suppression" narrative. It condemns efforts such as voter ID laws, cutting voting times, restricting voter registration, and "purging voter rolls" as attempts at "suppression."[26] In reality, these election integrity efforts help ensure that only citizens who have the legal right to vote do so, and they often help establish a chain-of-custody for ballots.

The Brennan Center also enjoys support from the Left's dark money network and access to the Biden White House. It has received:

- $1.6 million from New Venture Fund between 2014 and 2022 (Arabella)[27]
- $1.9 million from the Proteus Fund between 2011 and 2022, with $586,253 specifically marked for "democracy" efforts[28]
- $1 million from the Tides Foundation between 2018 and 2022[29]
- $4.8 million from the Open Society Foundations between 2016 and 2021[30]

Brennan Center leaders and staff have visited the White House at least twelve times. The center's president, Michael A. Waldman, attended a small gathering with President Biden in 2022.[31]

Lawrence Norden, the center's senior director of elections and government, met at the White House with left-leaning security

---

26 "Vote Suppression." Brennan Center for Justice. https://www.brennancenter.org/issues/ensure-every-american-can-vote/vote-suppression Accessed March 22, 2024.

27 "New Venture Fund." Form 990, Schedule I for 2014–2022, accessed on April 20, 2024.

28 "Proteus Fund Inc." Form 990, Schedule I for 2011–2022, accessed on April 22, 2024.

29 "Tides Foundation." Form 990, Schedule I for 2018–2022, accessed on April 22, 2024.

30 "Awarded Grants" page search results for "William J. Brennan." Open Society Foundations. https://www.opensocietyfoundations.org/grants/past?filter_keyword=William+J.+Brennan Accessed March 22, 2024.

31 White House Visitor Logs.

experts who helped silence concerns about mail-in voting during the 2020 election. In February 2023, Norden met with two staffers at the Bipartisan Policy Center—Matthew Weil, executive director of the center's democracy program, and William Adler, associate director of its elections project—and Amy Cohen, executive director of the National Association of State Election Directors.

Pay no attention to the name—the Bipartisan Policy Center slants to the Left, especially on election integrity. The Center's elections and democracy programs have stated that "mail voting is a safe, secure, and reliable voting method."[32] In September 2020, YouTube announced that it would label videos warning about mail-in voting as "misinformation," relying on resources from the Bipartisan Policy Center.[33]

As for Cohen, a November 2023 report from the House Judiciary Committee and its Select Subcommittee on the Weaponization of the Federal Government found that she was involved in a scheme with the Cybersecurity and Infrastructure Security Agency (CISA) to censor concerns about election integrity in 2020. This scheme involved the creation of an email address which CISA officials would use to report "misinformation" to social media platforms, copying on the email those who manage the address—such as Amy Cohen. The Election Integrity Partnership would urge social media platforms to remove content raising questions about mail-in voting, and to label posts "clarifying that vote by mail is secure."[34]

---

32   "Mail Voting is Safe and Secure." Bipartisan Policy Center Elections Project. Last updated March 13, 2024. https://bipartisanpolicy.org/report/mail-voting-is-safe-secure/ Accessed April 22, 2024.

33   Bergen, Mark. "YouTube Will Label Videos on Mail Voting to Blunt Misinformation." Bloomberg News. September 24, 2020. https://www.bloomberg.com/news/articles/2020-09-24/youtube-will-label-videos-on-mail-voting-to-blunt-misinformation Accessed April 22, 2024.

34   Committee on the Judiciary and the Select Subcommittee on the Weaponization of the Federal Government. *The Weaponization of 'Disinformation' Pseudo-Experts and Bureaucrats: How the Federal Government Partnered With Universities to Censor Americans' Political Speech. Interim Staff Report.* U.S. House of Representatives. November 6, 2023. https://judiciary.house.gov/sites/evo-subsites/republicans-judiciary.house.gov/files/evo-media-document/EIP_Jira-Ticket-Staff-Report-11-7-23-Clean.pdf Accessed April 22, 2024.

According to the report, this scheme "disproportionately targeted conservative-oriented speech."

The fact that the administrative state is relying on these biased sources for advice on voter registration raises serious concerns about the effort.

THE 'ZUCKERBUCKS' CONNECTION

Critics have branded Biden's executive order "Bidenbucks," echoing the 2020 presidential election scandal about "Zuckerbucks."

Many on the Left warned that fears about the COVID-19 pandemic would suppress voter turnout, so local election officials implemented new rules to expand voting by mail. Some of them also partnered with a group called the Center for Tech and Civic Life (CTCL), which doled out nearly $350 million to local election offices. The center received hefty funding from the Zuckerberg-Chan Initiative, so opponents branded the funding for election offices "Zuckerbucks."

According to the Foundation for Government Accountability, counties or cities that leaned Democratic disproportionately received Zuckerbucks grants, as did states with the greatest impact in the 2020 presidential election.[35]

After the 2020 election, the Center for Tech and Civic Life established the U.S. Alliance for Election Excellence, which provides grants for election offices.[36] Yet the first version of Zuckerbucks directly involved a project of the Arabella nonprofit New Venture Fund.

In 2016, New Venture Fund launched the Center for Secure and Modern Elections (CSME), which pushed for automatic voter

35 "'Zuckerbucks' Were a Problem in the 2020 Election." Foundation for Government Accountability. April 13, 2022. https://thefga.org/one-pagers/zuckerbucks/ Accessed May 24, 2024.

36 Lucas, Fred. "'Unprecedented Intrusion Into Our Election System': Tech-Backed, Left-Leaning Group to Invest in Election Training in Battleground States." *The Daily Signal.* November 28, 2022. https://www.dailysignal.com/2022/11/28/tech-backed-left-leaning-group-to-invest-in-election-training-in-battleground-states/ Accessed May 24, 2024.

registration, looser penalties for falsifying voter registration applications, and expanding vote-by-mail. CSME received a $600,000 grant to help support "elections jurisdictions" in the battleground states of Wisconsin, Michigan, Minnesota, and Ohio "for the November 2020 election."[37]

Numerous ties between CMSE and CTCL suggest that the Arabella group inspired the larger Zuckerberg initiative. Former CMSE employee Ashish Sinha advised the Center for Tech and Civic Life and election officials in Green Bay, Wisconsin, about the use of private drop boxes and "targeting communities" with absentee ballots. Sam Oliker-Friedland, chief council for CSME, previously worked for the digital campaign group that birthed CTCL: the New Organizing Institute.

"Emails from Green Bay and Philadelphia clearly show the CSME was operating hand in hand with the CTCL at the earliest stages on these grants while calling it the Cities Project," Todd Shepherd, an investigative journalist writing for the Pennsylvania outlet Broad + Liberty, told the Capital Research Center. "Even months after the election, persons working for the CSME were still talking to election officials about the CTCL grants while using the name Cities Project."

"Because of this evidence, I think it's a very fair question to ask to what degree the CSME may have actually been the originator of the entire effort, and whether the CTCL was just a better front for the project because they had 501(c)(3) status," Shepherd added.[38]

The Left's dark money network has bankrolled and may have helped coordinate both the Zuckerbucks and the Bidenbucks scandals, this time enlisting every federal agency in the effort.

---

37 Walter, *Arabella*. Chapter 4. Ebook pp. 98–104.

38 Ludwig, Hayden. "The Origins of 'Zuck Bucks': Center for Tech and Civic Life." Part 4. https://capitalresearch.org/article/the-origins-of-zuck-bucks-part-4/ Capital Research Center. January 26, 2023. Accessed May 24, 2024.

GOVERNMENT EFFORT UNNECESSARY

Even if the federal government's effort to increase voter registration and voter turnout were not tainted by collaboration with woke organizations that seem intent on undermining election integrity in a likely attempt to elected Democrats, is it necessary for the federal government to launch such an initiative?

Hans von Spakovsky, manager of the Election Law Reform Initiative at The Heritage Foundation, argues that this effort is not necessary to ensure access to the ballot box. "We had the highest voter registration rate in 2020 than we've had in the last five or six presidential elections," von Spakovsky told *The Daily Signal.* "When federal agencies are involved in voter registration, the real fear is that the party that controls the White House will use federal agencies to engage in partisan registration."[39]

It may sound noble to mobilize bureaucrats to help making voting easier, but this effort is unnecessary and tainted with extreme bias. The fact that Biden signed the executive order after failing to achieve similar results by legislation only adds insult to injury.

Make no mistake: this executive order and the whole-of-government effort to bolster voter registration amounts to a bureaucratic get-out-the-vote effort aimed at mobilizing the Left's preferred constituencies to keep their cronies in power. It represents the Woketopus' final gambit to maintain control as the American people wake up to its schemes.

---

39   Lucas, Fred. "Biden Bureaucracy Secretly Plans to Turn Out Voters After Failure of Election Takeover Bills." *The Daily Signal.* February 10, 2022. https://www.dailysignal.com/2022/02/10/biden-bureaucracy-secretly-plans-to-turn-out-voters-after-failure-of-election-takeover-bills/ Accessed March 22, 2024.

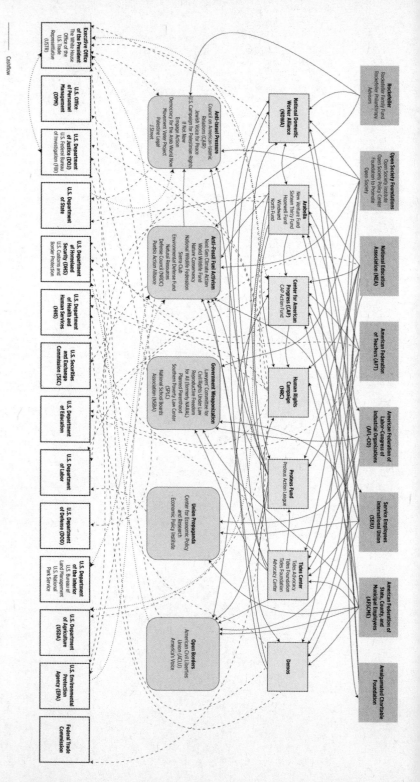

Conclusion

In the previous chapters, we've seen that the Left's dark money network funds a cabal of woke nonprofits that manipulate federal policy, often circumventing Congress and the president.

This Woketopus impacts education policy, pushing a pro-CRT agenda and urging student debt bailouts that prop up an increasingly woke higher education system. It corrupts labor law to favor unions at the expense of employers, workers, and the American people. It feasts on the ill-gotten gains of workers' union dues funneled to left-wing causes without their knowledge or consent.

The Woketopus uses legal loopholes to force its green agenda on the American people through a sue-and-settle strategy, while lobbying for wind and solar energy, which empower America's greatest geopolitical rival, China. It spreads its tentacles through the bureaucracy to push transgender orthodoxy and force the American people to reject basic truths about biological sex. It uses accusations of terrorism to weaponize federal law enforcement and scare its critics into silence.

The Woketopus has even launched a "deep state" in the Biden administration, undermining the president's policy on Israel from within and propping up a pressure campaign from without. At the same time, it has meddled in federal elections by turning the administrative state into a get-out-the-vote machine in an apparent attempt to keep its cronies in power.

This Woketopus did not start with Biden. The Left's tentacles have infiltrated the federal bureaucracy for decades, only becoming most obvious in the last few years.

Its influence will not end with his presidency, either—regardless of the results of the 2024 election. Even if a conservative president replaces Biden, the Woketopus will maintain close ties to bureaucrats throughout the administration, and many of Biden's political appointees will go to work at left-wing nonprofits, waiting for another woke president to usher them back into the bureaucracy.

What can the American people do to counter this nefarious influence campaign?

ELECTIONS HAVE CONSEQUENCES

While the Woketopus will continue to stretch its tentacles through the administrative state no matter who sits in the Oval Office, Americans can minimize and hopefully defeat it eventually.

We still have the opportunity to elect a new president every four years.

Voters should not just consider the man or woman at the top of the ticket—they should think about the interest groups that will gain more access to the administration if that person wins. Each candidate does not represent only himself; he represents a network of political and ideological allies who will affect policy.

If you don't want the federal government using your tax dollars to "forgive" student loans, that might affect how you vote. If you don't want the federal government forcing schools to let biological males compete against girls in sports, that may factor into your decision. If you don't want federal law enforcement to prosecute pro-life protesters for standing outside abortion clinics, or to cite the far-left and dishonest SPLC—which demonizes the moral position of the entire Roman Catholic Church—that might inform your choice.

Unfortunately, the administrative state's increasing control over the rest of the country has turned many moral and social issues that should be decided on an individual, community, or state level into matters of federal policy. It has also enabled the woke movement to weaponize the government into an ideological enforcement mechanism, punishing Americans who dare to dissent from an increasingly stifling leftist agenda.

This woke agenda is abetting the destruction of our country, all in the name of "social justice" and "inclusion." It is pitting parents against teachers, workers against their employers, and races against one another in the name of a "justice" that seems to favor the Left's preferred constituencies at the expense of everyone else.

Unfortunately, the Woketopus' tentacles inside the administrative state prevent a return to sanity on these and so many other issues. Breaking the Left's stranglehold on the bureaucracy must be a high priority for commonsense voters.

REINING IN THE ADMINISTRATIVE STATE

Many administrative agencies are not fully accountable to the people through our elected representatives in Congress, or even the presidency.

The Constitution gives Congress the ultimate authority to make law, which includes deciding how much money goes to which federal agencies, and even determining whether those agencies should exist. Congress needs to take this authority back from administrative agencies that now effectively make law. It also needs to consider reforming legislation, such as the Clean Air Act, that enables the corrupt sue-and-settle process we discussed in Chapter 4.

Congress needs to reassert its role under the Constitution and take responsibility for actually making law. Otherwise, the lawmaking process will remain bureaucratic and corrupt. If Americans truly want a more *democratic* form of government, we must insist that our elected representatives—not faceless, unaccountable bureaucrats—write the rules we must live by.

In the meantime, certain rules restrict a president's ability to hire and fire administrative staff, even though the Constitution gives him (or her) ultimate authority over the executive branch.

Civil service regulations protect administrative staff from being treated like at-will employees who can be fired for poor performance. These regulations exist to protect civil servants, based on the idea that these staffers do not make policy like the heads of agencies, whom presidents can appoint and fire more or less at will. Yet these civil servants often *do* make decisions that impact policy, and the regulations effectively entrench left-leaning bureaucrats, making them impossible to fire.

In October 2020, then-President Donald Trump issued an executive order to make the civil service protections more accurately reflect the reality. His Schedule F policy directed agency heads to prepare a list of federal employees in "positions of a confidential, policy-determining, policy-making, or policy-advocating character that are not normally subject to change as a result of a presidential transition." His order then created exemptions from civil service rules in these cases, allowing agency heads to make these staff at-will employees and easier to fire.[1]

In April 2024, the Office of Management and Budget proposed a new rule aimed at preventing a return to Trump's Schedule F. Robert Moffit, a senior research fellow for health and welfare policy at The Heritage Foundation and an OPM staffer under President Ronald Reagan, warned that "if such a rule were allowed to stand, it would tie a future president's hands—at least temporarily—in carrying out his responsibilities to make and implement his policies."[2]

Schedule F is not an inherently partisan issue. Both conservatives and liberals should agree that the executive branch should answer to the president, as the Constitution stipulates. Yet under both Trump and Biden, administrative staff have acted as a "deep state," undermining the duly elected president. During the Trump

1   Lucas, Fred. "EXCLUSIVE: Trump Executive Order Aims to Rein in Bureaucracy's Role in Policymaking." *The Daily Signal.* October 21, 2020. https://www.dailysignal.com/2020/10/21/exclusive-trump-executive-order-aims-to-rein-in-bureaucracys-role-in-policymaking/ Accessed May 17, 2024.

2   Lucas, Fred. "Biden Protects Deep State Bureaucrats With 'Anti-Democratic' Rule." *The Daily Signal.* April 8, 2024. https://www.dailysignal.com/2024/04/08/bidens-anti-democratic-personnel-regulation-could-insulate-deep-state/ Accessed May 17, 2024.

administration, an anonymous official penned an op-ed in *The New York Times*, bragging about working to undermine Trump's policies from within.[3] As we saw in Chapter 7, under Biden, anti-Israel officials have taken public and private actions to undermine the administration's policies on the Jewish state.

Schedule F will not be enough, however. Americans with common sense need to develop solutions to undermine the worst excesses of the administrative state. The Supreme Court recently cleared the way for Americans to bring lawsuits against federal agencies that overstep their bounds. In *Loper Bright v. Raimondo*, the court struck down the doctrine of "Chevron deference," by which courts had to defer to an administrative agency's interpretation of the law in cases where the law is ambiguous. This ruling will allow Americans to sue for damages when agencies abuse their power.[4] We must develop the intestinal fortitude to exercise this power when necessary.

Unfortunately, Supreme Court also upheld a funding scheme that insulates the Consumer Financial Protection Bureau (CFPB) from the requirements most federal agencies face—the need to secure funding from Congress every year. While I believe the Supreme Court made a mistake in that ruling, I believe it is essential for Congress to pass a law reasserting its rightful authority over that agency.[5]

---

3 O'Neil, Tyler. "New York Times Publishes Evidence of a Deep State 'Resistance' Inside the Trump Administration." *PJ Media.* September 5, 2018. https://web.archive.org/web/20191114072742/https://pjmedia.com/trending/new-york-times-publishes-evidence-of-a-deep-state-resistance-inside-the-trump-administration/ Accessed via Web Archive on May 17, 2024.

4 Stepman, Jarrett. "Supreme Court Throws Back 'Chevron Deference' in Ruling on Fishermen's Case Against Government." *The Daily Signal.* June 28, 2024. https://www.dailysignal.com/2024/06/28/supreme-court-throws-back-chevron-deference-in-ruling-on-fishermens-case-against-government/ Accessed July 11, 2024.

5 O'Neil, Tyler. "BREAKING: Supreme Court Upholds Consumer Financial Protection Bureau." *The Daily Signal.* May 16, 2024. https://www.dailysignal.com/2024/05/16/breaking-supreme-court-upholds-financial-agencys-funding-scheme-insulating-congress/ Accessed May 20, 2024.

Paring back the Woketopus will be no easy feat—and even if a conservative wins a presidential election, conservatives need to be prepared with executive orders and policy prescriptions to help that president balance the nefarious impacts of the radical Left in the administrative state.

Project 2025, a coalition of more than one hundred conservative-leaning organizations working with The Heritage Foundation to develop those policy prescriptions, represents an excellent place to start.

IN THE MEANTIME...

Those who dissent from the Left's woke orthodoxy need to realize what time it is in America. Trump's trial and conviction—only an example of the weaponization of law enforcement—underscore just how far the country has gone. Dissenters of all stripes—be they conservative, reactionary, moderate liberals, or apolitical working-class folks—need to realize that the woke agenda will do whatever it can to silence and ostracize them.

The Woketopus succeeds in part because cultural Marxists have captured the commanding heights of American culture. The Left's entrenchment in Hollywood, the universities, and corporate boardrooms gives the illusion that the only respectable—and therefore, the only true—perspective is the woke orthodoxy. This gives the illusion that the science is settled on climate change, that acceptance is the only allowable response to transgender orthodoxy, that America is fundamentally racist and oppressive, or that election integrity represents "Jim Crow 2.0."

None of this is true, and Americans need to continue to speak out against it.

In recent years, we have seen heartening signs that everyday Americans are pushing back on these deceptive narratives, and we need to celebrate and encourage that resistance.

Missouri Attorney General Andrew Bailey has helped reveal and unravel the Biden administration's censorship scheme to silence dissent on COVID-19. Former *New York Times* editor Bari Weiss has launched *The Free Press*, a powerful news outlet to platform liberals, conservatives, and independents who dissent from the woke narrative. Florida Governor Ron DeSantis has elevated common-sense critics of woke ideology like Chris Rufo to university boards, launching a less woke iteration of Florida's New College. The Daily Wire and Angel Studios have launched conservative alternatives to the increasingly woke Hollywood.

Colleges and universities are rejecting Diversity, Equity, and Inclusion policies, slashing DEI budgets. The legislatures in Florida, Texas, and Utah have banned DEI in higher education.[6] The University of North Carolina at Chapel Hill—which had hired *1619 Project* founder Nikole Hannah-Jones as a professor—eliminated $2.3 million in DEI funding, diverting it to police and campus safety.[7] As they reject this woke ideology, more universities should look to the example of my alma mater, Hillsdale College, in teaching more of the positive aspects of America's heritage and the principles behind the Constitution.

America needs more New Colleges and more Hillsdales. It needs more outlets like *The Free Press*. It needs more TV and movie companies like Angel Studios and The Daily Wire.

We must demand that powerful search engines like Google stop skewing their search results to bury dissenting and conservative opinions. We must demand that social media companies stop adding automatic "fact-checks" that force the woke narrative down our throats.

We also desperately need more moderate liberals to stand up and say, "Enough." These are not "conservative" positions, but an

---

6   Adams, Char and Nigel Chiwaya. "Map: See which states have introduced or passed anti-DEI bills." NBC News. March 2, 2024. https://www.nbc-news.com/data-graphics/anti-dei-bills-states-republican-lawmakers-map-rcna140756 Accessed May 20, 2024.

7   Kabbany, Jennifer. "UNC Chapel Hill to slash $2.3M in DEI funding, divert money to police, campus safety." *The College Fix.* May 14, 2024. https://www.thecollegefix.com/unc-chapel-hill-to-slash-2-3m-in-dei-funding-divert-money-to-police-campus-safety/ Accessed May 20, 2024.

attempt to save the spirit of America from an ideology that is suffocating it. The woke orthodoxy that stifles dissent by branding it hatred isn't interested in debate and fair play, and if the noble idea of America is to survive, we must rescue it from this behemoth.

Defeating the Woketopus isn't about taking power, it's about restoring our ability to be a free people again. Understanding that threat is half the battle, and with any luck, I've painted a picture that spurs you into action.

Acknowledgments

This book grew out of my efforts to further expose The Southern Poverty Law Center, which I still see as the tip of the spear in demonizing those who dare dissent from the Left's increasingly stifling ideology. As I covered the Biden administration, I realized that it had not only worked with the SPLC in ways that should shock Americans, but that the SPLC represents part of a vast network of far-left groups, propped up by a dark money network on a far grander scale than the Kochtopus.

My wife, Katie, deserves credit not just for helping me write this book, but for providing essential feedback that made it stronger than it would have been otherwise.

I also owe a debt of gratitude to my publisher, Post Hill Press, and David Bernstein in particular, for convincing me that it was still possible for me to begin the process of writing an election-themed book in March 2024. I cranked out this book in just over two months; I have always found deadlines a welcome challenge.

I also heartily thank Scott Walter, Parker Thayer, and the Capital Research Center for their help exposing the Arabella Advisors network and the Left's dark money apparatus. This book would not be possible without their hard work paving the way.

Americans for Public Trust also deserves special thanks for providing me background information on Hansjörg Wyss, and for exposing Randi Weingarten's influence on the Centers for Disease Control and Prevention.

Perhaps most importantly, my colleagues at *The Daily Signal* and my former colleagues at The Heritage Foundation deserve hearty thanks for their efforts to help me research these important topics and their feedback on some chapters of the book.

Beyond all else, I am indebted to my parents and to God, who inspired in me the desire to write, and the values that led me to uncover the truth. Soli Dei Gloria.

About the Author

Tyler O'Neil is a husband, father, and Eagle Scout. He graduated from Hillsdale College in 2012 and has written and edited articles for numerous conservative outlets, including the Christian Post, PJ Media, Fox News, and the *Daily Signal*. His first book, *Making Hate Pay: The Corruption of the Southern Poverty Law Center*, exposed how a civil rights organization became a threat to America's free speech culture. He enjoys board games, Indian food, and talking ceaselessly about politics, religion, and culture.